Permission to Develop

Aboriginal Treaties, Case Law and Regulations

Permission to Develop

Aboriginal Treaties, Case Law and Regulations

Jerry P. White, Paul Maxim and Nicholas Spence
University of Western Ontario

THOMPSON EDUCATIONAL PUBLISHING, INC.
Toronto, Ontario

Information on how to obtain copies of this book may be obtained from:

Website: www.thompsonbooks.com
E-mail: publisher@thompsonbooks.com
Telephone: (416) 766-2763
Fax: (416) 766-0398

Library and Archives Canada Cataloguing in Publication

White, Jerry Patrick, 1951-

  Permission to develop : Aboriginal treaties, case law and regulations / Jerry P. White, Paul Maxim and Nicholas Spence.

ISBN 1-55077-145-0

  1. Native peoples—Canada—Treaties. 2. Native peoples—Canada—Economic conditions. 3. Native peoples—Canada—Government relations. 4. Natural resources—Law and legislation—Canada. 5. Native peoples—Land tenure—Canada. 6. Native peoples—Canada— Claims. 7. Native peoples—Legal status, laws, etc.—Canada.

  I. Maxim, Paul S., 1950- II. Spence, Nicholas III. Title.

Copy Editing: Elizabeth Phinney
Interior Design: Danielle Baum
Cover Design: Elan Designs
Cover Illustration: Daphne Odjig, *Spiritual Legacy of the Western Wall* (1976).
                       Reproduced by permission of Daphne Odjig.

We acknowledge the support of the Government of Canada through the Book Publishing Industry Development Program for our publishing activities.

Printed in Canada.

1 2 3 4 5   09 08 07 06 05 04

Table of Contents

Foreword

This volume is the result of research carried out under the auspices of the First Nations Cohesion Project (FNCP), Sociology Department, The University of Western Ontario. The FNCP was developed out of a strategic grant received from the Social Sciences and Humanities Research Council of Canada (SSHRCC) and has resulted in many publications including *Aboriginal Conditions: Research as a Foundation for Public Policy* (White, Maxim and Beavon et al. 2003).

In 2001 we put a team in place to begin the basic legal research. The team had a mandate to review all legislation and legal agreements that could directly and/or indirectly impact the economic development of First Nations in Canada. The result is this volume, which is intended to be a primer for all who are interested in the frameworks that influence and/or determine development.

We believe that Aboriginal legal judgements, treaty agreements and negotiations in Canada have important implications for a diverse body of people. First Nations people and the workers who provide services for them are affected directly by the legislative frameworks that order their work. Lawyers represent and/or defend Aboriginal Peoples in an institution with much ambiguity and uncharted territory. For researchers, any fruitful research must acknowledge the interplay of the legal, political, social and economic dimensions of society and their net effects on the status of Aboriginal People. In the case of policy-makers, the development, administration and efficacy of policy depends on the legal context in which this process occurs. This work is designed to cover an integrated spectrum of the legal framework that affects development, work and economic activity.

The Aboriginal condition continues to change as does the wider society in which it is embedded. Thus, those whose responsibilities lie in researching and developing policy have a stake in knowledge about the past and present principles, legislation and treaties that impact Aboriginal People in Canada. Understanding the legal framework in Canada will also benefit those who specialize in Aboriginal affairs. This work attempts to provide a resource that serves as a basis for understanding the complexities of legislation and treaty agreements at the federal and provincial/territorial levels. It addresses development work and economic activity particularly.

This volume has many weaknesses, not the least of which is that it is inevitably out of date. Decisions are constantly being made by the courts and governments that alter the terrain. We are current to the end of summer 2002. We plan to revise and update in 2005. A second weakness of this volume is that it focuses on First Nations, particularly Status or Registered Indians and their communities. The authors do not wish to convey a lack of interest or concern for other Aboriginal peoples. This is merely our starting place and we hope to take our understandings forward to deal with all Aboriginal People in the next publication.

We want to express our deepest gratitude to Lisa Braid, who, as a visiting law student from Australia, worked as a researcher on this project. Her insight and legal skill, not to mention tenacity, has been instrumental in this project.

We wish to thank Professor Michael Coyle in the Faculty of Law at the University of Western Ontario for his review of the original manuscript. We also wish to acknowledge the many graduate and undergraduate students, Aboriginal and non-Aboriginal, as well as the post-doctoral fellows who have worked on the First Nations Cohesion Project.

References

White, Jerry P., Paul Maxim, and Dan Beavon. 2003. *Aboriginal Conditions: Research as a Foundation for Public Policy*. Vancouver: University of British Columbia Press.

Introduction

Understanding The First Nations Legal Framework

From the Royal Proclamation of 1763, to the *Constitution Act* of 1982, through to the present day, the issue of Aboriginal rights and Aboriginal title has been important and perplexing. For governments, communities, researchers, social activists and other stakeholders, the complexity and salience of this framework is no surprise. Indeed, the rights of Aboriginal People, as dictated through the legal framework of Canadian society, have profound social implications that garner great attention in a multitude of sectors.

The high standard of living in Canadian society is well recognized in the international community, whether in commendations from the United Nations or praise from human rights groups. Canada has placed at or near the top of the United Nations Human Development Index for several years (Beavon and Cook 2003). Although the standard of living in our society is no doubt laudable, it is not fully realized by all groups in society, including Aboriginals (ibid). This comes as no surprise, given that a high proportion of Aboriginals differ in their capacity to participate fully in society. Although Aboriginal problems and social ills tend to overwhelm much of mainstream media, there is much to celebrate among the Aboriginal population in Canada. Aboriginal Canadians continue to improve their standard of living on numerous indicators, including educational attainment and taking charge of their own affairs on an increasing scale. Despite the many positive gains, everyone, both Aboriginal and non-Aboriginal, acknowledges that there is much to be done.

Social scientists such as ourselves are puzzled by the observation that First Nations people face common socio-economic problems, despite being ethnically and geographically diverse. Social and economic development is at the heart of much discussion among stakeholders. This is understandable, given that our life experiences are related directly to the degree of development in our provinces and/or territories, and in our communities.

Many of us who have shared in the process of understanding the issues facing First Nations people of Canada are cognizant of their complex socio-economic situation nationwide. Moreover, we realize that there is no simple formula to solve the manifold socio-economic issues facing these communities. There are, however, some basic understandings that are necessary for informed socio-economic decision-making processes to occur.

What is the underlying context in which Aboriginals relate with one another, the natural environment and the wider society? First Nations in Canada are governed by legislation unique to them. Treaties, as well as provincial and federal arrangements, make the legal framework of First Nations a challenging one to grasp. It is the enumeration of this framework that forms this volume.

It is fair to say that the legal framework provides us with some possibilities while limiting others. Humans are social beings; hence, the way a society organizes itself structures our social relations and participation in its various institutions. The legal framework is, indeed, one of the foundations of our civilization. For example, the right to own private property, the right to free speech, the right to vote, the right to medical care and all the *Charter* rights and freedoms mould our social institutions, political structure and economic system. These rights reflect the principles of our society, enshrine our fundamental values and influence our social relations. While we recognize that the laws of society often lag behind our social consciousness and even reflect our less than perfect power relations, they nonetheless play a conditioning role. Thus, laws, treaties and agreements set the structural frame in which other processes occur, including economic and social development. From our legal framework come policies and programs that affect the day-to-day lives of Aboriginal Canadians. As participants in a society led by formal laws, an understanding of the basic framework sheds much light on the motivations and principles guiding the complex processes at work, both progressive and reactionary.

Demographics: Snapshots of Social Processes

We noted above that as social scientists we find similarities in the conditions that face First Nations in Canada and all Aboriginal groups, including Métis, Inuit and non-Status Indians. We want to introduce a snapshot of the demography of Aboriginal Canada. While we have done extensive studies of the data available from the first Aboriginal Peoples Survey (APS), the Census of 1996 and data held by the Department of Indian and Northern Development (DIAND), we are keenly aware that in the next two years, the new Census and new APS data will be released. However, it is not available now. We have opted for securing some summary data from Statistics Canada and DIAND researchers who are currently looking at the unreleased data. These researchers have worked with and published with the First Nations Cohesion Project at Western University.

Demographics impact greatly on the socio-economic capacity of a population. In recent years, the value of demographic analysis has been underscored as key in guiding program planning, research and policy initiatives. Demographic analysis has been used to assist various stakeholders in making informed policy decisions. Statistics are merely simplified descriptions and measured products of complex social processes. They allow us to assess change over time and give us baseline understandings of conditions.

Consistent with our goal of providing the legal framework in which socio-economic development takes place, we offer a brief, albeit informative, overview of the demographical information of Aboriginal Canadians to complement the discussion.

A Demographic Profile

The Aboriginal population has reached its highest level in 160 years in Canada. According to recent data released from the 2001 Census, 1.32 million people reported having at least some Aboriginal ancestry. In fact, over the course of one hundred years, 1901-2001, there has been a massive increase in the number of Aboriginal People, as illustrated in Figure 1.

Figure 1: Population reporting Aboriginal ancestry (origin), Canada, 1901-2001

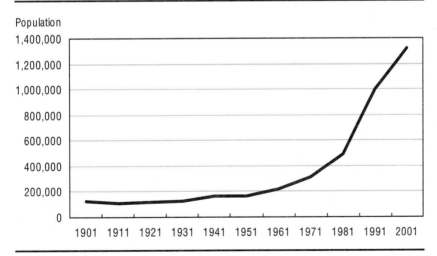

Source: Statistics Canada (2003a).

Table 1 illustrates the magnitude of percentage growth of the Aboriginal ancestry category over the 1996-2001 period–19.8 percent. The Aboriginal population is composed of three main groups: Inuit, Métis and North American Indian. These groups are very diverse and culturally different from one another. North American Indian identity is the largest Aboriginal group in Canada, followed by Métis, Inuit and Multiple and Other Aboriginal (i.e., persons who reported more than one Aboriginal identity group and those who reported being a Registered Indian and/or band member without reporting an Aboriginal identity) response categories. Table 1 also shows the growth of Aboriginal Peoples by identity. The Métis posted the highest growth rate over the 1996-2001 period at 43.2 percent, followed by the Multiple and Other Aboriginal (17.3 percent), North American Indian (15.1 percent) and Inuit (12.1 percent). We should note that the Status Indian population, that is, those who qualify to register and have registered as Status Indians, numbered approximately 554,900 persons in 1996.

Table 1: Size and growth of the population reporting Aboriginal ancestry and Aboriginal identity, Canada, 1996-2001

	2001	1996	Percentage growth 1996-2001
Total: Aboriginal ancestry[1]	1,319,890	1,101,960	19.8
Total: Aboriginal identity	976,305	799,010	22.2
North American Indian[2]	608,850	529,040	15.1
Métis[2]	292,310	204,115	43.2
Inuit[2]	45,070	40,220	12.1
Multiple and other Aboriginal responses[3]	30,080	25,640	17.3

1. Also known as Aboriginal origin.
2. Includes persons who reported a North American Indian, Métis or Inuit identity only.
3. Includes persons who reported more than one Aboriginal identity group (North American Indian, Métis or Inuit) and those who reported being a Registered Indian and/or band member without reporting an Aboriginal identity.

Source: Statistics Canada (2003a).

The Aboriginal population is 3.3 percent of the total Canadian population. This varies dramatically by province and territory as seen in Table 2. The Aboriginal population comprises a majority of the population in Nunavut (85.2 percent) and the Northwest Territories (50.5 percent), as well as a significant proportion of the Yukon (22.9 percent), Manitoba (13.6 percent) and Saskatchewan (13.5 percent). In contrast, this population makes up a small proportion of those living in Prince Edward Island (1.0 percent), Quebec (1.1 percent) and Ontario (1.7 percent) (Statistics Canada 2003a).

Table 2: **Population reporting Aboriginal identity, Canada, provinces and territories, 2001**

	Number	%
Canada	976,310	100.0
Newfoundland and Labrador	18,780	1.9
Prince Edward Island	1,345	0.1
Nova Scotia	17,015	1.7
New Brunswick	16,990	1.7
Quebec	79,400	8.1
Ontario	188,315	19.3
Manitoba	150,040	15.4
Saskatchewan	130,190	13.3
Alberta	156,220	16.0
British Columbia	170,025	17.4
Yukon Territory	6,540	0.7
Northwest Territories	18,725	1.9
Nunavut	22,720	2.3

Source: Statistics Canada (2003a).

While Ontario has one of the lowest proportions of Aboriginal People in Canada, according to their percentage of the total Ontario population, it has the highest percentage of Aboriginal People in Canada (19.3 percent). On the other hand, Nunavut (2.3 percent), Northwest Territories (1.9 percent) and the Yukon Territory (0.7 percent) make up a small proportion of all Aboriginal People in Canada.

According to 2001 Census data, the majority of the non-Aboriginal population resides in urban areas (80.4 percent), with 18.7 percent in urban non-census metropolitan areas and 61.7 percent in urban census metropolitan areas (Statistics Canada 2003b). Further, 19.5 percent reside in rural non-reserve areas, and 0.1 percent on reserve. In contrast, 49.1 percent of the Aboriginal population lives in urban areas. The most popular areas of residence of the Aboriginal population are reserves (31.4 percent) and urban census metropolitan areas (27.8 percent) (Norris and Siggner 2003). Over the 1996-2001 period, however, the percentage of the Aboriginal population living on reserve and in rural non-reserve areas declined by 1.3 percent and 0.9 percent respectively, while those residing in urban non-census metropolitan areas and urban census metropolitan areas increased by 0.6 percent and 1.5 percent respectively. Reserve populations are for all intents and purposes Registered Indians given issues of rights, but there are some non-Status and non-Aboriginal persons that live on reserve.

Age Distribution

The age distribution of the Aboriginal population is markedly different from the non-Aboriginal population. Indeed, the Aboriginal population is significantly younger than the non-Aboriginal population. This is the case for all Aboriginal groups. The median age for the population reporting Aboriginal identity is 13 years younger than the median age for the non-Aboriginal population in 2001, at 24.7 and 37.7 years respectively. Table 3 provides a useful breakdown of the median age of Aboriginal and non-Aboriginal populations throughout Canada. Although the Aboriginal population is younger than the non-Aboriginal population, the former is not homogeneous. In fact, Nunavut has the youngest Aboriginal population in Canada with a median age of 19.1 years, while the Yukon Territory has the oldest Aboriginal population with a median age of 28.6 years.

Table 3: Median age[1] for population reporting Aboriginal identity and non-Aboriginal population, Canada, provinces and territories, 2001

	Median age (years)	
	Aboriginal	Non-Aboriginal
Canada	**24.7**	**37.7**
Newfoundland and Labrador	27.7	38.5
Prince Edward Island	24.6	37.4
Nova Scotia	25.3	38.7
New Brunswick	28.2	38.5
Quebec	27.9	38.5
Ontario	27.9	37.1
Manitoba	22.8	38.5
Saskatchewan	20.1	38.8
Alberta	23.4	35.4
British Columbia	26.8	38.7
Yukon Territory	28.6	37.7
Northwest Territories	24.0	34.5
Nunavut	19.1	35.2

1. Median age is the point at which exactly one-half of the population is older, and the other half is younger.

Source: Statistics Canada (2003a).

As noted, the Aboriginal population is younger than the non-Aboriginal population, with over half of the former population between 0 and 24 years as seen in Table 4. Over the 1996-2001 period, however, there has been an increase in the 25-64 years category (43.4 percent to 45.4 percent) and the 65 years and over category (3.5 percent to 4.1 percent), which indicates that the Aboriginal population is ageing.

Table 4: Population reporting Aboriginal identity, by age groups, Canada, 1996 and 2001

	2001		1996	
	Number	%	Number	%
Total	**976,305**	**100.0**	**799,010**	**100.0**
0 to 14 years	323,960	33.2	280,420	35.1
15 to 24 years	169,065	17.3	143,795	18.0
25 to 64 years	443,600	45.4	346,485	43.4
65 years and over	39,680	4.1	28,310	3.5

Source: Statistics Canada (2003a).

Fertility and Life Expectancy

Fertility levels are much higher among Aboriginal women than for the general population. As of the 2001 Census, the total Canadian population fertility rate is 1.56, which is below replacement level. When we examine fertility by Aboriginal identity group, estimated births per woman are highest for the Inuit (3.21), followed by the North American Indian (2.81) and Métis (2.15), as seen in Figure 2. The fertility levels have, however, decreased for all Aboriginal identity groups between the 1986-1991 and 1996-2001 periods.

Figure 2: Estimated births per woman, by Aboriginal identity group and total Canadian population, Canada, 1986-1991 and 1996-2001

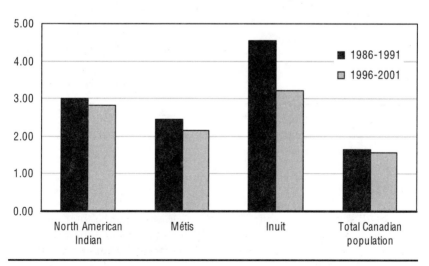

Source: Norris and Siggner (2003).

Although the life expectancy of the Registered Indian population is lower than the total Canadian population, there are key differences between the two sexes. In the total Canadian population, females outlive males. The life expectancy at birth among the Aboriginal population follows the same pattern as the total Canadian population, with females outliving males. Figure 3 indicates that, since 1975, the life expectancy at birth of the Aboriginal population has increased. Registered Indian males fare worse than their female counterparts, with the former's life expectancy at birth being 69 years and the latter's, 76 years. Registered Indian females have caught up to the total Canadian male population, but still lag behind the total Canadian female population by over 5 years. Registered Indian males are far behind the total Canadian population, with a life expectancy at birth of about 13 years less than the female population and about 7 years less than the male population. In terms of within-group differences, Registered Indian females have gained slightly more in life expectancy over the 25-year period than Registered Indian males, and they also hold a 7-year advantage over the latter.

Figure 3:   Life expectancy at birth, by gender, Registered Indian and total Canadian populations, Canada, 1975-2000

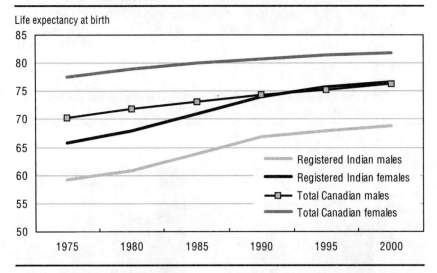

Source: Norris and Siggner (2003).

Health

The health status of Aboriginal Peoples is lower than the total Canadian population, when examined subjectively and objectively. In terms of self-rated health, the Aboriginal population is less likely to report excellent or very good health than the total Canadian population at all ages. There is a striking pattern in the data: Aboriginal Peoples on reserves are the least likely to report excellent or very good health; and Aboriginal Peoples residing in non-reserve areas are more likely to report excellent or very good health than the on-reserve population but less likely to report excellent or very good health compared to the total Canadian population. Thus, while the Aboriginal population rate their own health lower than the general population, there is heterogeneity in the Aboriginal population by area of residence.

Objective measures of health are a useful complement to subjective measures. The objective data concur with the self-rated health trends discussed above and show that rates of chronic conditions, including arthritis or rheumatism, high blood pressure, asthma and diabetes are for the most part higher among the Aboriginal population than the total Canadian population (see Figure 4). Especially noteworthy is the gap between the Aboriginal population on reserve and the total Canadian population with respect to diabetes. The on-reserve population has a rate of diabetes nearly 3.7 times that of the national population. Interestingly, the percentage of Aboriginal people reporting asthma on reserves is 3 percent less than the total Canadian population, while the percentage of non-reserve Aboriginal population reporting asthma is 2 percent higher than the total Canadian population. This might indicate that environmental issues connected to urban living may play a role in the differential percentages of reported asthma.

Figure 4: Aboriginal identity population in selected reserves and non-reserve areas compared to the total Canadian population reporting selected chronic conditions, Canada, APS 2001 and CCHS 2000/01

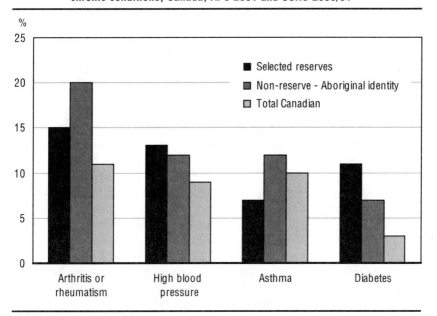

Source: Norris and Siggner (2003).

Migration and Mobility

Migration by area of residence for the Aboriginal population illustrates a high churn effect, as seen in Figure 5 for the year 2000-2001. The on-reserve and urban census metropolitan areas were the recipients of migrants from rural non-reserve and urban census metropolitan areas, which both had negative net migration rates of 1.8 percent and 0.4 percent respectively. Rural non-reserve and urban non-census metropolitan areas have the highest churn effects.

Figure 5: **Rate of in-, out-, and net migration in the population reporting Aboriginal identity, by area of residence, Canada, 2000-2001**

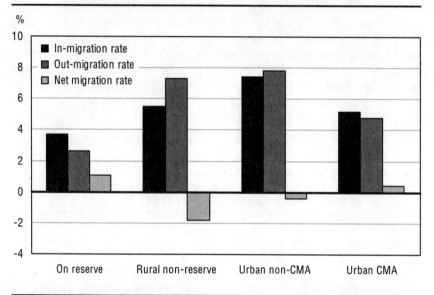

Source: Norris and Siggner (2003).

The Aboriginal population is very mobile. While 14.3 percent of the total Canadian population moved over the twelve-month period before the 2001 Census, this figure was much higher for the Aboriginal population at 22 percent. Most of the movement (14 percent) was within the same census subdivision, followed by 6.2 percent within the same province and/or territory or from a different census subdivision, and 1.8 percent from a different province and/or territory or country. The Aboriginal population in Saskatchewan (25.3 percent), Alberta (24.8 percent) and British Columbia (24.8 percent) posted the highest rates of mobility and the lowest in Newfoundland/Labrador (13.8 percent), Quebec (15.3 percent) and New Brunswick (16.2 percent) (Statistics Canada 2003c).

Culture

There are few if any accurate ways of measuring cultural retention among any peoples. One blunt measure can be the retention of traditional language. The Census gives us data on the number of people reporting knowledge of a traditional language. We have no way of knowing what the level of knowledge actually is for those reporting; therefore, this has to be taken as a simple indicator. What the 2001 Census does tell us is that Aboriginal respondents reporting knowledge dropped from 29.2 percent in 1996 to 24 percent in 2001 for all age categories. Data indicates that the younger the age group, the smaller the percentage of people reporting knowledge of an Aboriginal language. This is the same finding reported in the study by Norris and Maccon (2003).

Similarly, when knowledge of Aboriginal language is examined by Aboriginal identity groups in Figure 6, it is found that all three groups, North American Indian, Métis and Inuit, report a decrease over the 1996-2001 period. There are, however, considerable differences between these three groups with the Inuit (70.8 percent) most likely to have knowledge of an Aboriginal language, followed by North American Indians (30.3 percent) and the Métis (5.2 percent), in 2001.

Figure 6: Knowledge of Aboriginal language among the Aboriginal identity groups, Canada, 2001 Census

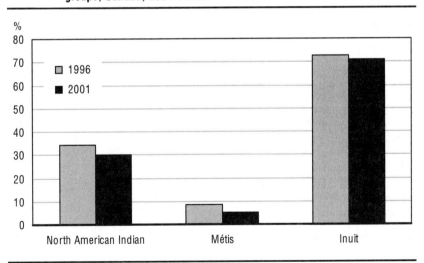

Source: Norris and Siggner (2003).

Family Structure

The living arrangements of Aboriginal children under 15 years of age are quite different than non-Aboriginal children. Data, reported in Table 5, indicate that the percentage of non-Aboriginal children living with two parents (82.5 percent) is considerably higher than Aboriginal children (60.5 percent), while a greater percentage of Aboriginal children live with a lone parent (35.4 percent) compared to non-Aboriginal children (16.9 percent). Under the category of "other living arrangements," which includes living with other relatives or non-relatives, Aboriginal children (4.0 percent) are more likely to live in these types of households than non-Aboriginals (0.6 percent). When broken down by area of residence, it is found that the lowest percentage of Aboriginal children living with two parents and the highest percentage of Aboriginal children living with a lone parent is in urban census metropolitan areas, while the opposite is true in rural non-reserve areas.

Table 5: Living arrangements of Aboriginal and non-Aboriginal children under 15 years of age, by area of residence,[1] Canada, 2001

	Aboriginal children[2]	Non-Aboriginal children
	%	%
All areas of residence		
Living with two parents	60.5	82.5
Living with a lone parent	35.4	16.9
Other living arrangements[3]	4.0	0.6
On reserve		
Living with two parents	65.0	...
Living with a lone parent	31.9	...
Other living arrangements[3]	3.2	...
Rural non-reserve		
Living with two parents	71.4	88.5
Living with a lone parent	23.3	10.9
Other living arrangements[3]	5.3	0.7
Urban non-CMA		
Living with two parents	56.9	79.5
Living with a lone parent	39.6	19.9
Other living arrangements[3]	3.5	0.5
Urban CMA		
Living with two parents	49.8	81.4
Living with a lone parent	45.6	18.0
Other living arrangements[3]	4.6	0.6

1. For a full description of area of residence, see <http://www12.statcan.ca/english/census01/products/analytic/ companion/abor/tables/definitions.cfm> for definitions of terms used in this document.
2. Those children reported as having an Aboriginal identity.
3. Includes living with other relatives, e.g., an uncle or aunt, or with non-relatives.
... Not applicable.
Source: Statistics Canada (2003a).

Housing Conditions

The living conditions of the Aboriginal population are at a lower standard than the total Canadian population. According to the 2001 Census, 7.6 percent of the total population in Canada lives in overcrowded dwellings[1] while 51.7 percent of Aboriginals residing in the North[2] report overcrowding, followed by 41.5 percent of those on reserves and over 12 percent in urban and other settings. It is important to note that the percentage of Aboriginal People living in overcrowded conditions has decreased significantly over the 1996-2001 period but remains too high (Norris and Siggner 2003).

Another indicator of living conditions, Aboriginal dwellings needing major repairs, reveals that the number of Aboriginal dwellings requiring repairs is 2.4 times higher than all dwellings in Canada (Norris and Siggner 2003).

Education, Employment and Income

Figure 7 indicates that over the 1996-2001 period, the percentage of Aboriginals aged 25-34 years completing less than high school has dropped by 6.4 percent, while the percentage of Aboriginals completing higher levels of education has increased across all categories, including high school and some post-secondary schooling not completed (1.8 percent), trades or college (2.1 percent) and university (2.4 percent).

Figure 7: Highest level of educational attainment for Aboriginal identity population aged 25-34 years, Canada, 2001

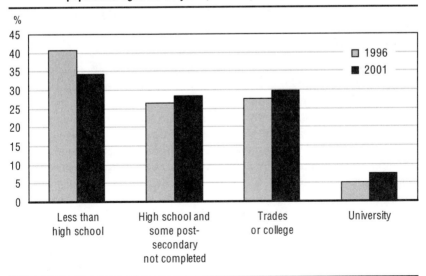

Source: Norris and Siggner (2003).

The primary reason cited for withdrawing from school differs between males and females. In 2001, the reason most cited for not finishing post-secondary schooling among males is financial (24.0 percent), and for females, family responsibilities (34.0 percent). A large number of females also report finances as a very important reason for dropping out (21 percent) (Norris and Siggner 2003).

The Aboriginal population has a lower employment rate than the non-Aboriginal population when examined by area of residence and age group. The data from 2001 show that, regardless of area of residence, the employment rate of Aboriginal People is lower than the non-Aboriginal population, with figures of 49.7 percent and 61.8 percent respectively. These figures, however, disguise key differences within the Aboriginal population. The magnitude of the disparity in employment rate between the two populations and within the Aboriginal population is, indeed, variable depending upon area of residence. In the case of Aboriginal people residing in urban census metropolitan areas, the employment rate within the Aboriginal group is highest at 56.7 percent, while on-reserve the rate is lowest at 37.7 percent – a 19 percent difference. Differences between Aboriginal and non-Aboriginal People are highest in rural non-reserve areas (8.9 percent), and lowest in urban non-census metropolitan areas (5.4 percent). The general trend is that employment rates increase in the following order for Aboriginal People: on-reserve (37.7 percent), rural non-reserve (52.1 percent), urban non-census metropolitan areas (52.9 percent), and urban census metropolitan areas (56.7 percent). When we examine Aboriginal employment rates relative to the non-Aboriginal population by age group, the data indicate lower levels of employment at all levels for the former compared to the latter. One last finding of note is that, as education increases, so does the employment level of the Aboriginal population (Norris and Siggner 2003).

The income of Aboriginal Peoples is significantly less than the total Canadian population, although this gap has decreased between 1995 and 2000, as indicated in Figure 8. In 1995, the median total income for the Aboriginal population was 58.4 percent of the total Canadian population median total income. By the year 2000, this figure had increased to 61.4 percent. Over the course of the five-year period, the median total income increased 13.2 percent for the Aboriginal population and 7.6 percent for the total Canadian population. Maxim, White and Beavon (2002) found there are differences between the Aboriginal groups. Registered Indians, particularly on-reserve, have the lowest incomes while Métis and non-Status Indians have higher incomes. All groups are below the income levels of the non-Aboriginal population (Maxim et al. 2002).

Figure 8: **Median total income of persons 15 years of age and older, Aboriginal identity and total Canadian populations, Canada, 1995 and 2000 (in constant 2000 dollars)**

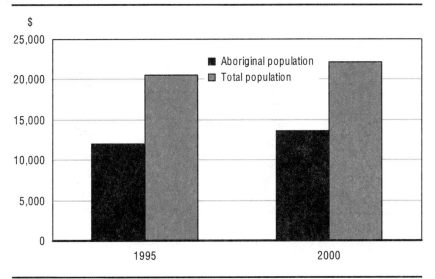

Source: Norris and Siggner (2003).

Total income is a product of numerous sources in Canadian society. It is common to differentiate between earned income and government transfers when discussing total income. In 1995 the total income for the Aboriginal population was composed primarily of earnings (70.2 percent), government transfers (26.1 percent) and other money (3.7 percent) (see Figure 9). Five years later in 2000, a larger percentage of Aboriginal income was received through earnings (75.1 percent) and other money (4.1 percent), while a lower percentage was derived from government transfers (20.8 percent). Aboriginal People receive a lower proportion of their income from earnings and other money than the total Canadian population, and a greater percentage of their income from government transfers; however this gap has closed (Norris and Siggner 2003; see also Maxim, White and Beavon 2002).

Figure 9: Major source of income distribution, Aboriginal identity and total Canadian populations, Canada, 1995 and 2000

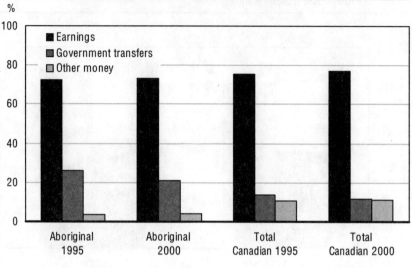

Source: Norris and Siggner (2003).

We have tried to give the reader a basic overview of key demographic and socio-economic circumstances facing all Aboriginal Peoples and Registered Indians in particular. We now will introduce the structure and basic contents of the book to help guide the reader.

Content Overview

This volume is organized with many sections and subsections to facilitate access and comprehensibility. In the first section of the book, the basic principles of Aboriginal rights are covered, with an examination of the history of the Aboriginal title, and the rights therein. Special attention is given to the *Constitution Act, 1982,* which for the first time articulated explicit constitutional recognition and affirmation of Aboriginal and treaty rights. Next, the connection between rights to land and resources and the notion of Aboriginal title is outlined. The idea of the treaty as a sacred exchange between the Crown and Aboriginal societies and related historical clarification outlining the nature, interpretation and grounds for infringement of treaty rights is discussed. The fiduciary relationship between the Crown and Aboriginal Peoples is described, and its impact on treaties, legislation and various documents relating to Aboriginal Peoples is given strict attention.

The second section addresses legislative authority and the division of powers at the federal and provincial and/or territorial levels. It covers the federal regulation of resources on reserve lands and provides an extensive look at the *Indian Act, Indian Oil and Gas Act,* Federal-Provincial Resource Agreements on Reserve Land, *Fisheries Act, Migratory Birds Convention Act,* and *First Nations Land Management Act.*

The third section of the book provides an in-depth, province-by-province breakdown of the major provincial and territorial legislation and treaties in Canada. Issues covered in this section revolve around natural resources, such as those related to hunting, fishing, forestry, water and mining and the relations between provinces and/or territories and Canada. There is a presentation of case law (i.e., law established by judicial decisions in particular cases, instead of by legislative action) throughout the book. Also, there are subsections provided that address issues unique to certain regions of Canada; for example, the subsections on Modern Agreements and Treaties (e.g., the Nisga'a of British Columbia) and Current Land Claims (e.g., Atikamekw and Montagnais Claims) identify the key modern treaty and legislative issues. Landmark cases that have affected subsequent decisions related to various First Nations legal issues are found throughout this work. Again, the world marches on and readers should be aware that these issues can change rapidly.

Conclusion

The socio-economic development of a nation or community can have profound effects on an individual's or community's quality of life. As alluded to in our discussion earlier, a critical component of this volume is to promote an approach to First Nations socio-economic development issues that is inclusive in scope. To discuss educational issues does not require advanced education in economics, sociology and political science, but it does require a willingness to be cognizant of economic, sociological and political issues in the process of contextualizing and understanding the impediments to increasing attainment and well-being. Similarly, understanding the basic legal framework of Aboriginal People in Canada does not require specialized training or education. What is necessary is a willingness to step back from our own areas of expertise and connect what may appear at first to be disjointed issues. This process leads one to see that one of the "ties that bind" socio-economic phenomena is the legal framework of society.

We again remind the reader that this volume is only current to 2002 (with some 2003 references). This book is unique in that legislative and treaty comparisons across geographical boundaries can be made. It captures the similarities between Aboriginal Canadians while acknowledging their diversity as reflected in the politico-legal milieu. The authors of this book are pleased to produce a resource for a diverse group of people, including scholars, students and policy-makers, which will assist them in their professional endeavours. The references in this book are invaluable with over one hundred rich sources, including books, reports, articles and online resources. Readers will find these sources useful and diverse, covering the legal framework as well as other salient topics. We hope this volume helps people come to a better understanding of the complexities involved in building community economic and social well-being.

References

Beavon, Dan, and Martin Cook. 2003. An Application of the United Nations Human Development Index to Registered Indians in Canada, 1996. In White, Jerry P., Paul Maxim and Dan Beavon. (Eds) *Aboriginal Conditions: Research as a Foundation for Public Policy*. Vancouver: University of British Columbia Press.

Maxim, P., Jerry White and Dan Beavon. 2002. "Dispersion and Polarization of Income among Aboriginal and Non Aboriginal Canadians." *Canadian Review of Sociology and Anthropology*.

Norris D., and A. Siggner. 2003. "What Census and the Aboriginal Peoples Survey Tell Us About Aboriginal Conditions in Canada." Presented at the 2003 Aboriginal Strategies Conference, Edmonton Alberta. Available online at <http://209.123.49.177/~statcan/presentations/dougnorris01.pdf>.

Norris, Mary-Jane, and Karen Maccon. 2003. Aboriginal Language Transmission and Maintenance in Families: Results of an Intergenerational and Gender-Based Analysis for Canada. In White, Jerry P., Paul Maxim and Dan Beavon. (Eds) *Aboriginal Conditions: Research as a Foundation for Public Policy*. Vancouver: University of British Columbia Press.

Statistics Canada. 2003a. "Aboriginal Peoples of Canada." Online at: <http://www12.statcan.ca/english/census01/products/analytic/companion/abor/canada.cfm>.

———. 2003b. "Aboriginal Identity, Age Groups, Sex and Area of Residence for Population, for Canada, Provinces and Territories, 2001 Census — 20 percent Sample Data." Ottawa: Statistics Canada. Catalogue number 97F0011XCB01001.

———. 2003c. "Aboriginal Peoples of Canada: Highlight Tables 2001 Census." Ottawa: Statistics Canada. Catalogue number 97F0024XIE2001007.

Endnotes

1. Overcrowding is defined as one or more persons per room per dwelling.

2. North includes Labrador, Nunavik/Quebec, Nunavut, Inuvialuit Region/NWT.

Part 1

Basic Principles

Chapter 1

Aboriginal Rights

For the most part, Aboriginal Peoples have been forced to rely on the courts to provide for recognition of their rights and to affirm their interests in Aboriginal tribal lands. The *Constitution Act, 1982*[1] provided, for the first time, explicit constitutional recognition and affirmation of Aboriginal and treaty rights. Section 35(1) gives constitutional validity to Aboriginal rights:

Section 35

(1) The existing Aboriginal and treaty rights of the Aboriginal Peoples of Canada are hereby recognized and affirmed.

(2) In this Act, "Aboriginal Peoples of Canada" includes the Indian, Inuit and Métis peoples of Canada.

(3) For greater certainty, in subsection (1) "treaty rights" includes rights that now exist by way of land claims agreements or may be so acquired.

(4) Notwithstanding any other provision of this Act, the Aboriginal and treaty rights referred to in subsection (1) are guaranteed equally to male and female persons.

This means that proven Aboriginal rights are supreme and will trump any inconsistent common law, federal or provincial legislation, subject to certain limits developed by the courts over the last decade.

R. v. Van der Peet[2] confirmed:

The doctrine of Aboriginal rights exists, and is recognized and affirmed by s. 35(1), because of one simple fact: when Europeans arrived in North America, Aboriginal Peoples were already here, living in communities, on the land, and participating in distinctive cultures as they had done for centuries.[3]

---

[1] R.S.C. 1985, App. II, No. 44, being Schedule B of the *Canada Act 1982* (U.K.), 1982, c.11.

[2] *R. v. Van der Peet*, [1996] 4 C.N.L.R. 177 (S.C.C.).

[3] *Ibid.* para. 30.

Aboriginal rights pre-existed the 1982 constitutional amendment, so the *Constitution Act, 1982* is not the legal origin or basis of Aboriginal rights. Such rights have been fully recognized at common law even in absence of the constitutional confirmation.

Origins of Aboriginal Title

Rights to land and resources are intertwined with the notion of Aboriginal title.

A starting point for understanding the nature and scope of Aboriginal title is the *Royal Proclamation of 1763*.[4] The *Royal Proclamation* effectively consolidated Great Britain's rule over North America, while recognizing the right of Aboriginal People to occupy their traditional lands.[5] Exclusive jurisdiction over the newly acquired territories in North America was claimed by imperial authorities, giving the Crown a monopoly on land transactions between Aboriginal nations and lands within their occupation. The Crown justified their exclusive jurisdiction by reason of the fact that "great Frauds and Abuses" had been committed against the Aboriginal People in the purchase of their lands, therefore the Crown prohibited settlers, and anyone else, from purchasing their land. The *Royal Proclamation* effectively gave the Crown the sole right of acquiring land from Aboriginal People.

This exclusive right of acquisition remains with the Crown today and has been given force of law as of 1982 in the *Canadian Charter of Rights and Freedoms*.[6] Section 25 of the *Charter* guarantees that the rights and freedoms contained within are not to be construed as to abrogate or derogate from an Aboriginal, treaty or other rights or freedoms, including those that were recognized by the *Royal Proclamation*. Until the *Charter* came into effect, the *Royal Proclamation* merely had the force of any other federal Act, and as such the rights and guarantees contained within it could be limited, altered or overridden by any subsequent federal legislation.

Three American decisions of *Johnson and Graham's Lesee v. M'Intosh*,[7] *Cherokee Nation v. Georgia*[8] and *Worcester v. Georgia*[9] involving breaches of the *Royal Proclamation* discussed the origins of Aboriginal title. The court in all three decisions affirmed both Aboriginal title to their traditional lands and also the Crown monopoly on land dealings, as derived from the *Royal Proclamation of 1763*.

---

[4] *Royal Proclamation of 1763*, R.S.C. 1985, App. II, No. 1.
[5] *R. v. Sparrow*, [1990] 1 S.C.R. 1075 at 177.
[6] Part I of the *Constitution Act, 1982, supra* note 1.
[7] *Johnson and Graham's Lessee v. M'Intosh* (1823), 8 Wheaton 543 (U.S.S. Ct.).
[8] *Cherokee Nation v. Georgia*, 30 U.S. (5 Pet.) 1 (1831).
[9] *Worcester v. Georgia*, 31 U.S. (6 Pet.) 515 (1832).

In the Privy Council decision of *St. Catherine's Milling and Lumber Co. v. R.*[10] in 1887, Lord Watson defined the right of Aboriginal Peoples to land as a "personal and usufructory right, dependent upon the good will of the Sovereign" that could be surrendered only to Crown authorities. The term "usufructuary right" has been defined as the right of temporary possession and enjoyment of the advantages of property belonging to another, so far as may be had without causing damage or prejudice to the land. Judicial authority on the ambit of usufruct in Canada is confined to *obita dicta*, or the mere opinion of the court. Such *dicta* have been consistent and have recognized the rudiments of the civilian notion of the usufruct.[11]

The existence of Aboriginal title in the common law was confirmed in *R. v. Calder*[12] where the court agreed that Aboriginal title existed independently of legislation, executive orders or treaties. Instead, this title is a legal right derived from traditional occupation and use of tribal lands. In *R. v. Guerin*[13] the court found that Aboriginal title is a special type of right that is *sui generis* in nature and best characterized by its "inalienability" coupled by an obligation on the Crown to "deal with the land on the Indians' behalf when the interest is surrendered."[14]

Roberts v. Canada[15] affirmed the common law basis of Aboriginal title and that the Federal Court of Canada has the jurisdiction to deal with such title. Furthermore, in the Supreme Court decision of *R. v. Smith*[16] the court held that, once Aboriginal title to land is surrendered, the rights associated with the title are extinguished, the land is no longer considered to be "reserve land" as per section 91(24) of the *Constitution Act, 1867*[17] and the land becomes Crown land.

Generally speaking, the issue of Aboriginal title only arises where land has not been the subject of a treaty signed between Aboriginal Peoples and the Crown, or where the issue of extinguishment is still a matter of contention. Lands that are not covered by an existing treaty remain open to Aboriginal title claims. In order to determine the existence of Aboriginal rights sufficient to give rise to Aboriginal title, continued use and occupancy of the land are important elements.

---

[10] *Saint Catherine's Milling and Lumber Co. v. R.*, 2 C.N.L.C. 541 (J.C.P.C.) at 549.

[11] See *Calder v. A-G of British Columbia*, [1973] S.C.R. 313; *R. v. Isaac* (1975), 8 C.N.L.R. 493 (N.S.C.A.); *A-G of Ontario v. Bear Island Foundation* [1991] 3 C.N.L.R. 79 (S.C.C.).

[12] *R. v. Calder*, [1973] S.C.R. 313.

[13] *R. v. Guerin*, [1984] 2 S.C.R. 335.

[14] *Ibid.* at 136.

[15] *Roberts v. Canada*, [1989] 2 C.N.L.R. 146 (S.C.C.).

[16] *R. v. Smith*, [1983] 3 C.N.L.R. 161 (S.C.C.).

[17] *Constitution Act, 1867*, 30 & 31 Vict., c. 3 (U.K.), (R.S.C. 1985, App II, No. 5).

The court has held that Aboriginal title is but one aspect of Aboriginal People's common law rights that are now protected by the Constitution. In *R. v. Van der Peet*,[18] Chief Justice Lamer affirmed that "Aboriginal title is a subcategory of Aboriginal rights which deals solely with claims of rights to land." Aboriginal rights are, therefore, not inexorably linked to Aboriginal title, but can exist independently. Aboriginal rights have been said to lie on a "spectrum."[19] Rights relating to traditional practices and customs of Aboriginal Peoples (whether associated to land or not) lie at one end of the spectrum and Aboriginal title to land lies at the other. Notably, the "occupation and use of the land" at the location of the activity is not "sufficient to support a claim of title to the land." However, constitutional protection is still afforded to those activities.

Aboriginal title can thus arise from the historic use and occupation of lands, from the Royal Proclamation of 1763 and from the common law. Aboriginal title is thus a burden on the Crown's title.

Identifying the Content of Aboriginal Rights

Prior to 1996, Canadian courts had not addressed the method of determining the *content* of Aboriginal rights. The Supreme Court of Canada had the opportunity to do so in a series of cases in the mid-1990s, the decisions of which have clarified, to some extent, the manner in which the content of Aboriginal rights is to be ascertained. In the first case of *R. v. Van der Peet*,[20] Van der Peet had been awarded an Aboriginal food-fishing licence under the *British Columbia Fishery (General) Regulations*,[21] which allowed her to catch salmon for food in accordance with the ancient traditions of her Sto:lo Nation Band. She was charged under the *Fisheries Act*[22] for selling fish contrary to the provisions of her licence. Van der Peet subsequently claimed that the restrictions contained in the licence were contrary to her Aboriginal rights as enshrined in the *Constitution Act* of 1982. The majority of the court found that a purposive approach is to be taken to identify which rights are recognized and affirmed under section 35. This section is to be afforded a generous and liberal interpretation on account of the fiduciary nature of the relationship between the Crown and Aboriginal Peoples. Chief Justice

---

[18] *Ibid.* para. 74.

[19] Mainville, R., *An Overview of Aboriginal and Treaty Rights and Compensation for their Breach*, Purich Publishers, Saskatoon, 2001, p. 25; determined in *R. v. Van Der Peet supra* note 2 and *R. v. Adams* [1996], 3 S.C.R. 101 (S.C.C.).

[20] *R. v. Van der Peet, supra* note 2.

[21] *British Columbia Fishery (General) Regulations*, SOR/84-248.

[22] *Fisheries Act*, R.S.C. 1970, c. F-14.

Lamer, rendering the majority opinion, held that any interpretation of section 35 must "aim at identifying the practices, traditions and customs central to the Aboriginal societies that existed in North America *prior to contact with the Europeans.*"[23] In order to determine whether the activity in question was central to the Aboriginal society that existed at that time, the activity or practice must be proven to be an integral part of the fibre of that society. As such, there is no such thing as a set of universal Aboriginal rights, as these must be determined on a case-by-case basis and will be specific to the community in question. Furthermore, upon the court's interpretation, the activity must still be an integral element of the personality of the community seeking constitutional protection of that right. The methodology adopted by the court led to a conclusion that the sale of fish by a member of the Sto:lo society was not a constitutionally protected right, as fish trading had only become an established practice *after* the arrival of Europeans to North America. This reasoning has been adopted and applied in various other cases since.

Content of Aboriginal Title

The leading case on determining the content of Aboriginal title is *Delgamuukw v. British Columbia.*[24] The case of *Delgamuukw v. British Columbia* involved the Gitksan and Wet'suwet'en people of northwestern British Columbia, who sought a declaration from the court affirming their ownership, jurisdiction and Aboriginal rights over 58,000 square kilometres of British Columbia territory.

Ultimately *R. v. Delgamuukw* was not decided and was sent back to a lower court for a new trial, having been rejected by the Supreme Court of Canada for determination due to procedural difficulties. The court did, however, affirm that Aboriginal title, being part of the wider conception of Aboriginal rights, is afforded constitutional protection. The interest in land cannot be understood under traditional property laws. Aboriginal title to land is not like fee simple, but is instead a *sui generis* interest in land.

The court identified the basic characteristics of this interest:

1. the inalienability of title, except to the Crown in right of Canada;
2. the origin of that interest stemming from prior occupation; and,
3. the collective nature of all the members of the Aboriginal society concerned and not by an individual.

---

[23] *R. v. Van der Peet, supra* note 2, para. 44.
[24] *Delgamuukw v. British Columbia*, [1998] 1 C.N.L.R. 14 (S.C.C.).

On the basis of the methodology adopted in *R. v. Van der Peet*, the court held that the right of Aboriginal title must be established by proof of occupation of land prior to the assertion of sovereignty by the Crown.

As Chief Justice Lamer noted in *Delgamuukw v. British Columbia*,[25] "the content of common law Aboriginal title...has not been authoritatively determined by the Court."[26] His Lordship summarized the content of the right as follows:

> ...the content of Aboriginal title can be summarized by two propositions: first, that Aboriginal title encompasses the right to exclusive use and occupation of the land held pursuant to that title for a variety of purposes, which need not be aspects of those Aboriginal practices, customs and traditions which are integral to distinctive Aboriginal cultures; and second, that those protected uses must not be irreconcilable with the nature of the group's attachment to that land.[27]

Once Aboriginal title has been established, the Aboriginal nation concerned is not constrained to practice solely those activities on which their title was established, but are free to use their land, including all resources pertaining to it, on an exclusive basis for any purpose that is not completely incompatible with their traditional practices on that land. In other words, activities that would sever the relationship of Aboriginal People to their land would not be justified by Aboriginal title. In practical terms, it is not absolutely certain what this means.

---

[25] *Ibid.*

[26] *Ibid.* para. 75.

[27] *Ibid.* para. 117.

Chapter 2
Treaty Rights

Nature of Treaty Rights

Treaty rights arise out of negotiations between Aboriginal Peoples and the Crown. Treaty rights have been given constitutional recognition and affirmation in section 35(1) of the *Constitution Act, 1982*. Treaty rights are not only afforded constitutional protection, but section 88 of the *Indian Act*[1] also protects treaty rights from incumbent provincial legislation.

Although many cases have dealt with clarification of treaty rights in recent times, with each decision the developing body of law has become increasingly complex on one hand and increasingly vague on the other. Accordingly there is much ambiguity surrounding the nature and scope of Aboriginal treaty rights. For the most part, treaties arising out of negotiations between Aboriginal Peoples and the Crown have been treated as legal instruments.

Canadian courts have held that each treaty is to be treated as unique and to be governed by public law rules.[2]

The courts have reiterated on many occasions that treaty rights are *sui generis* in nature and are held collectively by Aboriginal societies, not individually.

Chief Justice Lamer in *R. v. Sioui*,[3] relying on the Ontario Court of Appeal decision in *R. v. Taylor and Williams*,[4] found five non-exhaustive questions to be considered when determining whether the parties intended to conclude an Aboriginal treaty:

1. Has the right been consistently exercised in both the past and present?

---

[1] *Indian Act*, R.S.C., 1985, c. I-5, s. 88.

[2] *R. v. Simon*, [1986] 2 S.C.R. 387 at 404, and *R. v. Sioui*, [1990] 1 S.C.R. 1025 at 1043.

[3] *R. v. Sioui*, Ibid.

[4] *R. v. Taylor and Williams*, [1981] 3 C.N.L.R. 114 (Ont. C.A.).

2. What are the reasons for the Crown's commitments?
3. What were the prevailing circumstances at the time of the signing of the document?
4. What evidence is available of relations between the parties at the time of the signing of the document?
5. What was the ensuing conduct of both parties?[5]

In *R. v. Sioui*, despite the fact that the document omitted the territorial scope of the treaty, the court derived from the contextual history surrounding the conclusion of the treaty that the document in question was intended to be limited to those parts of the territory frequented by the Huron nation where exercise of traditional activities did not conflict with the Crown's alternative land use.[6]

Treaty rights are not restricted to actual rights documented in the written text of the treaty, but also extend to incidental rights. In *R. v. Sundown*,[7] Mr. Sundown was charged for entering a provincial park, cutting down trees and building a log cabin, a prohibited act without permission under provincial bylaws. In his defence, Mr. Sundown raised Treaty 6, which secured Aboriginal Peoples' right to hunt, fish and trap. Treaty 6 had been modified by the *Natural Resources Transfer Agreement* of 1930, which had transferred ownership of natural resources from the federal to the provincial government of Saskatchewan. The Agreement (constitutionally recognized in the *Constitution Act, 1930*[8]) effectively extinguished the treaty right to hunt commercially, but the area in which the right to hunt for food could be exercised was expanded. The principle established by Chief Justice Dickson in *R. v. Simon* was applied: "[t]he right to hunt to be effective must embody those activities reasonably incidental to the act of hunting itself."[9]

The court took into evidence the traditional practices of the Joseph Bighead First Nation, which had included expeditions that could last for weeks at a time. The court found that building a hunter's cabin was reasonably incidental to the right of members of that First Nation to hunt. The court discussed the nature of treaty rights, emphasizing the *sui generis* and collective elements of such rights.

---

[5] *R. v. Sioui, supra* note 2, at 1045.
[6] *Ibid.* at 1071.
[7] *R. v. Sundown*, [1999] 1 S.C.R. 393.
[8] *Constitution Act*, 1930, R.S.C., 1985, app. II, no. 26.
[9] *R. v. Simon, supra* note 2, at 403 cited in *R. v. Sundown, supra* note 7, at 408-409, para. 27.

Treaty Interpretation

Treaties have been found interpreted as constituting a solemn exchange of promises between the Crown and Aboriginal societies. The treaty is sacred and places an important obligation on the Crown to fulfil its side of the undertaking.

Special principles of interpretation apply to Aboriginal treaties.

- Treaties are to be interpreted broadly and liberally.[10]
- Treaties are not to be interpreted in a vacuum — all contextual and historical information must be taken into account to aid in their interpretation — that includes any historical and oral traditions.[11]
- Any oral evidence surrounding the negotiations can be used to aid interpretation of the treaty.[12]
- Evidence of conduct or discussions at the time of negotiations as to how the parties understood the treaty is to be of assistance in giving it content.[13]
- The fiduciary relationship extends to treaties, and in interpreting and applying the terms of a treaty, the courts will always consider the underlying fiduciary relationship. Where the Crown assumes certain obligations in executing those obligations, the Crown will normally be held to the standards of execution required under that relationship.[14]
- Treaties should be interpreted in a manner that upholds the honour of the Crown and does not sanction the appearance of "sharp dealing."[15]
- Any ambiguities as to the terms of the treaty are to be interpreted in favour of the Aboriginal Peoples concerned.[16]
- Treaties should not be interpreted to the prejudice of the First Nations society concerned if another construction is reasonably possible.[17]

---

[10] *R. v. White and Bob*, 6 C.N.L.L.C. 684 (S.C.C.).

[11] *R. v. Taylor and Williams*, *supra* note 4.

[12] *Ibid.*

[13] *Claxton v. Saanichton Marina Ltd.*, [1989] 3 C.N.L.R. 46 at 50 (B.C.C.A.).

[14] *Ontario (A-G) v. Bear Island Foundation*, *supra* note 11 in ch. 1; *Ontario v. Dominion of Canada and Quebec: In Re Indian Claims* (1898), 30 S.C.R. 151.

[15] *R. v. Taylor and Williams*, *supra* note 4.

[16] *Ibid.*

[17] *Claxton v. Saanichton Marina Ltd.*, *supra* note 13.

- The onus of proving that treaty rights have been extinguished resides with the Crown.[18]
- Strict proof of extinguishment and a clear and plain intention to do so is required.[19]
- Prior to the *Constitution Act, 1982*, treaty rights could be unilaterally extinguished by the federal government.[20]
- Treaty rights are not absolute. They are subject to reasonable and statutory limitations.[21]
- Treaty rights are to be interpreted in an evolutionary way — for example, Aboriginal Peoples are not constrained to using traditional weapons for fishing but can facilitate technological innovations to exercise their treaty rights.[22]
- Treaties are to be interpreted, not according to their technical meaning, but in the manner in which they would be naturally understood by the Aboriginal People concerned.[23]
- Extinguishment of a treaty right is not deemed to have occurred where the treaty rights have not been exercised for an extended period of time.[24]

There are currently many treaties that are vulnerable to litigation for the purpose of reinterpretation. Since the court ruled in *R. v. Delgamuukw* that oral evidence is submissible to support the Aboriginal understanding of the treaty and what was promised during negotiations, many treaties are likely to be hauled through the courts for reanalysis.

Infringement of Aboriginal and Treaty Rights

Aboriginal rights are not absolute and may be infringed by both federal and provincial governments if the infringement furthers a "compelling and substantial" legislative objective and is consistent with the special fiduciary relationship between the Crown and the Aboriginal Peoples.[25] *R. v. Sparrow*

---

[18] *R. v. Horseman*, [1990] 3 C.N.L.R. 95 (S.C.C.); *Calder v. Attorney-General of British Columbia*, [1973] *supra* note 11 in ch. 1 at 402-04; *Guerin v. The Queen, supra* note 13 in ch. 1 at 375; *R. v. Sparrow, supra* note 5 in ch. 1 at 1099; *R. v. Gladstone*, [1996] 2 S.C.R. 723 at 750-51 (para. 34); *Delgamuukw v. British Columbia, supra* note 1 at 1122-23 (para. 183); *Watt v. Canada (Minister of Citizenship and Immigration)*, [1999] 2 C.N.L.R. 326 (F.C.A.) at 334-36 (paras. 13-16); *R. v. Jacob*, [1999] 3 C.N.L.R. 239 (B.C.S.C.) at 266-67 (paras. 107-09).

[19] *R. v. Badger*, [1996] 2 C.N.L.R. 77 (S.C.C.).

[20] *R. v. Horseman, supra* note 18.

[21] *R. v. Machatis*, [1991] 1 C.N.L.R. 154 (Alta. Q.B.); *R. v. McGillivary*, [1990] 1 C.N.L.R. 124 (Sask. Q.B.); *R. v. Horseman, supra* note 18.

[22] *R. v. Simon, supra* note 2.

[23] *Claxton v. Saanichton Marina Ltd., supra* note 13.

[24] *R. v. Simon, supra* note 2.

[25] *Per* Lamer C.J. and Cory, McLachlin and Major JJ. at 160.

laid down a two-part test for justifying infringements of constitutionally protected Aboriginal rights. Such infringements are lawfully justified only if the Crown can show that there is a valid legislative objective behind the infringing measure and that the government action upheld the honour of the Crown.

In *R. v. Gladstone*,[26] Mr. Chief Justice Lamer explained that infringement is best defined as any real interference with or diminution of an Aboriginal right.[27] Once infringement is established, the question becomes whether or not government interference with the Aboriginal right is justified.

The test for justification has two parts. First, the Crown must establish that the legislation or government action that infringes the constitutionally protected right pursues a valid objective.[28] Conservation and management of a natural resource is one example given. Valid objectives are any purposes that are found to be "compelling and substantial." The Supreme Court in *R. v. Gladstone*[29] interpreted "compelling and substantial objectives" as those that strike at the purposes behind the recognition and affirmation of Aboriginal rights in section 35(1). Therefore, the development of "agriculture, forestry, mining and hydroelectric power, the general economic development of the interior of British Columbia, protection of the environment or endangered species, and the building of infrastructure and the settlement of foreign populations to support those aims" are objectives consistent with this purpose.[30] As seen in the earlier case of *R. v. Sparrow*, conservation was held to be a valid legislative purpose since it seeks to address both the Aboriginal and legislative interests.

The second part of the test compels the Crown to act in a manner that upholds its fiduciary duty towards Aboriginal Peoples.[31] Regulatory regimes that impact upon the exercise of Aboriginal rights must demonstrate that priority is given to the exercise of Aboriginal rights over other rights or privileges.[32] To establish whether the second part of the test is satisfied, the court held that three aspects of Aboriginal title are relevant:[33]

---

[26] *R. v. Gladstone, supra* note 18.

[27] *Ibid.,* para. 43.

[28] *R. v. Sparrow, supra* note 5 in ch. 1 at 1113.

[29] *R. v. Gladstone, supra* note 18.

[30] *Delgamuukw v. British Columbia,* [1988] 1 C.N.L.R. 14 (S.C.C.)

[31] *Guerin v. The Queen, supra* note 13 in ch. 1.

[32] *R. v. Sparrow, supra* note 5 in ch. 1 at 1116.

[33] *Delgamuukw,* op. cit. at 202-203.

1. First, the degree of scrutiny of the infringing measure or action will depend on the extent to which the land is subject to the right to exclusive use and occupation.

2. Second, that land cannot be put to a use that destroys the ability of the land to sustain future generations of Aboriginal Peoples. Incorporated in this element of the test is that there is a duty of consultation—possibly a duty with a heavier onus—with the Aboriginal People affected by the activity on their traditional lands.

3. Third, that compensation is relevant to the question of justification, given that Aboriginal title has an "inescapable economic component," and "fair compensation" will be required wherever land is taken away from Aboriginal People or used for a purpose that is not for their benefit.[34] Justices La Forest and L'Heureux-Dubé held that section 35(1) rights are not absolute, but like other *Charter* guaranteed rights, would be subject to the test of justification as laid out in section 1 of the *Charter*. Accordingly, legislation permitting the development of the British Columbia interior are valid objectives and are satisfied if a degree of consultation took place and fair compensation was paid to those Aboriginal People concerned and affected.

One other concern that is relevant to the justification of infringements of Aboriginal rights is whether the infringement minimally impairs the Aboriginal right when viewed in light of the desired outcome.

---

[34] *Ibid.* para. 168.

Chapter 3

Crown Monopoly, Fiduciary Duty and Legislative Authority

Crown Monopoly and Fiduciary Duty

The right to acquire land from Aboriginal People, having been reserved to the Crown by virtue of the Royal Proclamation of 1763, empowered the Crown with the capacity to enter into treaties and agreements with the Aboriginal landholders. The court has determined that in connection with the Crown monopoly on transactions involving land held by Aboriginal Peoples, the Crown is under a correlative duty as a fiduciary to that relationship.

The fiduciary relationship between the Crown and Aboriginal Peoples has its roots in the concept of Native or Aboriginal title. The fact that Aboriginal Peoples have a certain interest in lands does not, however, in itself give rise to a fiduciary relationship between the Aboriginal Peoples and the Crown. The conclusion that the Crown is a fiduciary depends upon the further proposition that the Aboriginal interest in the land is inalienable except upon surrender to the Crown.

An Aboriginal band is prohibited from directly transferring its interest in land to a third party. Any sale or lease of land can only be carried out after a surrender has taken place, with the Crown then acting on the band's behalf. The Crown first took this responsibility upon itself in the Royal Proclamation in 1763. It is still recognized in the surrender provisions of the *Indian Act*. The surrender requirement, and the responsibility it entails, are the source of a distinct fiduciary obligation owed by the Crown to the Aboriginal People.[1]

---

[1] *Guerin v. The Queen, supra* note 13 in ch. 1 at 379.

The nature of the legal relationship between Aboriginal People and the Canadian government has been characterized as a *sui generis* fiduciary relationship. The fiduciary relationship is to be taken into account by the courts in most circumstances where Aboriginal or treaty rights are at issue. This fiduciary relationship gives rise to certain duties and obligations for the government in its dealings with Aboriginal Peoples. The relationship also flavours interpretation of treaties, legislation and other documents relating to Aboriginal Peoples.

The Supreme Court in *R. v. Sparrow*[2] stated:

> In our opinion, *Guerin* together with *R. v. Taylor and Williams*[3] ground a general guiding principle for section 35(1). That is, the Government has the responsibility to act in a fiduciary capacity with respect to Aboriginal Peoples. The relationship between the Government and Aboriginals is trust-like, rather than adversarial, and contemporary recognition and affirmation of Aboriginal rights must be defined in light of this historic relationship.

The fiduciary relationship can lead to judicially enforceable fiduciary duties on the Crown, particularly when the Crown assumes or exercises a discretionary power over the rights or interests of Aboriginal Peoples. In the case of *Guerin v. The Queen,*[4] $10 million was awarded against the Canadian government for mishandling land transactions involving the lease of lands reserved to the Musqueam Indian Band.

The full range of circumstances in which the fiduciary duties of the Canadian government remains uncertain, but there are a range of cases in which the courts have found that the fiduciary duty does not apply. It is, however, incontestable that the relationship between Aboriginal Peoples and the Canadian government is governed by legal principles of the fiduciary duty.

Where the Crown assumes or exercises a discretionary power over the rights or interests of Aboriginal Peoples it is under an obligation to protect them in the enjoyment of their Aboriginal rights, in particular, in the possession and use of their lands.[5] In *Blueberry River Indian Band v. Canada*[6] the scheme of the *Indian Act* was found by the court to impose a duty on the Crown to prevent exploitative bargains in regard to reserve land

---

[2] *R. v. Sparrow, supra* note 5 in ch. 1 at 1108.

[3] [1981] 3 C.N.L.R. 114 (Ont. C.A.).

[4] *Guerin v. The Queen, supra* note 13 in ch. 1.

[5] For a discussion see Slattery, B., "Understanding Aboriginal Rights" (1987) 66 *Canadian Bar Review* 727.

[6] 130 D.L.R. (4th) 193 (S.C.C.).

surrender transactions. However, this duty does not impose on the Crown a duty to ensure that the *best* surrender arrangement for the band is obtained. The court has indicated that they will not interfere in a surrender transaction if it is not exploitative and if its terms are clearly and fairly explained to the concerned Aboriginal Peoples by the Crown representatives. This obligation does require that the Crown examine a proposed transaction and ensure that it is not an exploitative bargain.[7]

In certain circumstances the provincial Crown will be held to the same fiduciary obligations. The relationship will be deemed fiduciary when the province places itself in the position of the federal Crown. This may occur for example where the provincial Crown assumes undertakings in a treaty or attempts to infringe on Aboriginal or treaty rights.[8]

Federal and Provincial Legislative Authority

Section 91(24) of the *Constitution Act, 1867* gives exclusive legislative authority to the federal government over "Indians, and Lands reserved for the Indians." The *Indian Act*[9] attempts to govern most aspects of Aboriginal life and affairs both on and off the land reserved for Aboriginal Peoples.

Provincial laws are incorporated into the *Indian Act* by virtue of section 88:

> Subject to the terms of any treaty and any other Act of Parliament of Canada, all laws of general application…in force in any province are applicable to…Indians in the province, except to the extent that such laws are inconsistent with this Act or any order, rule, regulation or by-law made thereunder.

Generally, provincial laws apply to Aboriginal Peoples and lands reserved for their benefit. However, this basic rule is encumbered by a number of conditions:

1. Provincial legislation must not apply to Aboriginal Peoples exclusively or to land reserved for their benefit as this would infringe upon an area of exclusive federal jurisdiction.[10]
2. Provincial laws cannot affect "an integral part of primary federal jurisdiction over Indians and lands reserved for the Indians."[11]

---

[7] *Semiahmoo Indian Band v. Canada (C.A.)*, [1998] 1 F.C. 3.

[8] *Halfway River First Nation v. British Columbia (Minister of Forests)*, [1999] 4 C.N.L.R. 1; *Perry v. Ontario* [1997] O.J. No. 2314; *Gitanyow First Nation v. Canada*, [1999] B.C.J. No. 1600.

[9] *Indian Act*, R.S.C. 1985, c. I-7.

[10] *R. v. Sutherland*, [1980] 3 C.N.L.R. 71; *Dick v. R.*, [1985] 4 C.N.L.R. 55; *Leighton v. British Columbia*, [1989] 3 C.N.L.R. 136 (B.C.C.A.).

[11] *Four B Manufacturing v. UGW*, [1979] 4 C.N.L.R. 21 at 25 (S.C.C.).

3.   The 1930 *Natural Resources Transfer Agreements* effectively prohibit provincial laws from depriving Aboriginal People of their right to hunt for game and fish for food.[12]

4.   If a provincial law of general application is inconsistent with a federal law in its application to Aboriginal Peoples or their lands, then the law is invalid to the extent of the inconsistency.

5.   A provincial law may be declared invalid and of not force or effect if it infringes an existing Aboriginal or treaty right that is protected by section 35 of the *Constitution Act, 1982.*

In *Re Stony Plains Indian Reserve No. 135*[13] the court held that provincial legislation is inapplicable to land reserved for Aboriginal People if it affects the use, enjoyment of and interests in reserve lands. This principle has subsequently been qualified by certain exceptions.

For a provincial law to be applicable to Aboriginal People, the laws must be "general" in nature and cannot relate exclusively or directly to Aboriginal People.[14] Dickson J. stated in *Kruger and Manuel v. R.*:

[There are] two indicia by which to discern whether or not a provincial enactment is a law of general application...If the Act does not extend uniformly throughout the territory, the inquiry is at an end...If the law does extend uniformly throughout the jurisdiction, the intention and effects of the enactment need to be considered. The law must not be in relation to one class of citizens in object and purpose...There are few laws which have a uniform impact. The line is crossed, however, when an enactment, though in relation to another matter, by its effect impairs the status or capacity of a particular group.[15]

The interpretation of "laws of general application" has since been expanded to include provincial legislation that impairs the status and capacity of an Aboriginal person without necessarily singling out an Aboriginal person or group.[16] One case concerned the British Columbia *Wildlife Act,*[17] which, by prevening hunting all year-round, impaired the traditions of an Aboriginal man who wished to pursue his traditional lifestyle of hunting.[18] The Supreme Court of Canada held that, as the legislation did not apply singly to the Aboriginal person concerned, it was a law of "general application" and was therefore valid and within the jurisdictional capacity of the provincial legislature.

---

[12]   For example, *R. v. Horseman*, *supra* note 18 in ch. 2.

[13]   Re *Stony Plain Indian Reserve No. 135*, [1982] 1 C.N.L.R. 133 at 151 (Alta. C.A.).

[14]   *Kruger and Manuel v. R.*, 9 C.N.L.C. 624 at 628 (S.C.C.).

[15]   *Ibid.*

[16]   *R. v. Dick*, *supra* note 10.

[17]   *Wildlife Act*, R.S.B.C. 1979, c. 433, ss. 3 and 8.

[18]   *R. v. Dick*, *supra* note 10.

Provincial legislation cannot extinguish Aboriginal rights and title.[19] In *Delgamuukw v. British Columbia*,[20] the majority opinion of the Supreme Court written by Chief Justice Lamer considered whether or not British Columbia had the power to extinguish Aboriginal rights after 1871, either by way of its own jurisdiction or by the application of section 88 of the *Indian Act*.[21] The majority reiterated the fact that the federal government has exclusive jurisdiction to extinguish Aboriginal rights and title by virtue of section 91(24) of the *Constitution Act, 1867*.[22]

Alberta, Saskatchewan and Manitoba are further restricted by the 1930 Natural Resources Transfer Agreements in which a clause is contained that preserves the right of Aboriginal People to hunt, trap and fish for food:

> In order to secure to the Indians of the Province the continuance of the supply of game and fish for their support and subsistence, Canada agrees that the laws respecting game in force in the Province from time to time shall apply to the Indians within the boundaries thereof, provided, however, that the said Indians shall have the right, which the Province hereby assures to them of hunting, trapping and fishing game for food at all seasons of the year on all unoccupied Crown lands and on any other lands to which the said Indians may have a right of access.

In *R. v. Horse*[23] the Supreme Court held that this clause must be given a wide and liberal interpretation in favour of the Aboriginal person or group concerned. However the right to hunt and fish for food is limited to the lands specified, and no right of access to private lands exist. The right has been held to exist all year-round and provincial laws to the contrary are invalid.[24]

Territorial Authority

The Yukon Territory and the Northwest Territories are creatures of the federal Parliament and do not have independent sovereign status like the provincial and federal legislatures. The *Northwest Territories Act*[25] and the *Yukon Act*[26] empower the respective commissioners in council of each territory and the governor in council to enact ordinances and make regulations dealing specifically with Aboriginal and Inuit People in a narrow range of matters.

---

[19] *Delgamuukw v. British Columbia, supra* note 24 in ch. 1.

[20] *Ibid.* para. 153.

[21] *Ibid.* paras. 172-82.

[22] *Ibid.* para. 173.

[23] *R. v. Horse*, [1988] 2 C.N.L.R. 112 (S.C.C.).

[24] *R. v. Sutherland, supra* note 10.

[25] *Northwest Territories Act*, R.S.C. 1985, c. N-27.

[26] *Yukon Act*, R.S.C. 1985, c. Y-2.

Section 18 of the *Northwest Territories Act* and section 19 of the *Yukon Act* provide that territorial legislatures may make such laws as are applicable to and in respect of Aboriginal and Inuit Peoples. However, such laws cannot restrict or prohibit Indians or Inuit from hunting for food on unoccupied Crown land unless the game has been declared by the governor in council as game that is in danger of becoming extinct.

Laws of general application in the Northwest Territories are not absolute. They are subject to federal legislative authority (section 35 protecting Aboriginal and treaty rights) and land claims agreements (which are constitutionally recognized under section 35(3)).

Part 2

Federal Regulation

Chapter 4

Federal Regulation of Resources on Reserve Lands

Under the *Constitution Act, 1867*, the federal government is given the full responsibility for legislating in respect of "Indians and Lands Reserved for the Indians."[1] Reserve lands are set apart for the band as a whole and individual band members do not have a right of individual possession. The land is not owned by the band but is retained by the Crown for the band's use and benefit.[2] The land is held for the use and benefit of the entire band; it is a collective right of the band members as a body and not a right of band members individually to enforce.[3]

Pursuant to section 109 of the *Constitution Act, 1867*, ownership of land and natural resources located in a province at Confederation belongs to the provincial Crown. Section 109 reads:

> All lands, mines, minerals and royalties belonging to the several provinces of Canada, Nova Scotia and New Brunswick at the union, and all sums then due or payable for such lands, mines, minerals or royalties, shall belong to the several provinces of Ontario, Quebec, Nova Scotia and New Brunswick, in which the same are situate or arise, subject to any trust existing in respect thereof, and to any interest other than that of the province.

Provincial proprietary interest in lands and resources under section 109 may be burdened by Aboriginal title. Aboriginal title is an underlying burden on provincial lands and, by extension, on the natural resources of the provinces.[4] This provision of the Constitution is becoming increasingly relevant to land claims in areas of Canada where land cession treaties have never been negotiated. In such instances, the First Nations have the

[1] *Constitution Act, 1867* 30 & 31 Vict., c. 3 (U.K.), (R.S.C. 1985, App II, No. 5), s. 91(24).

[2] *R. v. Stevenson*, [1986] 5 W.W.R. 737.

[3] *Joe v. Findlay*, [1981] 3 W.W.R. 6.

[4] *St. Catherines Milling and Lumber Co. v. The Queen*, *supra* note 10 in ch. 1; *Haida Nation v. British Columbia and Weyerhaeuser*, [2002] B.C.C.A. 147.

opportunity to lay claim to all resources that were being used prior to contact with non-Aboriginal settlers within their traditional territories of occupation.

Indian Act[5]

The *Indian Act* is not a document that conveys rights, but instead defines the federal government's relationship with Canadian Aboriginal People in administrative terms. The Minister of Indian and Northern Affairs has his or her regulatory capacities and obligations defined in the statute. Under section 18 of the Act, the federal government is under a fiduciary obligation to administer reserve land in the best interest and use of the First Nation affected.

The federal Parliament is given broad powers under the *Indian Act* to make regulations for resource use on First Nations' reserve lands. In particular, the Canadian legislature may make regulations

- authorizing the Minister to grant treefelling licences, conditional or restricted if deemed necessary with the consent of the "council of the band" on reserve lands;
- providing for the disposition of surrendered mines and minerals underlying reserve lands;[6]
- to dispose of sand, gravel, clay and other non-metallic substances on or under lands in a reserve, with the consent of the council of the band, or where that consent cannot be obtained without undue difficulty or delay, they may issue temporary permits for removal of such substances which are renewable only with the band council's consent; full proceeds of the transactions being credited to band funds for equal division amongst the members of the band concerned.[7]

For minerals, stone, sand, gravel, clay, soil, trees, saplings, shrubs, underbrush, timber, cordwood or hay to be removed from a reserve, under section 93 permission of the Minister or a duly authorized representative must first be obtained.

Canada does, however, have the power to grant to the band in occupation the right to exercise such control and management over lands in the reserve.[8]

The federal Parliament has enacted regulations to govern both mining and timberfelling on First Nation reserve land.

---

[5] R.S., c. I-6.
[6] *Indian Act*, R.S., 1985, c. I-6, s. 57.
[7] *Ibid.* s. 58.
[8] *Ibid.* s. 61(1).

Indian Mining Regulations[9]

The *Indian Mining Regulations* administer exploration and development of minerals and mining on reserve lands. These Regulations specifically exclude mines and minerals underlying reserve lands in British Columbia from their application, which continue to be governed by British Columbia, but apply to all other reserve lands under federal jurisdiction.[10] Under section 4 of the Regulations, provincial laws regarding exploration for development, production, treatment and marketing of minerals are incorporated to the extent that no conflict arises with the Regulations.

Who obtains the rights to mine on reserve land will depend primarily on the administrator's method of obtaining tenders. The administrator of the Regulations is to invite tenders for mineral rights by public advertisement or by other means, on such terms and conditions as he or she deems appropriate.[11] The administrator is under no obligation to accept the highest tender.[12]

The lessee is entitled to all minerals found within his lease area, subject to any terms and conditions attached to his or her permit.[13] Note that, under the Regulations, the term "minerals" includes "naturally occurring metallic and non-metallic minerals and rock containing such minerals," but does not include "petroleum, natural gas and other petroliferous minerals or any unconsolidated minerals such as placer deposits, gravel, sand, clay, earth, ash, marl and peat."[14]

Indian Timber Regulations[15]

The *Indian Timber Regulations* give the Department of Indian and Northern Affairs absolute discretion in respect of harvesting timber on reserve lands, including timber used by First Nations residents. Obtaining a licence is mandatory for cutting timber on reserve lands.[16] Such permits may be issued free of charge by the Minister to a band. However, the Regulations state that such permits are to be granted to a band "for band purposes, or to a member or group of members of a band, to cut timber and fuel wood for his or their individual use."[17] A licence to cut timber for sale may be issued to a band or

---

[9]   *Indian Mining Regulations*, C.R.C., c. 956.
[10]   *Ibid.* s. 3.
[11]   *Ibid.* s. 5(1).
[12]   *Ibid.* s. 5(2).
[13]   *Ibid.* s. 20.
[14]   *Ibid.* s. 2(1).
[15]   *Indian Timber Regulations*, C.R.C., c. 961.
[16]   *Ibid.* s. 3.1.
[17]   *Ibid.* s. 4.

to a member or group of members of a band with the consent of the band council concerned.[18] Consent of a band council is required for a timber permit issued to any person for operations on First Nation land.[19] Where concerned with forest management, watershed protection, fire protection, preservation of the beauty of the landscape, game or game shelters, the Minister can order the marking of trees to be left standing.[20]

The Timber Regulations (and the *Indian Act*[21]) only provide for logging. No mention is made of forestry planning, reforestation or preservation of ecosystem values.

Stuart-Trembleur Lake Band (Tanizul Timber Ltd.) Timber Regulations[22]

Notwithstanding the *Indian Timber Regulations,* the Minister of Indian Affairs and Northern Development can, with the consent of the council of the Stuart-Trembleur Lake Band, grant a licence to cut timber on the reserve lands of the band to Tanizul Timber Ltd.[23] Rights under the licence are to be exercised in accordance with the *Forest Act, Ministry of Forests Act* and *Range Act* of British Columbia, as though the licence were issued on private lands, within the meaning of the *Forest Act.*[24]

Forestry Exploitation on Reserve Lands

Currently, Aboriginal communities can exploit timber in several ways. Contracts can be entered into by Aboriginal groups and the government, or forestry corporations for various forest management activities.[25] An example of this is the Siwash Silviculture Company that has been run by five bands of the Fraser Canyon Indian Administration for the last 10 years. By agreement with the federal and provincial governments, the company manages 41,000 hectares at the Chilcotin Military Block of the Department of National Defence. An example of a contract relationship between an Aboriginal group and a logging corporation is that between the Cheslakee people and the Cheslakee Logging Ltd., which has logged on the Cheslakee reserve and nearby Crown lands for 59 years.

---

[18] *Ibid.* s. 5(1).

[19] *Ibid.* s. 9.

[20] *Ibid.* s. 22(2).

[21] *Indian Act,* s. 57.

[22] *Stuart-Trembleur Lake Band (Tanizul Timber Ltd.) Timber Regulations,* SOR/82-171, as am. SOR/93-244; SOR/95-531.

[23] *Ibid.* s. 3.

[24] *Ibid.* s. 6(1).

[25] See the Task Force on Native Forestry, *Native Forestry in British Columbia: A New Approach Final Report,* Victoria, 1991.

Another method whereby First Nations can exploit timber resources and be involved in its management is by joint venture initiatives between corporations and First Nations.[26] Crown tenures can also be activated; however, Aboriginal People have traditionally found it difficult to access the forestry tenure regime as it currently exists.[27]

Finally, the department of Natural Resources Canada is managing the implementation of 11 model forests in British Columbia, Alberta, Saskatchewan, Manitoba, Eastern Ontario, Quebec, New Brunswick and Newfoundland.[28] The model forests are designed to enable First Nations involvement in forest resource management. Inventories of current and historical cultural activities are to be developed on traditional lands.

First Nation Forestry Program[29]

The First Nation Forestry Program applies to timber harvesting on reserve lands and off-reserve on traditional lands. This program was designed to conclude on 31 March 2002,[30] whereupon First Nations were allowed to continue with the harvesting activities that were assisted by the federal program, but without continued federal funding. However, the program has been extended. The program is designed, primarily, to assist Aboriginal People to actively pursue economic development opportunities. In particular, it is to enable Aboriginal groups to amass knowledge of the industry and thereby assume control of the management of their forest resources. A secondary goal of the program is to encourage Aboriginal groups to enter into partnerships with the government and industry groups for the management of forest resources. Under the program, an Aboriginal group would compose an application for funding, which would be approved provided it met certain criteria.[31]

---

[26] See the Burns Lake Development Corporation which owns 10 percent of the Babine Forest Products located on the Burns Lake Reserve in British Columbia. The First Nation has a seat on the management committee and 70 jobs, or over one-third of the workforce. See also initiatives of the Carrier Sekani Tribal Council, the Stellawuo, Nadleh and Stoney Creek Bands (the Ne-Du-Chun Forest Company), and the Gitxsan Nation, Hunter, J., "Consent and Consultation After *Delgamuukw*: Practical Implications for Forestry and Mining in British Columbia," Aboriginal Title Update, Continuing Legal Education Society of British Columbia, Vancouver, 1998.

[27] But see the Tree Farm Licence 42 tenure held by the Tlazten Nation in British Columbia; and the tenure held by the Meadow lake Tribal Council in Saskatchewan.

[28] See Natural Resources Canada, The Backgrounder: The Canadian Model Forest Program, Ottawa, 1997.

[29] First Nation Forestry Program, online: <http://www.fnfp.gc.ca/>.

[30] See 10 April 2001, "Government Of Canada First Nation Forestry Program Extended," online: http://www.nrcan.gc.ca/css/imb/hqlib/200124e.htm.

[31] See also the National Forest Strategy, Direction 7: *Aboriginal Peoples: Issues of Relationship*, online: <http://www.nrcan.gc.ca/cfs/nfs/strateg/control_e.html>.

According to the First Nation Forestry Program website, there are over 2,300 First Nation reserves located throughout Canada with a total area of over 3 million hectares, of which 1.4 million are forested. Approximately 80 percent of First Nations are located within the boreal and temperate forest regions. Eighty-five percent of the Bands in Canada on 1,172 reserves have forests totalling 1,122,000 hectares. Two hundred and forty bands have productive forest areas that are larger than 1,000 hectares.[32]

The federal government committed $4.5 million to the First Nations Forestry Project for 2001-02. The Department of Indian and Northern Affairs provided $2.75 million, while Natural Resources Canada promised $1.75 million. This extension to the life of the program is designed to be an interim measure while the Government of Canada develops an approach that encompasses a broader agenda for First Nations people.

Forestry Exploitation and Management on Traditional Lands

Section 91(24) of the *Constitution Act, 1867*, assigns jurisdiction to the federal government over "Lands reserved for the Indians"; however, forest management comes under provincial regulation. This division of legislative powers creates a complex management structure whereby both the federal and provincial governments dictate use of timber on traditional Aboriginal lands. Since *R. v. Delgamuukw*, lower court rulings have challenged Crown authority over forested lands. In *R. v. Peter Paul*,[33] a lower New Brunswick court upheld an Aboriginal right to access Crown land and fell timber. The four men, members of the Mi'kmaq First Nations, were charged with unlawfully cutting and removing timber from Crown land under the *Crown Lands and Forests Act*.[34] The court found in favour of the accused, ruling that the Act did not apply to the Mi'kmaq of New Brunswick because it found a treaty right, guaranteed by Mascarene's Treaty of 1726 and the Treaty of the Peace with the Eastern Mi'kmaq Tribes of 1752, to harvest and sell forest-derived products. Widespread logging ensued in the province, and on appeal, the New Brunswick Court of Appeal found that Judge Turnbull of the Court of Queen's Bench had undertaken independent research, outside of the rules of evidence, which led to his conclusion that a right to harvest timber for commercial purposes existed. Accordingly, the Crown had had no opportunity to respond to this evidence, and the accused's case failed on this

---

[32] See Notzke, C., *Aboriginal People and Natural Resources in Canada*, Captus University Press, North York, 1994, pp. 86-87.

[33] (1996), 182 N.B.R. (2d) 270 (Prov. Ct.), aff'd (sub nom. *R. v. Paul* (T.P.) (1997), 193 N.B.R. (2d) 321 (Q.B. T.D.), rev'd (1998), 196 N.B.R. (2d) 292 (C.A.), leave to appeal to S.C.C. refused (1998), 204 N.B.R. (2d) 400n.

[34] S.N.B. 1980, c. C-38.1.

basis. However, in *R. v. Bernard*,[35] a majority of the Court of Appeal set aside the decision on the basis that the accused has an established treaty right that had been infringed upon.

The case of the *Haida Nation v. British Columbia (Minister of Forests)*[36] dealt with a challenge by the Haida Nation as to a decision by the Ministry of Forests to renew a tree farm licence that applied to the traditional territory of the Haida Nation to which the Haida people claim Aboriginal title. The forestry legislation under which such a licence can be issued describes a tree farm licence as being applicable to an area of Crown land that is not otherwise encumbered. Accordingly, the Haida Nation claimed that Aboriginal title was such an encumbrance. This issue was considered only as a preliminary issue of law, and the Court of Appeal ruled that Aboriginal title, if it is proven to exist, would be an encumbrance on Crown title.

In the Court of Appeal, the court found unanimously that Aboriginal title is indeed an encumbrance on provincial ownership of resources as per section 109 of the *Constitution Act, 1867*. The court held that, although it has not yet been determined whether or not the Haida people have a legitimate claim to the land and forest in question, upon the strength of their application it seemed to the court that this was sufficient for a duty of consultation to arise. The court stressed that the land claim process is a long one and it could be more than a decade before the land claim issue is resolved. Again, the court indicated that the strength of the Haida people's application was enough to forewarn the government that it was likely that they do have a lawful claim to the land in question and for that reason the government should proactively seek to consult with such nations in the future. This may involve a negotiations process whereby the government, industry and First Nations discuss use of resources on land where a claim is likely or possible. The strength of the First Nation's land claim application will determine the weight of the obligation on the Crown to consult with those Aboriginal People. If the government fails to do so and Aboriginal title in that land is later recognized, the government will face hefty compensatory obligations to the First Nation(s) affected.

One other case worth considering is *British Columbia (Minister of Forests) v. Westbank First Nation*[37] where the Westbank First Nation challenged provincial jurisdiction over forestry by cutting over one hundred truckloads of trees on Crown land. The Minister of Forests was seeking to enforce a stop work order, issued under the *Forest Practices Code of British Columbia Act*,[38] against the Westbank First Nation that had allegedly

---

[35]   *R. v. Bernard*, [2003] N.B.C.A. 55.

[36]   [1997] B.C.J. No. 2480, leave to appeal to the S.C.C. refused [1998] S.C.C.A. No. 1.

[37]   [1999] B.C.J. No. 2161 (B.C.S.C.).

[38]   R.S.B.C. 1996, c. 159.

removed Crown timber unlawfully. The Westbank First Nation countered with an Aboriginal rights and title claim and sought clarification of the constitutionality of the law under which the stop work order was issued on the basis that it infringed Aboriginal rights and title. The court held that there was a constitutionality issue to be heard as the Westbank First Nation had its constitutional rights put in jeopardy by the Forest Practices Code insofar as it might infringe on pre-existing rights and title should Aboriginal rights be found to exist. On appeal, the decision of the lower British Columbia Court was upheld that a trial should be ordered to consider the constitutionality of the legislation and a freeze be placed on the logging licence in question.[39]

The Supreme Court decision in *R. v. Delgamuukw* appears to have wide-ranging implications for forestry, particularly forestry practices on Aboriginal title lands. The court recognized that First Nations could have Aboriginal title to traditional practices and commercial uses, so long as they are consistent with the continued enjoyment of historic uses of the land. The potential for Aboriginal People to realize resource exploitation rights post-*Delgamuukw* is, however, tempered by the fact that there is no legal recognition of Aboriginal title without first establishing that it exists. This means that title must be established by a court decision or treaty settlement on a case-by-case, nation-by-nation basis. At a minimum, *R. v. Delgamuukw* has created an environment where decision making is shared and cannot be undertaken solely by either level of government without prior, meaningful consultation with affected First Nations and possible payment of compensation where Aboriginal rights are found to be infringed.[40] Following the *Haida* decision, at the very least, Aboriginal title is an encumbrance on Crown title and therefore must be taken into account.

A direct result of the lack of Crown action affirming Aboriginal rights has been that Aboriginal Peoples have developed model federal legislation, namely the *First Nations Forest Resources Management Act*. The legislation establishes a framework for First Nations to manage and control their forest resources on reserve and traditional lands.[41]

---

[39] *British Columbia (Minister of Forests) v. Westbank First Nation,* [2000] B.C.C.A. 99.

[40] See *Cheslatta Carrier Nation v. British Columbia (Environmental Assessment Act, Project Assessment Director)* (1998), 53 B.C.L.R. (3d) 1 (S.C.) decided after *R. v. Delgamuukw* where the Cheslatta Carrier people sought judicial review of decisions made under provincial environmental assessment legislation accepting an application for the development of a mine in their traditional territory. The court found that meaningful consultation had not taken place and that the Crown is under a duty to fully inform, discuss issues and take the concerns of the affected First Nation seriously. Whereupon the First Nation seeks relevant information from the Crown, it is obliged to comply. The affected First Nation is then under a duty to cooperate in the consultation efforts.

[41] See the National Aboriginal Forestry Association, A Proposal to First Nations, National Aboriginal Forestry Association, Ottawa, 1994.

Indian Oil and Gas Act[42]

The *Indian Oil and Gas Act* vests the Department of Indian Affairs and Northern Development with the power to regulate and manage exploitation of oil and gas on "land reserved for the Indians."[43] The Act is merely the legislative framework to enable and authorize the *Indian Oil and Gas Regulations*.[44] Under the *Indian Oil and Gas Act*, the governor in council can make regulations with respect to

- granting leases, permits and licences for the exploitation of oil and gas in First Nations land and issues incidental to oil and gas exploitation in those lands;
- seizing and forfeiture of any oil or gas taken in contravention of regulations or terms and conditions attached to any interest that has been granted;
- determining royalties payable on oil and gas obtained from First Nations lands;
- imposing penalties for failure to comply with any lease, permit or licence granted by the department.[45]

The First Nations people to whom this Act may apply have little control over exploitation of oil and gas on First Nations land, apart from the condition in section 6(1) of the Act, which requires the Minister to consult, on a continuing basis, the persons representative of First Nations bands most directly affected by determinations under this Act. The manager of Indian Oil and Gas is vested with immense discretionary power in the development of oil and gas on reserve land.

Indian Oil and Gas Regulations[46]

The *Indian Oil and Gas Regulations* set out the procedures that must be followed by any person seeking to mine for minerals on land reserved for Aboriginal People. The Regulations provide for exploratory licences, permits, leases, royalties, drilling monitoring and regulation, surface rights and other activities relating to mining. The Regulations are administered by Indian Oil and Gas Canada, specifically by the executive director of that organization. The power bestowed to the executive director to grant licences, permits or leases in respect of oil and gas on reserve lands is fettered by an obligation to seek the consent of the First Nation council who will be affected by activity on its lands.[47] The relatively recent amendments to the

---

[42] *Indian Oil and Gas Act*, 1974-75-76, c. 15, s. 1.

[43] *Constitution Act, 1862*, s. 91(24).

[44] *Indian Oil and Gas Regulations,* 1995 [SOR/94-753].

[45] *Indian Oil and Gas Act*, s. 3.

[46] *Indian Oil and Gas Regulations, 1995*.

[47] *Ibid.* s. 6(4) & s. 10.

Regulations provide for comprehensive guidelines relating to consultation and consent processes in relations to the First Nation concerned. Nonetheless, Aboriginal People are still denied substantive control of oil and gas operations on reserve land, and there are no provisions to promote Aboriginal ownership of an oil and gas venture on reserve land.

Federal-Provincial Resource Agreements on Reserve Land

Agreements concerning resource exploitation and management on reserve lands have been concluded by the federal government and the governments of each province.

Canada-Ontario Agreement[48]

By virtue of the agreement between Canada and Ontario, the federal government administers not only reserve lands but also surrendered lands that are the subject of a specific agreement. Under the *Indian Lands Agreement (1986) Act* a specific agreement may be entered into by Ontario, Canada, and any Band or group of Bands relating to lands or natural resources, including

(a)   any matter dealt with in the 1924 Agreement;

(b)   administration and control;

(c)   the exercise, allocation or transfer or disposal of any interests in lands or natural resources;

(d)   minerals, mineral rights and royalties, and the disposition or taxation of any of them;

(e)   hydro powers;

(f)   disposition of lands or natural resources;

(g)   consequences of extinction or enfranchisement of a Band;

(h)   disposition of any monies;

(i)   the non-applicability of any section or sections of the 1924 Agreement;

(j)   any other provision required for the implementation of a specific agreement.[49]

---

48   *An Act for the Settlement of Certain Questions Between the Governments of Canada and Ontario Respecting Indian Reserve Lands,* S.C. 1924, c.48; *Indian Lands Agreement (1986) Act,* S.C. 1988, c.39.

49   *Ibid.* ss. 2 & 3.

Alberta, Manitoba and Saskatchewan

Mineral rights on reserves are governed under the Natural Resource Agreements[50] that were concluded with each of the Prairie provinces in 1930.[51] Each agreement contained the following clause:

> All lands included in Indian reserves within the Province, including those selected and surveyed but not yet confirmed, as well as those confirmed, shall continue to be vested in the Crown, and administered by the Government of Canada for the purposes of Canada, and the Province will from time to time, upon the request of the Superintendent General of Indian Affairs, set aside, out of the unoccupied Crown lands hereby transferred to its administration, such further areas as the said Superintendent General may, in agreement with the appropriate Minister of the Province, select as necessary to enable Canada to fulfill its obligations under the treaties with the Indians of the Province, and such areas shall thereafter be administered by Canada in the same way in all respects as if they had never passed to the Province under the provisions hereof.

All moneys amassed from mining on reserved lands are to go to the Aboriginal People concerned in the Prairie provinces.

Aboriginal People in Alberta,[52] Manitoba[53] and Saskatchewan[54] are also provided with a right to take fish, trap and hunt for food on unoccupied Crown land:

> In order to secure to the Indians of the Province the continuance of the supply of game and fish for their support and subsistence, Canada agrees that the law respecting game in force in the Province from time to time shall apply to the Indians within the boundaries thereof, provided, however, that the said Indians shall have the right, which the Province hereby assures to them of hunting, trapping and fishing game for food at all seasons of the year on all unoccupied Crown lands and on any other lands to which the said Indians may have a right of access.

The impact of the Natural Resource Agreements on exercising Aboriginal rights to resources will be discussed below under the chapter devoted to the Prairie provinces.

---

[50] *Constitution Act*, 1930.

[51] *Alberta Natural Resources Act* S.C. 1930, c.3, *Saskatchewan Natural Resources Act*, S.C. 1930, c.41, *Manitoba Natural Resources Act*, S.C. 1930, c.29.

[52] *Alberta Natural Resources Act*, cl. 12.

[53] *Manitoba Natural Resources Act*, cl. 14.

[54] *Saskatchewan Natural Resources Act*, cl. 12.

British Columbia-Canada Agreement[55]

The British Columbia-Canada Agreement requires that half of the mineral revenues derived from reserve lands goes to the federal government for the benefit of the First Nations affected and the other half goes to the provincial government. Apart from the First Nation's right of veto, the province administers and disposes of reserve minerals.

Atlantic Provinces[56]

In Nova Scotia and New Brunswick the transfer of title of reserves from the province to Canada results in the proceeds of mineral disposition on reserves going to the federal government for the benefit of Aboriginal People. Minerals and mining developments are done under the *Indian Act*.

Quebec

There are no agreements regarding minerals on reserves in Quebec, apart from the James Bay and Northeastern Quebec Agreements.[57] For the most part, Quebec has title to most reserve land within its province. Upon surrender of land to the Crown, the province thus receives the benefits of the mineral in the province subject to the *Indian Act* veto over land.

Northwest Territories and Yukon

Recent land claims that are discussed below generally clarify who has mineral rights to lands reserved for Aboriginal People.

Fisheries Act[58]

In the absence of conflicting treaty rights, the *Fisheries Act* is deemed to apply to fishing activities of Aboriginal People in Canada. The federal fisheries legislation sets up a regime whereby the Minister has absolute discretion, wherever the exclusive right of fishing does not already exist by law, to issue or authorize to be issued leases and licences for fisheries or

---

[55] S.C. 1943, c. 19; *Indian Reserves Mineral Resources Act,* R.S.B.C. 1979, c.192.

[56] *An Act to Confirm an Agreement between the Government of Canada and the Government of the Province of Nova Scotia Respecting Indian Reserves,* S.C. 1959, c.50; *An Act to Confirm an Agreement between the Government of Canada and the Government of the Province of New Brunswick Respecting Indian Reserves,* S.C. 1954, c.4.

[57] *James Bay and Northern Quebec Native Claims Settlement Act,* S.C. 1976-77, c.32; James Bay Agreement, S.Q. 1976, c.32; Northern Quebec Agreement, Order in Council, February 23, 1976, F.C. 1978-502; Northern Quebec Agreement S.Q. 1978, c.98.

[58] *Fisheries Act,* R.S., c. F-14.

fishing, regardless of where such activities are conducted.[59] This power extends to the power to regulate lobster fishing and fisheries.[60] No person can destroy, purchase, sell or possess any fish that has been caught in contravention of the *Fisheries Act* and associated regulations.[61] The Minister has the power to make regulations, including the power to regulate for

(a)   management and control of the sea-coast and inland fisheries;

(b)   conservation and protection of fish;

(c)   catching, loading, landing, handling, transporting, possession and disposal of fish;

(d)   operation of fishing vessels;

(e)   use of fishing gear and equipment;

(f)   suspension and cancellation of licences and leases;

(g)   terms and conditions under which a licence and lease may be issued;

(h)   obstruction and pollution of any waters frequented by fish;

(i)   conservation and protection of spawning grounds;

(j)   export of fish or any part thereof;

(k)   taking or carrying of fish or any part thereof from one province to any other province;

(l)   where a close time, fishing quota or limit on the size or weight of fish has been fixed in respect of an area under the regulations, authorizing government persons to vary the close time fishing quota or limit in respect of that area or any portion of that area.[62]

The Minister also has the sole right to regulate the harvesting of marine plants in the coastal waters of Canada.[63] Accordingly, the Minister is vested with the power to make regulations prohibiting, subject to the conditions of any licence,

(a)   the harvest of marine plants or any class of marine plants;

(b)   the harvest of marine plants or any class of marine plants in quantities in excess of quantities specified in the regulations, or

(c)   the harvest of marine plants or of any class of marine plants in a manner specified in the regulations;

(d)   harvest of marine plants during particular periods of time in the coastal waters of Canada.[64]

---

[59]   *Ibid.* s. 7.

[60]   *Ibid.* s. 18.

[61]   *Ibid.* ss. 32 & 33.

[62]   *Ibid.* s. 43.

[63]   *Ibid.* s. 44.

[64]   *Ibid.* s. 46.

The Act preserves the traditional harvesting of marine plants by Indians for food under section 48, which restrains the Minister from regulating to hinder Aboriginal harvesting rights.

Aboriginal Communal Fishing Licences Regulations[65]

Pursuant to section 43 of the *Fisheries Act*, the federal government enacted the *Aboriginal Communal Fishing Licences Regulations.* The Regulations are deemed to apply to fisheries in Canadian waters

- in and adjacent to Ontario, Quebec, Nova Scotia, New Brunswick, Prince Edward Island, Newfoundland and the Northwest Territories;
- fisheries in the tidal waters in and adjacent to Manitoba;
- fisheries in tidal waters in and adjacent to the Yukon Territory and fisheries in the Yukon for fish of an anadromous stock of chum salmon, coho salmon, pink salmon, chinook salmon, pink salmon, rainbow trout, the family *Coregonidae* (whitefish and cisco or Arctic char); and
- fisheries in the waters of the Areas enumerated and described in Schedule II to the *Pacific Fishery Management Area Regulations* and salmon fisheries in British Columbia.[66]

The Regulations give the federal Minister of Fisheries and Oceans the power to issue communal licences to Aboriginal organizations for the purposes of carrying on fishing and fishing related activities. Under the regulations, the Minister of the Environment and Wildlife of Quebec is able to issue licences in respect of fisheries and species of fish described in section 3(1) of the *Quebec Fishery Regulations, 1990*, and the Minister of Natural Resources for Ontario is empowered to issue such licences for fisheries in the non-tidal waters of Ontario. The regulations are deemed inapplicable to fisheries in national parks.[67]

The Minister is also permitted to specify in a licence any condition respecting any of the matters set out in paragraphs 22(1)(b) to (z.1) of the *Fishery (General) Regulations* (pertaining to harvestable species, locations of harvest and so on) and also matters including:

(a) the species and quantities of fish that are permitted to be taken or transported;

(b) the locations and times at which landing of fish is permitted;

---

[65] *Aboriginal Communal Fishing Licences Regulations*, SOR/93-332

[66] *Ibid.*, s. 3(1).

[67] *Ibid.* ss. 2 & 4.

(c)   the method to be used for the landing of fish and the methods by which the quantity of fish is to be determined;

(d)   the information that a designated person or the master of a designated vessel is to report to the Minister or a person specified by the licence holder, prior to commencement of fishing, with respect to where and when fishing will be carried on, including the method by which, the times at which and the person to whom the report is to be made;

(e)   the maximum number of persons or vessels that may be designated to carry on fishing and related activities;

(f)   the maximum number of designated persons who may fish at any one time;

(g)   the type, size and quantity of fishing gear that may be used by a designated person;

(h)   the disposition of fish caught under the authority of the licence.[68]

The Regulations state that no person who is authorized to fish under the authority of a communal fishing licence is able to fish for or catch and retain any species of fish in any regulated area during closed fishing seasons.[69]

Fisheries Agreements

Fisheries agreements are made pursuant to the *Fisheries Act* and the *Aboriginal Communal Fishing Licences Regulations*. Several types of agreements can be made pursuant to section 4 of the Regulations.

Communal Licenses

Communal licences are issued to various Aboriginal organizations to enable them to undertake fishing and fishery-related activities.

- A *"Single Species" Communal Licence.* This type of licence is granted to permit and regulate the harvest of a single species (usually salmon). This type of licence is used to licence all fisheries on the Fraser River, for the Yukon and Northern British Columbia. They are also issued for spawn-on-kelp fisheries in the North Coast.

- A *"Multi Species" Communal Licence.* This type of licence delineates amounts of a number of different fish species that may be harvested by the Aboriginal organization to which it applies. This type of licence is generally used for coastal fisheries.

---

[68]   *Ibid.* s. 5(1).
[69]   *Ibid.* s. 9(1).

- *"Dry Rack" Licence.* A Dry Rack Licence may be issued to an Aboriginal organization that has historically wind-dried fish. To be eligible for this licence, the Aboriginal organization must have appropriate fishing and drying sites and have erected structures along the Fraser River. The fish are subsequently dried or canned and will then be used for food, social and ceremonial purposes.
- *"Ceremonial" Licences.* A Ceremonial Licence can be issued by the Department where fishing has been restricted or prohibited where local stocks are depleted to a level that an open fishery is unsustainable. The Aboriginal organization to whom the licence applies may be allowed to fish for ceremonial purposes where such limited fishing will not threaten the fishery stocks.

Fishery (General) Regulations[70]

The *Fishery (General) Regulations* require that every person who wishes to buy, sell, trade, barter or offer to buy, sell, trade or barter any fish have a licence. A licence obtained under the *Aboriginal Communal Fishing Licences Regulations* satisfies this criterion.[71]

Marine Mammal Regulations[72]

No person in Canada is permitted to fish for marine mammals except under the authoriy of a licence issued under the *Marine Mammal Regulations* or under the *Aboriginal Communal Fishing Licences Regulations.*[73]

Notwithstanding, an Indian or Inuk may fish for food, social or ceremonial purposes for

- seals;
- cetaceans, except beluga in certain areas, bowhead whales, right whales and narwhal; and
- four walrus per year.[74]

This section does not apply to beneficiaries under an agreement or treaty whereby other harvesting may be permitted.[75]

No person is permitted to buy, sell, trade or barter the edible parts of a cetacean or walrus except with a permit issued by the Department of Fisheries and Oceans Canada. This provision does not apply, however, to an

---

[70] SOR/93-53.

[71] *Fishing (General) Regulations*, s. 35(2).

[72] SOR/93-56.

[73] *Marine Mammal Regulations*, s. 5.

[74] *Ibid.* s. 6(1).

[75] *Ibid.* s. 6(2).

Aboriginal Person or Inuk (who is not subject to an agreement or treaty) within the Northwest Territories, the Yukon Territory, Quebec or Newfoundland, or to a beneficiary under an agreement or treaty if the purchase, sale, trade or barter is carried out in accordance with the terms of the applicable agreement.[76]

Atlantic Fishery Regulations[77]

The *Atlantic Fishery Regulations* provide licensing, registration and quota requirements for people fishing in federally governed waters. The Regulations are deemed not to apply to any person who is designated fishing authority of a licence issued under the *Aboriginal Communal Fishing Licences Regulations* who may engage freely in fishing in accordance with the conditions of that licence without being registered and without the need to register their vessel.[78]

Pacific Fishery Regulations, 1993[79]

Subject to these Regulations, no person is permitted to fish in the federally regulated waters of the Pacific without the authority of a licence. Licences issued under the *Aboriginal Communal Fishing Licences Regulations* will be honoured.[80]

Alberta Fishery Regulations[81]

Under the *Alberta Fishery Regulations*, Aboriginal People are permitted to engage in sportfishing without a licence.[82] The provincial Minister can issue a licence to an Aboriginal person to engage in fishing solely for the purpose of catching fish for food for their personal use or for the use of their immediate family.[83]

---

[76] *Ibid.* s. 13(1).
[77] 1985, SOR/86-21.
[78] *Atlantic Fishery Regulations,* s. 15(3).
[79] SOR/93-54.
[80] *Pacific Fishery Regulations, 1993,* s. 26(1).
[81] 1998, SOR/98-246.
[82] *Alberta Fishery Regulations,* s. 13(2).
[83] *Ibid.* s. 13(3).

British Columbia Sport Fishing Regulations[84]

Under the *British Columbia Sport Fishing Regulations*, no person can harvest herring spawn on kelp other than under the authority of a licence issued under the *Aboriginal Communal Fishing Licences Regulations*.[85]

Manitoba Fishery Regulations[86]

The Minister of Natural Resources in Manitoba may issue a General Fishing Permit to a person if its issuance will not adversely affect the conservation and protection of fish in the fishery.[87] Where the Minister is issuing a permit to a person who has an existing treaty or Aboriginal fishing right, the Minister is under an obligation to ensure the permit authorizes the person to fish in accordance with and to the extent of that right and that the permit respects the priority of the holders of the treaty or Aboriginal right to exercise that right.[88]

Maritime Provinces Fishery Regulations[89]

No person fishing in waters controlled by the federal government in the Maritimes is permitted to catch or retain fish, other than where fishing on a recreational basis, unless the person is authorized to do so under the authority of a licence issued under these Regulations, the *Fishery (General) Regulations* or the *Aboriginal Communal Fishing Licences Regulations*.[90]

Newfoundland Fishery Regulations[91]

The *Newfoundland Fishery Regulations* establish a regulatory and licensing scheme that does not apply to the Inuit and Aboriginal Peoples in Labrador who may catch and take fish for food at any time in inland waters by means of nets, traps or spears but such fish are not to be sold or used for any commercial purpose.[92] Certain net size restrictions still apply to the Inuit and Indians of Labrador when fishing in inland waters. Restrictions also apply to fishing in the coastal waters of Southern Labrador. However, such restrictions are deemed not to apply to a Native who lives in that area who holds a commercial trout fishing licence or a trout food fishing licence. Such people

---

84 1996, SOR/96-137.
85 *British Columbia Sport Fishing Regulations*, s. 20.
86 1987, SOR/87-509.
87 *Manitoba Fishery Regulations*, s. 6(1).
88 *Ibid.* s. 6(2).
89 SOR/93-55.
90 *Maritime Provinces Fishery Regulations*, s. 4(1).
91 SOR/78-443.
92 *Newfoundland Fishery Regulations*, s. 10(4).

may food fish for trout or char in such waters by means of gill nets at any time.[93]

Northwest Territories Fishery Regulations[94]

Under the *Northwest Territories Fishery Regulations* no person is to fish except with the authority of a licence issued under these, or under the *Aboriginal Communal Fishing Licences Regulations*.[95] Notwithstanding this provision, an Aboriginal, Inuk or person of "mixed blood" may fish without a licence by angling or by means of gill nets, set lines, spears, snares or dip nets, for food for himself or herself, his or her family and his or her dogs.[96]

Ontario Fishery Regulations, 1989[97]

No person is permitted to fish in Ontario without a recognized licence such as a licence issued under the *Aboriginal Communal Fishing Licences Regulations*.[98]

Quebec Fishery Regulations, 1990[99]

An Aboriginal person must be authorized by a licence issued under the *Aboriginal Communal Fishing Licences Regulations* or otherwise to fish lawfully in federally governed fisheries in Quebec.[100]

Yukon Territory Fishery Regulations[101]

A licence for food, social and ceremonial purposes must be obtained for an Aboriginal person to fish lawfully in the Yukon Territory or he or she must be authorized by a licence issued under the *Aboriginal Communal Fishing Licences Regulations*.[102] This restriction does not apply to beneficiaries fishing for subsistence purposes under a treaty or other agreement.[103]

Aboriginal Fisheries Strategy

---

[93] *Ibid.* s. 75(2).
[94] C.R.C., c. 847.
[95] *Northwest Territories Fishery Regulations*, s. 5(1).
[96] *Ibid.* s. 22(1).
[97] 1989, SOR/89-93.
[98] *Ontario Fishery Regulations, 1989*, s. 4(1).
[99] SOR/90-214.
[100] *Quebec Fishery Regulations, 1990*, s. 5(1).
[101] C.R.C., c. 854.
[102] *Yukon Territory Fishery Regulations*, s. 9(2.1)(b).
[103] *Ibid.* s. 9(2.1)(d).

The landmark Supreme Court ruling in the *R. v. Sparrow*[104] decision established Aboriginal Peoples' right to fish for food, social and ceremonial purposes.[105] The court determined that this right takes priority over all other fishery uses subject only to overriding considerations relating to conservation of the resource. An additional obligation was imposed on the government to consult with Aboriginal groups when their fishing rights have the potential to be affected. In response to this decision, the Department of Fisheries and Oceans Canada launched the Aboriginal Fisheries Strategy in 1992, an organization that receives $32 million in federal funding per year. The program set out in the Aboriginal Fisheries Strategy is deemed to apply where a fisheries management regime has not already been established by land claims settlements. The Department can thus enter into agreements with Aboriginal groups to set in place a regulatory framework for the management of their fishery.

Where an agreement can be reached with Aboriginal groups, time-limited fisheries agreements between the Department of Fisheries and Oceans Canada and Aboriginal groups may be issued. Fisheries agreements negotiated under the Aboriginal Fishing Strategy will specify

- a harvest allocation to the Aboriginal group;
- terms and conditions, for example, provisions relating to enforcement and data collection; and
- a framework for the co-management by the Department of Fisheries and Oceans Canada and the Aboriginal group of the Aboriginal fishery, including projects designed to manage and improve fisheries generally.

The Aboriginal Fishing Strategy is committed to providing commercial fishing licences and other economic development opportunities to Aboriginal groups. One of the fundamental goals of the organization is to contribute to the economic self-sufficiency of Aboriginal communities. Licences are being issued in such a way as to minimize impact on the resource, and one of the integral parts of ensuring minimal impact is the Allocation Transfer Program that is facilitated by the Department of Fisheries and Oceans Canada. This program allows for commercial licenses to be voluntarily retired, which will then be transferred to a requesting Aboriginal group. Since 1994, 250 commercial fishing licences have been transferred to Aboriginal groups

---

[104] *R. v. Sparrow*, *supra* note 5 in ch. 1.
[105] For a discussion of the case, see Binnie, W., "The Sparrow Doctrine: Beginning of the End or End of the Beginning?" (1991), 15 *Queen's Law Journal* 217; Elliot, D., "In the Wake of *Sparrow*" (1991) 40 *University of British Columbia Law Journal* 23; Asch, M. and Macklem, P., "Aboriginal Rights and Canadian Sovereignty" (1991) 26:2 *Alberta Law Review* 502.

under the program.[106] Where an agreement cannot be concluded, a communal fishing licence will be given to the group allowing them to fish for food, social and ceremonial purposes.

The Aboriginal Fishing Strategy applies only to fisheries over which Canada exerts jurisdiction. The bulk of concluded agreements have occurred with the groups in the Department of Fisheries and Oceans "Pacific Region" while the remainder have been established in Quebec and Atlantic Canada.

Agreements were initially concluded with the following First Nations. The original agreements expired on 31 March 2001. Some of these First Nations are now authorized to fish under fisheries agreements concluded with the Department of Fisheries and Oceans Canada.

- Abegweit
- Acadia
- Afton
- Annapolis Valley
- Bear River
- Big Cove
- Buctouche
- Burnt Church
- Chapel Island
- Eel Ground (Natuaguanek)
- Eel River Bar
- Eskasoni
- Fort Folly
- Gesgapegiag
- Gespeg
- Horton
- Indian Brook

- Indian Island
- Kingsclear
- Lennox Island
- Listiguj
- Madawaska Maliseet
- Malécites de viger
- Membertou
- Millbrook
- Oromocto
- Pabineau
- Pictou Landing
- Red Bank
- Saint Mary's
- Tobique
- Wagmatcook
- Waycobah
- Woodstock

The Aboriginal Fisheries Strategy was recently challenged by the Chippewas of Nawash First Nation in the Federal Court before Mr. Justice Dawson in *Chippewas of Nawash First Nation v. Canada (Minister of Fisheries and Oceans).*[107] The Chippewas argued that the Aboriginal Fisheries Strategy was discriminatory in that most Aboriginal groups that pursue inland fishing have been denied access to the program. The Federal Court considered whether the exclusion of Aboriginal groups in non-coastal

---

[106] Aboriginal Fish Strategy Fact Sheet, Department of Fisheries and Oceans Canada, online: <http://www.dfo-mpo.gc.ca/COMMUNIC/FISH_MAN/AFS_e.htm>, as at 10/11/01.

[107] [2001] 1 C.N.L.R. 20.

areas of Canada violates the plaintiffs' right to equality under section 15(1) of the *Canadian Charter of Rights and Freedoms*, and also whether the alleged discrimination constitutes a breach of any fiduciary duty owed by the Crown to the plaintiffs. The court found no such breach and the application was subsequently dismissed. Fundamentally, the Ontario government has the legislative and regulatory capacity to govern the inland fisheries of Ontario and for that reason, the plaintiffs' claims were thrown out.

First Nations Affected by the Decision in *R. v. Marshall*[108]

Since the Supreme Court decision in *R. v. Marshall*, the Department of Fisheries and Oceans has set about negotiating new fishing agreements with First Nations. This case involved an appeal by Marshall from a Nova Scotia Court of Appeal decision that had upheld his convictions for selling eels without a licence, fishing without a licence and fishing during the close of season with illegal nets, contrary to the federal fishery regulations. Marshall is a Mi'kmaq from Membertou Band of Cape Breton Island who was convicted of fishing for eels contrary to federal fishing laws. He was charged with fishing without a licence and selling eels without a licence as well as fishing in a closed season. Marshall claimed that he had a right to fish and to sell his catch as such a right had never been surrendered to the British Crown. The treaty argument was based on treaties signed with the Crown in 1760 and 1761. Marshall alleged that these agreements guaranteed to the Mi'kmaq the right to fish for commercial purposes. Under those treaties, the Crown placed an obligation on the Mi'kmaq of Nova Scotia to "traffic and barter commodities with the persons or the managers of such Truckhouses as shall be established for that purpose by His Majesty's Governors." The federal government set aside $160 million for this task. The agreements are broadly similar in structure. However, the contents of the agreements vary according to certain factors, for example, agreement particulars depend on such factors as the population size of the First Nation and what its particular interests are.

The agreements serve two purposes. They can provide infrastructure for commercial and food fishing, including boats, fishing equipment and so on. They can also provide for government-run courses involving training, capacity building and other fishery-related economic development initiatives such as aquaculture or ecotourism. The content of such an agreement will depend upon the goals and planning ideas of the First Nation concerned.

---

[108] *R. v. Marshall (Marshall No. 2)*, [1999] 3 S.C.R. 533 (reconsideration refused).

Under the scheme, First Nations who already have an arrangement under the Aboriginal Fishing Strategy have an option to maintain two separate agreements or of negotiating one comprehensive agreement. Again, this depends on the individual First Nation's preference.

The federal government made the following statement as to the "success" of the initiative:

> To ensure the viability of the fishery, which is fully subscribed, the Department created a space for this increased access through voluntary retirement of licences held by non-Aboriginal fishers. As a result of these initiatives, Mi'kmaq and Maliseet communities have increased their participation in the Atlantic fishery. More than 130 fishing vessels have been allocated to Aboriginal communities. There has been a 174% increase in the number of commercial lobster enterprises owned and operated by First Nations. Prior to the *Marshall* decision, First Nations held one tuna licence. They now have 10. In 2000, 5% of the shrimp in Quebec was harvested by First Nations, and 7% of the crab quota for the southern Gulf of St. Lawrence and Scotian Shelf was allocated to First Nation fishers.[109]

The government initiative did not dissipate the frustration and anxiety of Aboriginal fishers affected by the *Marshall* decision. In February 2000, the Department of Fisheries and Oceans confiscated two crab-fishing boats from the members of Indian Brook. Seven more Indian Brook fishing vessels were seized later in 2000 and 18 people were charged with illegally fishing lobster. Burnt Church rejected an interim fishing agreement proposed by the Department and the Burnt Church people were raided with 700 traps being seized and four people arrested.[110] Two short-term agreements were negotiated with the Burnt Church people in 2001 to temporarily suppress conflict.

Some First Nations affected by *Marshall* interpret the decision as evidence of a judicially recognized right for them to self-regulate their share of the fishery. In the actual judgement, the court was very careful to state their decision in fact-specific terms and did not address Aboriginal self-government or the federal government's claims to exclusive regulation of the fishery. It is clear that the federal government's capacity to regulate the Mi'kmaq treaty right to fish is limited to actions that are capable of being shown by the Crown to be justified. Such justification will require a "compelling and substantial objective" and may include such objectives as regulation for the purpose of conserving a resource.

---

[109] Indian and Northern Affairs Canada, "Backgrounder: The *Marshall* Judgment and the Federal Government's response" (B-HQ-01-09(149), February 2001) at 2.

[110] See Isaac, T., *Aboriginal and Treaty Rights in the Maritimes: The Marshall Decision and Beyond*, Purich Publishing Limited, Saskatoon, 2001, p. 151.

On the west coast, the Douglas Treaties were relied upon by 14 First Nations to support their claims to an Aboriginal fishery. Fishing licences along with fishing equipment were offered to them to prevent litigation.

The Department of Oceans and Fisheries Canada promised funds for Aboriginal fishing-related activities. The Department pledged contributions designed to support increased Native participation in commercial fisheries, co-operative fisheries management arrangements and consultations respecting Aboriginal fisheries agreements. The Department committed $34.7 million for 2001-02 and a further $34.7 million for 2002-03.

One insightful article highlights the infringements of Aboriginal fishing rights by the Pacific Salmon management system as a whole and suggests that a fundamental revision is required.[111] The legal basis for the Aboriginal rights to harvest fishery resources was affirmed in *R. v. Sparrow.*[112] In *R. v. Gladstone*[113] the court recognized that Aboriginal People have the right to special consideration in some commercial fisheries. *R. v. Sparrow* further determined that Aboriginal People with a legal right to fish have the right to exercise their rights by preferred means and are not restricted to traditional methods or equipment to do so. To date, fishing rights have been construed narrowly to mean the right to harvest, a right that is seen as separate and distinct from management of the resource. This, according to the article's authors, is problematic and does not give full and rightful protection to the Aboriginal People to whom the fishing right has been recognized and affirmed.

Generally speaking, the Western approach to economic exploitation of natural resources has separated the concepts and activities of exploitation and management. On one hand, resource users are expected to apply their legal rights to compete and prosper and, in so doing, to behave according to market pressures. Responsibility for preventing overuse of a resource, on the other hand, relies with public institutions and regulatory agencies. This notion of resource use and management is a deeply ingrained concept in Western society. This concept contrasts starkly, however, with the Aboriginal concept. The authors of the article refer to extensive sources indicating a consensus among anthropologists, historians and Aboriginal commentators that complex systems of fisheries use and management existed before Aboriginal Peoples experienced contact with non-Aboriginal settlers.

---

[111] Walter, E., M'Gonigle, M., and McKay, C., "Fishing around the Law: the Pacific Salmon Management System as a "Structural Infringement" of Aboriginal Rights" (2000), 45 *McGill Law Journal* 263.

[112] [1990] 1 S.C.R. 1075, 70 D.L.R. (4th) 648.

[113] [1996] 2 S.C.R. 723, 137 D.L.R. (4th) 648.

By referring extensively to principles expounded in recent Supreme Court decisions, the authors conclude that the current Pacific Salmon management system unlawfully imposes upon and detracts from Aboriginal fishing rights. Such infringements are "unnecessary to achieve either conservation, reconciliation, or economic and regional fairness."[114] Accordingly, the authors suggest that community-based management according to clean production principles would impair Aboriginal fishing rights to a lesser degree and would be a sustainable regime. Moreover, the Government of Canada would be fulfilling its fiduciary obligations to the Aboriginal People adversely affected by the current Pacific Salmon management system.

The Migratory Birds Convention Act[115]

Great Britain became a signatory to the Migratory Bird Convention on behalf of Canada in 1916. The Convention purports to preserve migratory birds and save them from indiscriminate slaughter by establishing closed hunting seasons, prohibiting the removal of nests and eggs belonging to protected species, and by preventing the sale of such species and their by-products. The agreement recognized that Aboriginal People had a right to "take at any time scoters for food but not for sale."[116] Under the current Act, "Eskimos and Indians" are allowed to "take at any season, auks, auklets, guillemots, murres and puffins, and their eggs for food and their skins for clothing, but the birds and eggs so taken shall not be sold or offered for sale."[117]

The *Migratory Birds Convention Act* recognizes that the Act does not detract from constitutionally guaranteed treaty rights.[118] Prior to the enactment of section 35, Aboriginal treaty rights were not guaranteed and the courts consistently found that the *Migratory Birds Convention Act* overrode any purported treaty rights.[119] Since 1982, Aboriginal and treaty rights to hunt migratory species are respected, but if conservation measures are found to be justified, then the Act will still apply to Aboriginal People. Rights to hunt migratory species may also be conveyed via modern land claim agreements and also provincial resource agreements with individual or groups of bands. Generally speaking, the Act takes away the rights to hunt migratory birds incorporated into Treaty No. 11 and other treaties.

---

[114] *Supra.* note 28 in ch. 2, para. 175.

[115] *Migratory Birds Convention Act*, R.S.C. 1970, c.M-12.

[116] *Ibid.,* Art. II, s. 2.

[117] *Ibid.,* Art. II, s. 3.

[118] *Migratory Birds Convention Act*, R.S.C. 1985, c. M-7, as am. R.S.C. 1985, c. 31 (1st Supp.), s. 38; c. 40(4th Supp.), s. 2 (Schedule, item 6); 1992, c. 1, s. 96; 1994, c. 22; 1995, c. 22, s. 18, Sched. IV, item 27.

[119] See for example, *R. v. Sikyea*, [1964] S.C.R. 642, and *Daniels v. White*, [1968] S.C.R. 517.

First Nations Land Management Act[120]

The *First Nations Land Management Act* was enacted to bring into effect the Framework Agreement on First Nation Land Management.[121] The Act was enacted to secure control by First Nations over First Nations lands and the right to govern those lands, including its own communities and any contained resources. The purpose of the Act is to lay to rest arguments that the land management provisions of the *Indian Act* have conferred immense power and authority on government officials, and has hindered land and economic development for First Nations. The proposed land management system was devised by 13 chiefs representing the First Nations of Westbank, Musqueam, Lheit-Lit'en, N'Quatqua, Squamish, Siksika, Muskoday, Cowessess, Opaskwayak Cree, Nipissing, Mississaugas of Scugog Island, Chippewas of Georgina Island and Chippewas of Mnjikaning. The Act applies only to those First Nations who sign the Framework Agreement. So far, only one other First Nation has signed the Agreement; namely, Saint Mary's. The Agreement provides a First Nation with the choice of subscribing to a process that will give it the option of governing its lands and resources under its own law.[122]

The Act does not alter Aboriginal title to First Nation land, which continues to be set apart for the use and benefit of the First Nation for which it was set apart, and therefore still falls within federal jurisdiction as included in section 91(24) of the *Constitution Act, 1867*.[123]

The Act anticipates the establishment of a "land code" that is to cover a range of land use issues.[124] Under section 18 of the Act, a First Nation is given a range of management powers over First Nations land. [125] The envisaged "land code" gives the First Nation concerned the right to exercise the powers, rights and privileges of an owner in relation to its land. This includes:

- the right to grant interests in and licences in relation to that land;[126]
- to manage the natural resources of that land;[127] and
- to receive and all revenue acquired under its land code on behalf of the entire First Nation.[128]

---

[120] *First Nations Land Management Act*, 1999, c. 24.

[121] Framework Agreement on First Nation Land Management, Land Advisory Board, online: <http://www.fafnlm.com/LAB.NSF/39e36a26f6235821852568c3005dc7af/c367db5e6523f58b852568e7006ed01b?OpenDocument>.

[122] *Backgrounder – First Nations Land Management Regime Framework Agreement*, Department of Indian Affairs and Northern Development, online: <http://www.ainc-inac.gc.ca/nr/prs/j-a1996/9550bk.html>.

[123] *Ibid.* s. 5.

[124] *Ibid.* s. 6.

[125] *Ibid.* s. 18(1)(a).

[126] *Ibid.* s. 18(1)(b).

[127] *Ibid.* s. 18(1)(c).

[128] *Ibid.* s. 18(1)(d).

The Act also makes clear that, for any purpose relating to its land, a First Nation is granted the legal capacity to exercise its powers and perform its duties and functions.[129] In particular, the agent or council of a First Nation, in accordance with its "land code," is empowered with the ability to enact laws in relation to

- interests in and licences in relation to its land;[130] and
- measures for the development, conservation, protection, management, use and possession of land and ancillary matters.[131]

These rights extend to enactment of enforcement measures to ensure compliance with these laws.[132]

The right to make laws in respect of land management is restricted only by bylaws made by a First Nations council itself under section 81 of the *Indian Act*. Where a conflict arises between the sets of laws, the land code is to prevail to the extent of that inconsistency or conflict.[133]

The *Indian Oil and Gas Act* is deemed still to apply in respect of any First Nation that was subject to the Act prior to the relevant land code enactment, and applies in respect of an interest in First Nation land that was granted to the Crown for the exploitation of oil and gas pursuant to a land code.[134] Where inconsistency or conflict between a land code or a First Nation law made under the code and a federal law exists, the federal law is deemed to prevail to the extent of the inconsistency or conflict.[135] The Act explicitly states that no law relating to migratory birds, endangered species, or fisheries is altered or can be overridden by the operation of this Act.[136] Nothing in the Act is deemed to limit the application of the *Nuclear Safety and Control Act*[137] and the *Nuclear Energy Act*.[138]

Several provisions of the Act assure that the existing land base of the First Nation parties cannot be diminished. The prohibition on the sale of land and the mandatory replacement of any lands expropriated are two examples of this general rule. A third is that a First Nation may consent to exchange a portion of its lands through a voluntary agreement with a third party. Again, the compensation must include replacement lands so the land base is not diminished.[139]

---

[129] *Ibid.* s. 18(2).
[130] *Ibid.* s. 20(1)(a).
[131] *Ibid.* sections 20(1)(a) & (b).
[132] *Ibid.* s. 20(3).
[133] *Ibid.* s. 20(4).
[134] *Ibid.* s. 39(1).
[135] *Ibid.* s. 40(1).
[136] *Ibid.* s. 40(2).
[137] *Nuclear Safety and Control Act*, 1997, c. 9.
[138] *Nuclear Energy Act*, R.S., 1985, c. A-16, s. 1; 1997, c. 9, s. 89.
[139] See sections 26–33, *First Nations Land Management Act*.

Although the *First Nations Land Management Act* would appear to empower First Nations to govern resource use and development on First Nations land to a much greater extent than permitted under the *Indian Act* and related legislation, general reluctance among First Nations to sign the Agreement is apparent. One review of the legislation has identified several reasons as to why this may be the case.[140] As a general observation, as currently structured, there is a limit as to the number of First Nations that can participate in the program. To many First Nations, commercially based land management is not worthwhile as land transactions are only occasional.[141] A report compiled by the Departmental Audit and Evaluation Branch of the Department of Indian Affairs and Northern Development summarizes the most commonly expressed complaints about the land management program:

1. There is general concern that Aboriginal land related interests will in fact be weakened by becoming a signatory to the Agreement. There is some fear that by accepting the delegation of ministerial authority that the government (as represented by the Minister) will relinquish its fiduciary obligation and statutory duty.[142]

2. The Agreement and Act requires that a referendum be held to establish to whom, or to which group, authority is to be delegated. A concern aired about this aspect of the Agreement is that political leadership is forced to submit itself to a vote of confidence that may result in a negative outcome. This places the political leadership in an awkward position.[143]

3. A further concern expressed by First Nations relates to the funding formula and conditions. Funding is made available to First Nations under the Agreement to provide land management services in lieu of services previously supplied by the Department of Indian Affairs and Northern Development. The formula by which funding is conferred is based primarily on the number of revenue-producing land transactions undertaken by First Nations. The formula used measures administrative, development and other types of workload, focusing on three types of land transactions, namely, leases, permits and allotments. This formula is criticized for being "inflexible, unresponsive to the diversity of land management activities, and too transaction driven."[144]

---

[140] Clarkson, B. and Goss Gilroy Inc., *Evaluation of Department of Indian and Northern Affairs' Lands Management* Program, Departmental Audit and Evaluation Branch, Department of Indian Affairs and Northern Development, Project 94/16, June 1997, online: <http://www.ainc-inac.gc.ca/pr/pub/ae/ev/94-16_e.pdf>.

[141] *Ibid.* p. ii.

[142] *Ibid.* p. 5.

[143] *Ibid.* p. 6.

[144] *Ibid.*

4. The formula used to measure funding arrangements is also alleged to be overly limited and inherently unfair. Effectively, the amount of funding received by each First Nation will depend on the number of leases, permits and allotments that have been issued. Commercial success is, therefore, rewarded with corresponding funding, while traditional land use is not taken into account. Moreover, there is little opportunity under the funding formula for planning, surveying and environmental assessments in relation to land use.[145]

5. A further complaint concerns the relative inequity among First Nations. Under the funding formula, as stated above, First Nations with high land transactions will attract the most government funding for land management. It is those First Nations who make money from such interests, and therefore can afford to establish and run a land management office already. In many circumstances, First Nations that are involved in a high volume of land transactions already have a land management office in place. It is these already financially advantaged First Nations who will receive the highest levels of funding under the program, while First Nations with a small volume of land transactions and less external transactions will attract considerably less funding and may not be able to afford to establish and operate a land management office.[146]

6. Another criticism has been levelled at the inadequacy of both funding and staff resources to provide adequate land management. Funding is considered insufficient to attract qualified people to the land management positions, leading to a high turnover rate. The report indicates that many First Nations people are returning to reside upon reserves, and as they do so, land management activity increases on First Nation land. There is a growing volume of work, with a lack of human resources to staff land management offices and inadequate remuneration to keep them for long.[147]

To date, four of the First Nation signatories to the Framework Agreement have developed land codes: Chippewas of Georgina Island, Lheidli T'enneh, Muskoday and Mississaugas of Scugog.[148]

---

[145] *Ibid.*

[146] *Ibid.*

[147] *Ibid.* p. 7.

[148] See Land Codes, Land Advisory Board, online: <http://www.fafnlm.com/LAB.NSF/vWebLand?OpenView>.

Part 3

Provincial Regulation

Chapter 5

Ontario

At Confederation, pursuant to section 109 of the *Constitution Act, 1867*, the Crown interest in public lands in specific regions passed to the provinces. In southern Ontario at the time, very few reserves had been established upon Ontario's entry into Confederation and much of the province had yet to be settled. In southern Ontario, Aboriginal title was considered to be extinguished by the Robinson Treaties of 1850, and for that reason, no express power was reserved for the federal government at Confederation for the purpose of creating reserves out of land taken from the province.

Since Confederation, occasionally Ontario has assented to additional public lands being set aside in order that reserves be created for First Nations people. The most common method of establishing reserve lands in southern Ontario has been by purchase of private land by the federal government.

Canada-Ontario Agreement[1]

By virtue of the agreement between Canada and Ontario, the federal government administers not only reserve lands but also surrendered lands that are the subject of a specific agreement. As noted earlier, under the *Indian Lands Agreement (1986) Act,* a specific agreement may be entered into by Ontario, Canada, and any band or group of bands relating to lands or natural resources (see page 32).

One half of proceeds from minerals goes to the province and the other half goes to the First Nation affected.

---

[1] *An Act for the Settlement of Certain Questions Between the Governments of Canada and Ontario Respecting Indian Reserve Lands*, S.C. 1924, c.48; *Indian Lands Agreement (1986) Act*, S.C. 1988, c.39.

Mineral Potential on Indian Reserve Lands in Ontario[2]

The Mineral Potential of Indian Reserve Lands report compiled by the Department of Indian and Northern Affairs Canada[3] provides overall rating measures of the economic mineral possibilities of each reserve as a whole, on a scale of low/moderate/good. Factors that affect this rating are the size of the reserve, the location with respect to markets, transportation, access, value and type of commodity, social and cultural barriers to mining on certain lands and areas, marketability of a commodity at any given time and other differentials.

The following rating applies in Ontario:

- 82 reserves were given a low rating;
- 69 reserves were given a moderate rating; and
- 38 reserves were given a good rating.

The report indicates that 59 reserves have at least one commodity that has potential for development. Of the total 189 reserves, at the time of this report, 27 had surrendered their minerals in some way.

Provincial Legislation

Note that provincial legislation and regulations are deemed to apply to Aboriginal People subject to two conditions:

- provincial legislation cannot apply exclusively to Aboriginal People or to land reserved for their benefit; and
- a provincial law may be declared invalid or inapplicable to Aboriginal People if it infringes upon an established Aboriginal or treaty right that is constitutionally protected.

Where an Aboriginal person has established an Aboriginal or treaty right to hunt or fish, then the provincial legislation cannot interfere with that right[4] unless the limitation can meet the test of justification and is in keeping with the honour of the Crown.[5] A limitation on the exercise of a treaty or Aboriginal right would need to be tested in the courts for clarification. It is clear that sufficient consideration must be given to the Aboriginal interest.

---

[2] See the Department of Indian and Northern Affairs, online: <http://www.ainc-inac.gc.ca/ntr/ont_e.html>.

[3] Keep in mind that although this site was last updated on the 30 April 2001, the report was actually completed in 1991.

[4] *R. v. White and Bob, supra* note 10 in ch. 2; *R. v. Simon, supra* note 2 in ch. 2; and, *R. v. Sioui, supra* note 2 in ch. 2.

[5] *R. v. White and Bob, supra* note 10 in ch. 2; *R. v. Simon, supra* note 2 in ch. 2; and, *R. v. Sioui, supra* note 2 in ch. 2; *R. v. Sparrow, supra* note 5 in ch. 1.

Apart from measures implemented by a province to conserve a resource, it is unlikely that any court in Canada would uphold any other provincial legislation that restricts an Aboriginal or treaty right. Recently, provincial laws designed to protect public safety have been permitted to override and limit Aboriginal resource rights.

Fishing in Ontario[6]

The administration and regulation of inland, non-tidal fisheries in Ontario was transferred to the province in 1899. The Department of Fisheries and Oceans Canada has retained little involvement in the management of the fisheries over the last century. The Minister of Natural Resources for Ontario is also empowered to grant licences for Aboriginal fishing in Ontario by virtue of the *Aboriginal Communal Fishing Licence Regulations* made pursuant to the federal *Fishery Act*.

To fish lawfully in Ontario, most Canadian residents need to obtain what is called an "Outdoors Card" that provides proof to a provincial fisheries officer that he or she is permitted to fish. Members of Aboriginal communities in Ontario that have already established Aboriginal and treaty rights to harvest fish do not need an Outdoors Card or an Ontario fishing licence tag to fish for "personal use" within their traditional lands or treaty territory. Personal use is fishing for food, social or ceremonial purposes only.

Hunting in Ontario[7]

The *Fish and Wildlife Conservation Act*[8] and the *Endangered Species Act*[9] restrict or prohibit the species that may be harvested in the province. It is an offence to hunt or trap any specially protected species in Ontario,[10] and a licence must be obtained to hunt or trap the following species:

(a) a black bear, white-tailed deer, moose, caribou or elk, and any other game mammal;
(b) a game bird;
(c) a furbearing mammal;
(d) a game reptile;

---

[6] See the Ontario Ministry of Natural Resources, online:
    <http://www.mnr.gov.on.ca/MNR/fishing/oc10.html>.
[7] See the Ontario Ministry of Natural Resources, Ontario Hunting Regulations Summary, online:
    <http://www.mnr.gov.on.ca/MNR/pubs/hr2001.pdf>.
[8] 1997, C.41.
[9] R.S.O. 1990, c. E-15.
[10] *Fish and Wildlife Conservation Act*, s. 5(1).

(e)   a game amphibian; and

(f)   particular types of birds.[11]

No person is permitted to take or possess the nest or eggs of a bird that belongs to a species that is wild by nature,[12] although authorization from the Minister may be sought. Migratory birds continue to be governed federally.[13] Hunting, trapping and possession of wildlife in a provincial park or Crown game preserve is prohibited.[14]

These laws and regulations are deemed to apply generally to Aboriginal people to the point that interference with an established right to hunt and trap is unjustified.

Ontario Treaties

- Numerous Pre-Confederation Treaties
- Post-Confederation Treaties
- Treaties No. 3, 5 and 9
- Williams Treaties, 1923

Pre-Confederation Treaties

Many of the pre-Confederation treaties make no mention of residual resource rights belonging to the Aboriginal People with whom the negotiations took place. Most of these treaties have never been the subject of judicial review and Aboriginal People have rarely tried to assert resource rights under these agreements. Recent decisions, including the case of *Chippewas of Sarnia Band v. Canada (Attorney General)*[15] indicate that Ontario courts are open to accommodating Aboriginal claims challenging the validity of these treaties. The Supreme Court of Canada decision in *R. v. Delgamuukw* has opened the way for oral evidence to be submitted in support of the Aboriginal understanding of the treaties and agreements, and these Ontario treaties may

---

[11]   See *Ibid.* s. 5(2).

[12]   *Ibid.* s. 7(1).

[13]   *Ibid.* s. 7(4).

[14]   *Ibid.* s. 9(1).

[15]   [2000] O.J. No. 4804.

well be vulnerable to Aboriginal claims that rights to hunt, fish and trap were intended to be protected by the Crown. At present, very few treaties make mention of or appear to protect Aboriginal rights to natural resources on surrendered tracts of land.[16] Litigation concerning the pre-Confederation treaties in Ontario will be considered below.

---

[16] See the following treaties where no guarantee of a positive right to resources in the surrendered land is mentioned: Treaty No. 116 of 1786 with the Ottawas and Chippewas of Detroit in relation to the area covered by Anderdon Township and West Sandwich in Lambton County; Treaty No. 3 (of the single payment cession treaties) of 1792 with the Mississaugas people in relation to the area between Lake Erie, Ontario and Thames River; Treaty No. 3 – of 1793 signed by the Six Nations in relation to the Bay of Quinte; Treaty No. 3 – of 1795 signed by the Mississaugas people in relation to the land between Burlington Bay and Lake Ontario; Treaty No. 4 (of the single payment cession treaties) of 1793 agreed to by the Six Nations in relation to land around the River Ouse; Sombra Township Purchase of 1796 by the Mohawk, Oghquaga, Onondaga, Seneca, Cayuga people in relation to land on Grand River; London Township Purchase – No. 7 of 1796 signed by the Chippewa people of Escunnisepe in relation to the area of land now covered by London; Land for Joseph Brant – No. 8 of 1797 signed by the Mississauga people of the Burlington Bay, Head of Lake Ontario district in relation to that land – the wording of this treaty is such that the Aboriginal People surrendered not just the tract of land in question, but also the "woods and waters thereon...free and clear...Hereby renouncing and forever absolving [them] of all title"; Penetanguishene Harbour – No. 5 of 1798 between the Chippewa of Simcoe County and the Crown whereby the Chippewa promised to renounce any claims that may have existed to both the land and to the woods and waters thereon; St. Joseph Island – No. 11 of 1798 between the Chippewa and the Crown in relation to St. Joseph's Island whereby the Chippewa promised to surrender any claims that may have existed to both the island and the woods and waters upon it; Treaty No. 12 of 1800 between the Ottawa, Chippewa, Potawatomie and Wynadot people concerning the Huron Church Reserve surrendering title to the land and to the woods and waters upon it; Lake Simcoe Land – No. 16 of 1815 between the Chippewa and the Crown concerning Simcoe County; Treaty No. 17 of 1816 between the Mississaugas and the Crown conveying 428 acres of land situated at the Bay of Quinte; Lake Simcoe-Notawasaga Purchase – No. 18 of 1818 between the Chippewa and the Crown concerning parts of Grey and Wellington Counties; Aietance Purchase – No. 19 of 1818 between the Mississagua and the Crown in relation to the area covered by the Peel and Wellington Counties; Long Woods Purchase 1819 – 27 – Western Ontario – No. 21 of 1819 between the Chippewa people and the Crown in relation to the land covered by Middlesex, Lambton and Kent counties; Treaty No. 24 of 1820 signed by the Mohawk (Six Nations) and the Crown in relation to the area of the River Shannon to Bowen's Creek; Treaty No. 27 – of 1822 between the Mississagua people and the Crown in relation to the area of land covered by the Midland and Johnstown Districts of Ontario; Treaty No. 30 of 1830 between the Six Nations and the Crown Concerning land in the County of Wentworth; Treaty No. 31 of 1831 between Six Nations and the Crown concerning land covered by the County of Haldimand; Treaty No. 37 of 1834 between the Chippewa people and the Crown in relation to the surrender of the land now covered by the township of Carradoc; Treaty No. 38 between the Six Nations and the Crown in relation to the surrender of 48,000 acres of land surrounding the Ouse River; Treaty No. 41 of 1835 between the Mohawk and the Crown in relation to the Hastings and Midland districts; Treaty No. 47 of 1836 between the Moravian people and the Crown in relation to the surrender of an area of land on the northern side of the Thames River; Treaty No. 53 – of 1843 concluded by the Ojibewa people and the Crown in relation to the land around the River Saint Clair; Treaty No. 47 of 1847 between the Iroquois and the Crown in relation to the surrender of the land of Saint Regis County of Glengarry; Treaty No. 96 of 1848 between the Chippewa and the Crown in relation to land covered by the Anderden township in Essex County; Treaty No. 53 – B of 1849 between the Chippewa people and the Crown, surrendering 4 acres situated in the town of Carrodoc, London for the purpose of the establishment of an industrial school by the Weslayan Methodist Conference and Missionary Society; an untitled agreement of 1849 between the Ojibewa people and the Crown surrendered land around the Saint Clair River.

No. 106

Negotiations were entered into in 1784 by the Six Nations (Mohawk) and the Crown in respect of land that was granted by Governor Haldimand to those Aboriginal People. The land, situated on the Banks of the Grand River flowing into Lake Erie, was designed to compensate the Six Nations who had been pushed out of their settlements. The land was to provide "a safe and comfortable retreat for them." Ontario courts have subsequently held that this transfer did not create a legal estate and the Aboriginal People or their descendants cannot therefore alienate the land.[17]

No. 2

This treaty was negotiated by the Ottawa, Chippewa, Pottowatomy and Huron Aboriginal People and the Crown in 1790 in relation to the land north and adjacent to Lake Erie. The Aboriginal People promised to "grant, give, enfeoff, alien and confirm...a certain tract of land; His Majesty...shall and lawfully may from henceforward and forever after peaceably and quietly have, hold, occupy and possess and enjoy the said tract of land...with all...appurtenances."

In *R. v. Riley*[18] an Ontario court found that Treaty No. 2 of the single payment cession treaties did not contain a reservation of the right to hunt and trap. The Ontario court examined the validity of a Memorial that was signed in 1794 that allegedly confirmed that the right to hunt and fish was preserved over the lands covered by the 1790 treaty. The court found, however, that the Memorial is a unilateral document made years after the treaty was signed and therefore had no weight in law. The right to hunt was protected by neither statute nor treaty. The Ottawa, Chippewa, Pottowatomy and Huron people from the north and adjacent to Lake Erie are therefore subject to provincial laws of general application, in this case to the Ontario *Game and Fish Act*.

No. 20

Treaty No. 20 was negotiated in 1818 whereby the Crown and the Chippewa people agreed to a land transaction in relation to certain areas within the Peel, Wellington and other counties. The Chippewa people agreed to "freely, fully and voluntarily surrender and convey [the land]...without reservation or limitation in perpetuity." The treaty makes no mention of resource or harvestation rights. Ontario courts considered this treaty and whether or not it had somehow preserved rights to hunt and fish in the case of *R. v. Taylor*

---

[17] *Jackson v. Wilkes* (1835), 4 U.C.K.B. 142, 1 C.N.L.C. 259; *Sheldon v. Ramsey* (1852), 9 U.C.Q.B. 105, 1 C.N.L.C. 439; *Bown v. West* (1946), 1 E. & A. 117.

[18] *R. v. Riley* (1983), [1984] 2 C.N.L.R. 154 (Ont. Prov. Offences Ct.).

and Williams[19] in the early 1980s (prior to the constitutionalization of Aboriginal and treaty rights). The respondents were convicted of harvesting bullfrogs out of season, contrary to the Ontario *Game and Fish Act*.[20] The frogs were retrieved from unoccupied Crown lands falling within the boundaries of Treaty No. 20. The minutes of the negotiations at the time of the treaty conclusion indicated that hunting and fishing rights were assured to the Chippewa people. The court found that the minutes from the meeting were also a part of the treaty and therefore held that the 1818 treaty preserved the right of the respondents to fish and hunt on Crown grounds in the area within the treaty boundaries. Treaty No. 20 Aboriginals exercising their rights under the treaty were therefore protected from the operation of the provincial legislation. The Supreme Court subsequently found that Treaty No. 23 had extinguished these rights.[21]

Huron Tract – No. 29

The Huron Tract Treaty No. 29 was concluded in 1827 by the Crown and the Chippewa people in relation to land in the Waterloo, Wellington, Huron and Middlesex counties. There is no mention in the treaty of residual resource rights in relation to the land that the Chippewa people agreed to "forever yield up" to the Crown.

This treaty was considered in *R. v. George*.[22] In this case a Chippewa man was convicted of killing two ducks, on reserve, out of season under the *Migratory Birds Regulations* passed under section 12(1) of the *Migratory Birds Convention Act*. The accused claimed that he had a right to hunt by virtue of the fact that such a right was guaranteed under the 1827 treaty. The court did not determine whether such a right existed under the treaty; rather, it found that section 87 (now section 88) of the *Indian Act* did not guarantee that parliamentary legislation would be subject to the terms of any treaty, merely that the intent of section 87 was to make Aboriginal People subject to the exclusive jurisdiction of the federal Parliament, subject only to provincial laws of general application. The *Migratory Birds Regulations* were therefore deemed to apply to the accused.

In a later case,[23] the accused was caught fishing with a gill net without a license and failing to return fish in violation of the *Ontario Fisheries Regulations*, enacted under the federal *Fisheries Act*. The court recognized the right of the Chippewa people of Kettle Point to fish in waters adjacent to

---

[19] (1981), 34 O.R. (2d) 360, 62 C.C.C. (2d) 227 (C.A.), affirming (1979), 55 C.C.C. (2d) 172, [1980] 1 C.N.L.R. 83 (Ont. Div. Ct.).

[20] R.S.O., c.186.

[21] *R. v. Howard* (1994), S.C.R. at 299.

[22] *R. v. George*, [1966] S.C.R. 267, 47 C.R. 382, reversing [1964] 2 O.R. 429, 45 D.L.R. (2d) 709, [1965] 2 C.C.C. 148 (C.A.), affirming [1964] 1 O.R. 24, 41 D.L.R. (2d) 31 (H.C.).

[23] *R. v. Jackson*, [1992] 4 C.N.L.R. 121 (Ont. Prov. Ct.).

the Kettle Point reserve using gill nets for their *own consumption* and *limited commercial purposes*. This right the court found to be "inherent" in the treaty of 1827 and bolstered by the *Royal Proclamation* of 1763. The Ontario court found that First Nations have a right to the allocation of any surplus fisheries after conservation measures are given consideration. The court held that the general government desire to place regulations that sought to preserve fish stocks was an insufficient reason to justify regulation of the First Nations fishery. The *Ontario Fisheries Regulations* were found not to apply to the right of the accused to fish with a gill net. This case indicates that, where reserve land is adjacent to bodies of water, the Aboriginal residents have a right to fish within that water, free from all provincial legislation that is not in force for conservation reasons. Where conservation measures are in place, these cannot fall primarily on Aboriginal fisheries.

The most recent litigation concerning interpretation of these pre-Confederation treaties was in the 2000 land rights litigation case of *Chippewas of Sarnia Band v. Canada (A.G.)*. In 1827 the Chippewa Nation had entered into an agreement (Treaty No. 29) with the Crown whereby certain land, now covered by the township of Sarnia, was to be conveyed to the First Nation as a reserve. In 1853 that land was then patented by the Crown to a non-Aboriginal man by the name of Cameron, despite the lack of surrender of that land by the Chippewa people. An informal land transaction then occurred in 1839 when Cameron paid a certain amount of money to the Chippewas in return for the conveyance of that land. The Chippewas thus alleged that, given that Aboriginal lands are only alienable to the Crown, the exclusive right to occupy the land in question, as specified in Treaty No. 29, had not been extinguished by the direct dealings with Cameron.

The Court of Appeal accepted that a surrender of Aboriginal land interest required a "voluntary, informed, communal decision to give up the land," and this had not occurred in the surrender of the land in question. Nonetheless, the court dismissed the Chippewas claim against the 2,000 occupiers of the surrendered land on the basis that they had hesitated for too long to take action to recover the land or seek a remedy from those land owners. Given that remedies in these types of circumstances are highly discretionary, the court decided not to award a remedy in favour of the Chippewas on the basis that, although the surrender of land was invalid, the First Nation had waited far too long to attempt to recover their land or recover damages in lieu of recovery. This case is important because it demonstrates that the court is at least willing to examine the possibility of nullifying land transactions that occurred by way of the pre-Confederation treaties. It will, however, only be in exceptional circumstances that courts will be willing to permit compensation for unlawful land surrender and subsequent occupation and it is unlikely that recovery of the land in question would ever be ordered by the court.

Recent litigation indicates that these pre-Confederation treaties are not closed to the possibility of reinterpretation. The courts in Ontario have been willing to read into the treaties certain resource rights, admittedly, to date, only in relation to resources situated on reserves and in adjacent water bodies. However, with the Supreme Court decision in *R. v. Delgamuukw*, these treaties that make no mention of resource rights may be reinterpreted on the basis of evidence produced by Aboriginal oral traditions. It may well be discovered that rights to resources on non-reserve land are preserved by virtue of promises made at the time of treaty negotiations or other historical evidence.

Post-Confederation Treaties

Robinson Treaty – With the Ojibewa Indians of Lake Superior Conveying Certain Lands to the Crown

The Robinson-Superior Treaty No. 60 was negotiated by the Crown and the Ojibewa Aboriginal People of Lake Superior in 1850. The Ojibewa people living on the Northern Shore of Lake Superior agreed to "freely, fully and voluntarily surrender, cede, grant and convey unto Her Majesty, Her heirs and successors forever, all their right, title and interest in the whole of the territory" save for those reservations set out in the schedule.

The Crown promised in return to allow the Aboriginal People the "full and free privilege to hunt" over the area of land surrendered and to "fish in the waters thereof as they [had] been in the habit of doing." This right is limited in the treaty to land that has not been "sold or leased to individuals, or companies of individuals, and occupied by them with the consent of the Provincial Government." Another qualification on the rights of the Ojibeways to the ceded territory was that they not hinder or prevent persons from exploring or searching for mineral or other valuable resources in any part of that territory.

Robinson Treaty – With the Ojibewa Indians of Lake Huron Conveying Certain Lands to the Crown

The second treaty, Robinson-Huron Treaty No. 61, was also concluded in 1850 by the Ojibeway people of Lake Huron and the Crown. The Ojibeway people of the eastern and northern shores of Lake Huron agreed to "fully, freely, and voluntarily surrender, cede, grant and convey unto Her Majesty, her heirs and successors for every, all their right, title, and interest to, and in the whole of, the territory" save for the reservations that were to be held and occupied by the chiefs and their tribes in common, for their own use and benefit, and to their best advantage.

In return, the Crown promised to allow the Ojibeway people the "full and free privilege to hunt over the Territory ceded by them, and to fish in the waters thereof, as they have heretofore been in the habit of doing." That privilege is subject to settlement or development of land that may be "sold or leased to individuals or companies of individuals" where those rights may not be exercised. Another qualification on the rights of the Ojibeway to the ceded territory was that they not hinder or prevent persons from exploring or searching for mineral or other valuable resources in any part of that territory.

The Robinson treaties were concluded in consequence of the discovery of minerals on the shores of Lake Huron and Lake Superior. Both treaties reserved the right of the signatory First Nations to continue to hunt and fish over the territory, subject only to private interests that would be granted in the Ojibeway peoples traditional lands in the future.

The report of Treaty Commissioner Mr. William Robinson to Colonel Bruce, superintendent-general of Indian Affairs, raises two issues worth considering. First, the treaty reveals that the intention of the Crown was to allow those First Nations to engage in commercial activities. Second, the treaty indicates that the Crown promised not to "take from their usual means of subsistence."[24]

Robinson infers that the Ojibeway would be quite entitled to engage in trade as an offshoot of their preserved right to hunt and fish. During the course of treaty negotiations, according to Robinson, several "extravagant terms" were placed on the table. In order to explain to the treaty First Nations why the terms of the Robinson treaties were different to terms that had been negotiated between the American government and Aboriginal People on the south side of Lake Superior, Robinson indicated that the land in question was of lesser value. He goes on to relate the explanation that he gave to the treaty First Nations:

> I explained to the chiefs in council the difference between the lands ceded heretofore in this Province, and those then under consideration, they were of good quality and sold readily at prices which enabled the Government to be more liberal, they were also occupied by the whites in such a manner as to preclude the possibility of the Indian hunting over or having access to them: whereas the lands now ceded are notoriously barren and sterile, and will in all probability never be settled except in a few localities by mining companies, whose establishments among the Indians, instead of being prejudicial, would prove of great benefit as they would afford a market for any things they may have to sell, and bring provisions and stores of all kinds among them at reasonable prices.[25]

---

[24] Reproduced in a reprint Morris, A., *The Treaties of Canada with the Indians of Manitoba and North-West Territories*, Belfords, Clarke & Co., Toronto, 1980, p. 17.

[25] *Ibid.*

The intention of the Crown to allow the treaty First Nations to trade wares for value is revealed in this paragraph. This right is somewhat tempered by the fact that the treaties impose an obligation on the treaty Indians to first seek the consent of the superintendent-general for the sale of "other valuable productions." Although this treaty clause may be interpreted as relating to products such as timber and other non-mineral resources, it is highly unlikely that this clause could be interpreted as relating to animals, fish, negligible forest resources and other non-mineral substances.

Later in the treaty report, Robinson indicates that a promise was made to the Lake Superior and Lake Huron First Nations that the government would not detract from their right to hunt and fish, and this would ensure that the Ojibeway would have no claims for assistance from the Crown:

> In allowing the Indians to retain reservations of land for their own use I was governed by the fact that they in most cases asked for such tracts as they had heretofore been in the habit of using for the purposes of residence and cultivation, and by securing these to them and the right of hunting and fishing over the ceded territory, they cannot say that the Government takes from their usual means of subsistence and therefore have no claims for support.[26]

In *R. v. Penasse and McLeod*[27] the Ontario Provincial Court considered treaty Indians who had been convicted of selling fish without a commercial licence contrary to the then gaming and fishing legislation, the Ontario *Game and Fish Act*.[28] The court found that there was no evidence to show that any acts of the accused went beyond the rights secured by the treaty and was subsequently acquitted. The court reiterated that the onus falls on the Crown to prove that the treaty is inapplicable beyond a reasonable doubt. The court in this case called for an urgent enactment of legislation (by the federal government or by the band councils) to conserve the resource. In response to this case the federal government enacted the *Ontario Fishery Regulations*,[29] designed to conserve the resource in question, which has the effect of overriding the treaty First Nations' right to fish commercially without a licence. Under the *Ontario Fishery Regulations*, fishing for commercial purposes cannot occur in Ontario without the issuance of an authorizing licence.

---

[26] *Ibid.* p. 19.

[27] (1971), 7 C.N.L.C. 375, 8 C.C.C. (2d) 569 (Ont. Prov. Ct.).

[28] *Game and Fish Act*, 1961-62 (Ont.), c. 48 as amended.

[29] S.O.R./89-93.

In the later case of *R. v. Agawa*[30] the court found that enactment of the Regulations was a valid exercise of federal legislative capacity and thereby prevails over treaty terms. The court in this case reiterated that restrictions on treaty rights must be reasonable and that the regulation in question was for conservation purposes and was therefore a reasonable limitation on the right to fish. *R. v. Chevrier*[31]also determined that an Aboriginal person who obtained hunting rights under the Robinson treaties could not be convicted under the provincial gaming and fishing Act as the province had no jurisdiction to override the rights conveyed by the treaties. Although the provinces cannot negate treaty rights, the federal government retains the right to do so, subject to section 35 justification.

Whether or not the harvestation clause created a trust relationship between the Crown and the Robinson-Huron Treaty Aboriginals was considered in *Pawis, McGregor et al. v. The Queen.*[32] The court held that the Crown did not guarantee hunting and fishing rights free from regulation and that no trust relationship could be established; therefore the Crown was not bound with respect to the treaty guarantee of hunting and fishing rights. By entering into a treaty, the court found that the Crown did not take upon itself a trust obligation. For a trust to exist there must be property, which is the subject matter of the trust. The court could find no such property. In the alternative, the plaintiffs argued that the Crown had breached the treaty's terms, and therefore a breach of contract had occurred. On this point the court found that an action for breach of contract could be taken only by the group with which the contract was negotiated. In this case a treaty was concluded with an Aboriginal community and not with individual members of that group. Although the court acknowledged that breach of treaty terms might, in some circumstances, give rise to an action for breach of contract against the Crown, breach of treaty terms by lawful legislation is not actionable.

Manitoulin Island Treaty No. 94

The Manitoulin Island Treaty was designed to be an agreement to bind the original Aboriginal occupants of Manitoulin to live within the confines of Manitoulin Island. The treaty documents the surrender of the better areas of Manitoulin by the resident First Nations people, including the shores and waterways of Manitoulin in return for certain promises from the Crown. The treaty provides for the "release, surrender, give up" by the First Nation occupants to the Crown forever. The treaty makes no mention of who can have access to the resources found on reserves, but does indicate that, upon

---

[30]   (1988), 28 O.A.C. 201, [1988] 3 C.N.L.R. 73, 65 O.R. (2d) 505.

[31]   (1988), [1989], 1 C.N.L.R. 128 (Ont. Dist. Ct.).

[32]   (1979), [1980] 2 F.C. 18, 102 D.L.R. (3d) 602.

ceded lands, the Aboriginal People concerned were to have the same fishing rights as non-Aboriginals. The full text of the treaty apparently does not exist. However, reference is made in the 1862 treaty to an earlier treaty of 1836. The 1862 treaty purports to be a modification of the earlier treaty.

The Bond Head Purchase-No. 45 was documentation of a land transaction in 1836 between the Ottawa and Chippewa people and the Crown in relation to Manitoulin Island. The treaty was an agreement that the First Nations would "relinquish [their] respective claims to these islands and make them the property (under [their] Great Father's control) of all Indians whom he shall allow to reside on them."

In return, the Crown was obligated to "from their facilities and from their being surrounded by innumerable fishing islands, they might be made a most desirable place of residence for many Indians who wish to be civilized, as well as totally separated from the whites."

The treaties of 1836 were written and signed by Sir Bond Head and the indigenous chiefs.[33] Whether or not the treaties conveyed an absolute and exclusive right to fish is a matter of debate.[34] Records show that Bond Head intended that the Manitoulin treaty make the Aboriginal People of Manitoulin "totally separate" from non-Aboriginal People. The treaty opens with the intent of the Crown to instate "new Arrangements" in order to protect the lands of the Manitoulin First Nation from "Encroachments" by white settlers. It was therefore proposed that the Manitoulin Aboriginal societies be relocated to the Island, which, the treaty states, is "surrounded by enumerable Fishing Islands" and would serve as a suitable domicile "for many Indians who wish to be civilized as well as totally separated from the Whites." Sixteen chiefs from the Ottawa and Chippewa societies agreed that their island could be used for such a purpose and signed the treaty. Thus an exclusive right to access the fisheries surrounding the "Fishing Islands" may be derived from the fact that the purpose of the treaty was to create a reserve in which the Aboriginal People could fish and hunt free from white encroachment. Such an interpretation appears to be supported by one of the Saugeen Ojibway signatories, Chief Metigwob, who, at a council conducted shortly after the treaty was signed, explained that during the negotiations period, the Saugeen chiefs had advised Bond Head that they preferred to remain on the Saugeen peninsula "as there were many fish in that place."[35]

---

[33] Recorded in Sir F. Bond Head, Lt. Gov. Upp. Can., to Lord Glenelg, Sec. of State (20 August 1836) Imperial Blue Books, 1839, No. 93 at 122-123 , printed as Treaty No. 45 (Ottawas and Chippewas of Manitoulin) and Treaty No. 45 1/2 "TO the Saukings" (Saugeen Ojibway) in *Canada, Indian Treaties and Surrenders*, Queen's Printer, Ottawa, 1891, vol. 1, pp. 112 – 113.

[34] See Walters, M., "Aboriginal Rights, Magna Carta and Exclusive Rights to Fisheries in the Waters of Upper Canada" (1998), 23 *Queen's Law Journal* 301.

[35] "Statement of Metigwob, one of the Sahgeeng Chiefs, made in a General Council held at the River St. Clair on the 13th September 1836 respecting the surrender of the Sahgeeng Territory to the British Government." Six Nations Land Research Office, cat. No. 836-9-13-1.

According to Chief Metigwob, Bond Head replied that the Saugeen owned "all the islands in the vicinity of that neck or point of land, he was about to reserve for them, and that he would remove all the white people who were in the habit of fishing on their grounds."[36]

It seems clear then that Bond Head's intention was to ensure exclusive Aboriginal fishing rights, protected from non-Aboriginal encroachment, which would be prevented. No payment was made to the Saugeen chiefs for the surrender of the Saugeen territory. Walters suggests that the Crown's consideration was its promise to protect Saugeen's exclusive rights to the islands and the fisheries.[37] Providing additional support to the premise that the Saugeen were under the impression that the treaty would preserve and protect their exclusive fishing rights is the fact that, prior to the conclusion of the treaty, some confusion existed about the terms under which a commercial fishing outfit that was non-Aboriginal owned could operate in the islands' fisheries. At that time the outfit obtained a licence of occupation from not only the Lieutenant Governor in council, but also from the Saugeen chiefs for use of the islands.[38]

There is also later evidence that supports the theory that the Manitoulin Island Aboriginals never ceded or surrendered their land to the Crown. In 1844 a commission of inquiry on Aboriginal affairs took notice of the continued encroachment of non-Aboriginal fishing on the Saugeen fisheries and the frustration of the Aboriginal People at what they considered to be a violation of their exclusive right to fish in the Saugeen fisheries.[39] A letter from Chief Wahbahdick to the colonial secretary reveals that the Saugeen sought written confirmation of their rights in 1843.[40] A proclamation issued

---

[36] *Ibid.*

[37] Walters, M., note 34, para. 13.

[38] Cited in Walters, M., note 34, Upper Canada, Office of the Lieutenant Governor, "Licence of Occupation to the Huron Fishery Company" (3 July 1834) (Lt. Govr. Sir. J. Colborne) NA RG10 vol. 55 at 58368. In 1834, the Huron Fishery Company obtained this licence of occupation for the islands from the Lieutenant Governor of Upper Canada Sir J. Colborne on the condition that the "Indian Tribes are not excluded from the right of fishing which they have always enjoyed" (Wm. Rowan, Sec. to the Lt. Govr., to Dr. Dunlop (22 May 1834) NA RG10, vol. 55 at 58367. Before commencing its operations on the islands the company therefore obtained the "sole use" of the islands from the Saugeen Chippewa, entering into a lease with the "Chiefs of the 'Chippewa Fisheries,'" Report of the Huron Fishery Company, E. C. Taylor, Secretary, Goderich (18 April 1835) NA RG 5 M vol. 152 at 83421-83426; Lease to the Huron Fishery Company from the Chiefs of the Chippewa Fisheries (2 September 1834) NA RG10, vol. 56 at 58707. However, it was later suggested that this lease was not necessary: see "Opinion of Attorney General in reference to Licence of Occupation &c of the fishing islands, 1834" (NA RG10, vol. 55 at 58370-58371). See also Blair, *supra* note 11 in ch. 1 at 129-130; and Jones and Nadjiwon, *supra* note 11 in ch. 1 at 437.

[39] Canada, Legislative Assembly of Canada, Report on the Affairs of the Indians in Canada (22 January 1844) in Journals of the Legislative Assembly of Canada (1845), Appendix EEE, s. 2, II.15 at 43.

[40] Letter of Chief Wahbahdick to the Colonial Secretary, (10 June 1843) NA RG1 L3 vol. 538 "W" Bundle 1843-44, 29m-29o.

by the Crown in 1847 in the form of letters patent defined the Saugeen territory and confirmed Ojibway title to it.[41] The deed stated that the Saugeen "for ever shall possess and enjoy" the land defined and its "rents, issues, and profits...without any hinderance whatever on our part or on the part of our heirs and successors, or of our or their servants and officers."

In later years most of the Saugeen reserve was actually surrendered. However, smaller reserves and the fishing islands were not ceded.[42] Despite the treaty and the Crown's assurance, the exclusive fishing right of the Manitoulin people was ignored, and in 1857, the province enacted legislation regulating fishing in the colony after which time the fishing islands were leased by officials without Ojibway consent.[43]

In 1862 the Crown and the Aboriginal People of Manitoulin entered into a second treaty. According to Morris, the treaty was designed to complement the former treaties, and had the objective of "rendering available for settlement the large tract of good land upon [Manitoulin] Island."[44]

There is a strong feeling, kept alive by the day-to-day oral tradition of the Manitoulin Aboriginal People, that the second treaty was not valid, and that the purpose of the first treaty was understood as preserving the entire island for them. There is some evidence that the island was intended by the Crown to be some kind of concentration camp to isolate the Manitoulin Aboriginal People. A surviving portion of the 1862 treaty states that

> whereas, the Indian title to said island was surrendered to the Crown on the ninth August, Anno Domini, 1836, under and by virtue of a treaty made between Sir Francis Bond Head, then Governor of Upper Canada, and the Chiefs and Principal Men of the Ottawas and Chippewas then occupying and claiming title thereto, in order that the same might "be made the property (under their Great Father's control) of all Indians whom he should allow to reside thereon."

> And whereas, but few Indians from the mainland, whom it was intended to transfer to the island, have ever come to reside thereon.

> And whereas, it has been deemed expedient (with a view to the improvement of the condition of the Indians as well as the settlement and improvement of the country) to assign to the Indians now upon the island certain specified portions thereof to be, held by patent from the Crown, and to *sell the other, portions thereof fit for cultivation to settlers,* and to invest the proceeds thereof, after

---

[41] Declaration by Her Majesty in favour of the Ojibway Indians respecting certain lands on Lake Huron (29 June 1847) NAC RG68, vol. LIBER AG. SPECIAL GRANTS 1841-1854, C-4158.

[42] Treaty No. 72 (13 October 1854) in *Indian Treaties and Surrenders, supra* note 226 in ch. 3 at 195-196.

[43] *Fisheries Act,* 1857, 20 Vict. c. 21 (Can.).

[44] Morris, A., 1880, p.22.

deducting the expenses of survey and management, for the benefit of the Indians.

And whereas, a majority of the chiefs of certain bands residing on that portion of the island easterly of Heywood Sound and the Manitoulin Gulf, have expressed their unwillingness to accede to this proposal as respects that portion of the island, but have assented to the same as respects all other portions thereof, and, whereas the Chiefs and Principal Men of the bands residing on the island westerly of the said sound and gulf, have agreed to accede to the said proposal.

The argument made is that, at the time of the second treaty, the Crown held the island in trust for the Aboriginal People of Manitoulin. For this reason, some argue, the Aboriginal People could not sell part of it to the Crown for settler use and occupation and the conveyance of title to settlers by virtue of the second treaty. Title in trust may, therefore, still exist.[45]

However, two cases involving Aboriginal defendants charged with fishing contrary to the *Ontario Fishing Regulations* made pursuant to the federal *Fisheries Act* were unsuccessful in asserting that they were protected by the treaties.[46]

Article 6 of the 1862 treaty reads: "Sixthly. All the rights and privileges in respect to the taking of fish in the lakes, bays, creeks and waters within and adjacent to the said island, which may be lawfully exercised and enjoyed by the white settlers there on, may be exercised and enjoyed by the Indians."

In both of these cases, the court held that the *Fisheries Act* overrode any treaty right, which may or may not have existed under the treaties. The court did not discuss what the content of what the rights guaranteed by this treaty may be. However, in neither case did the accused attempt to argue that the 1864 treaty was invalid.

Since the Supreme Court decision in *R. v. Delgamuukw* permitting the use of evidence from the Aboriginal oral tradition, there is certainly the opportunity for the Manitoulin Aboriginal People to contest the validity of the treaties. It would seem that contestants would have a strong case based on historical and ethnological evidence. A challenge to the Manitoulin treaties and Crown "ownership" of the Manitoulin Islands is in fact currently pending in the lower courts of Ontario.

---

[45] Native American Resources, online: <http://www.kstrom.net/isk/maps/cantreaty/manitoulin.html>, as at 14 January 2002.

[46] *R. v. Hare and Debassige* (1985), 9 O.A.C. 161, [1985] 3 C.N.L.R. 139, 20 C.C.C. (3d) 1, reversing (1983), [1984] 1 C.N.L.R. 131 (Ont. Dist. Ct); *R. v. Commanda* (1985), 9 O.A.C. 161.

In *R. v. Jones and Nadjiwon*[47] the court determined that the treaty had affirmed a right of the Ottawa and Chippewa people to fish for commercial purposes that has not been extinguished. Accordingly, what the treaty did was record the right of access and use of the Saugeen Band's traditional fishing grounds, but did not convey rights of ownership and possession. They found that the Saugeen had a collective right to fish for sustenance purposes in their traditional fishing grounds, but that this right was not a right to pursue a commercially profitable enterprise. The court held that the Crown had failed to give sufficient consideration to the Aboriginal right to fish in those waters when allocating surplus fishery resources. The Regulations therefore did not apply to the accused.

Treaties No. 3, 5 and 9

Treaty No. 3 – Between Her Majesty the Queen and the Salteaux Tribe of the Ojibeway Indians at the Northwest Angle on the Lake of the Woods with Adhesions

Treaty No. 3 covers an area of land primarily situated in the Province of Ontario although the treaty also covers a small portion of land in Manitoba.

Treaty No. 3, the Northwest Angle Treaty, was negotiated with the Saulteaux and Ojibeway in 1873. The treaty states explicitly that

> ...the said Indians, shall have right to pursue their avocations of hunting and fishing throughout the tract surrendered as hereinbefore described, subject to such regulations as may from time to time be made by Her Government of Her Dominion of Canada, and saving and excepting such tracts as may, from time to time, be required or taken up for settlement, mining, lumbering or other purposes by Her said Government of the Dominion of Canada, or by any of the subjects thereof duly authorized therefor by the said Government.

This provision appears to indicate that, although the Aboriginal right to hunt and fish is protected, the federal government retained a right to regulate those rights. This issue was discussed in *R. v. Bombay*[48] where the Ontario Court of Appeal held that the treaty provision permitting government regulation of treaty rights is not an unfettered right. The federal government must justify any regulation of treaty rights by fulfilling the justification test laid out by the Supreme Court of Canada in the *R. v. Sparrow* decision; that is, that any infringement of Aboriginal treaty rights must have a valid objective; that the Crown must fulfil its fiduciary duty; that Aboriginal People are to be given priority over other groups where rights to access resources are being allocated; and that consultation with the Aboriginal People affected is

---

[47]   [1993] 3 C.N.L.R. 182, (Ont. Prov. Div.).

[48]   [1993] 1 C.N.L.R. 92 (Ont. C.A.).

necessary prior to proceeding with the project. Legislation and regulations can therefore regulate Aboriginal and treaty rights providing that this test is met.

Historical evidence shows that the Anishinabe of the Lake of the Woods, English River, Rainy River and Rainy Lake region used many subsurface materials including dyes, pigments, pipestone, clay and stone. Moreover, the Treaty No. 3 First Nations used copper, silver and lead for the purpose of making pipes and weapons. Records from the treaty negotiations show that the Aboriginal People affected knew the value of the minerals underlying the treaty lands. Morris writes:

> They are well informed as to the discovery of gold and silver to the west of the watershed, and have not been slow to give us their views as to the value of that discovery. "You offer us," said they, "$3 per head and you have only to pick up gold and silver from our rocks to pay it many times over." The Chief of the section where the discoveries have taken place was emphatic in expressing his determination to keep miners from his country until he had been paid for his land.[49]

No provision is made for the use of reserve resources; however, the official letter from the lieutenant governor dated 14 October 1873, which contains a full narrative of the treaty negotiation proceedings, states: "They asked if the mines would be theirs; I said that if they were found on their reserves it would be to their benefit, but not otherwise,"[50] and: "If any important minerals are discovered on any of their reserves the minerals will be sold for their benefit with their consent."[51]

Promises were made to the Treaty No. 3 First Nations that they would be awarded the entire benefit of mineral development on their reserves and, furthermore, that they could explore mineral potentials off their reserves. The promise concerning minerals was recorded in various documents, including reports by the Treaty Commissioners, a newspaper account and in a record kept by an employee of the chiefs.

Neither the federal nor provincial governments lived up to this promise. The guarantee was never printed in the written text of the treaty and Ontario, for many years, denied the Treaty No. 3 Aboriginals rights to any part of the reserves, including minerals. In accordance with the assurance that was made by the Treaty Commissioners, the treaty First Nations went about prospecting and participated in associated mineral exploration activities. The Ontario government subsequently issued patents to reserve lands where Treaty

---

[49] Morris, A., *The Treaties of Canada*, Belfords, Clarke and Co, Toronto, 1880, reprinted by Coles Publishing Company, Toronto, 1971, p. 45.

[50] *Ibid*. p. 50.

[51] *Ibid*.

No. 3 Aboriginals had discovered gold, and took such lands without paying any compensation. The largest mine in northwestern Ontario was, in fact, established on a reserve.

There is very strong evidence in support of a challenge to the operation of Treaty No. 3 with respect to revenue distribution from mineral resources exploitation.

The Treaty No. 3 First Nations claim that any development in the Treaty No. 3 area, such as forestry, mining, hydro, highways and pipeline system developments, requires their consent, agreement and participation. Where proponents seek to develop in the Treaty No. 3 area, the Grand Council of Treaty No. 3 acts on behalf of the member First Nations to hold discussions or potential negotiations in order to express the opinions and concerns of the Aboriginal People of the area. One of the council's priorities is to establish a negotiation strategy for addressing Crown governments and industry on the issues of natural resource revenue sharing and management.

Treaty No. 5 – Between Her Majesty the Queen and the Saulteaux and Swampy Cree Tribes of Indians at Beren's River and Norway House with Adhesions

Note that this is discussed in the chapter devoted to Alberta, Saskatchewan and Manitoba.

The James Bay Treaty – Treaty No. 9

Treaty No. 9 was negotiated and signed in 1905 and 1906 by representatives of the federal and provincial governments and by a number of leaders of the Cree and Ojibwa people. In return for the surrender of approximately 208,000 square kilometres of ancestral lands, the federal government made a series of promises to the Aboriginal People concerned. That land mass was extended by several adhesions in the late 1920s to cover an additional 204,8000 square kilometres. The land covered by Treaty No. 9 amounts to roughly two-thirds of the total land mass in Ontario.

The Aboriginal parties to the treaty agreed to "cede, release, surrender and yield up to the Government of the Dominion of Canada, for His Majesty the King and His successors forever, all their rights, titles and privileges" to the land covered by the treaty. Another of the treaty's terms provided that the Aboriginal signatories agreed to "conduct and behave themselves as good loyal subjects of His Majesty the King" and "in all respects, obey and abide by the law." In return, the government promised an annuity for each Aboriginal person: it agreed to support education of the treaty Aboriginals and to provide other miscellaneous items. The traditional hunting, fishing and trapping rights of the Aboriginal People are explicitly recognized in the treaty: "His Majesty the King hereby agrees with the said Indians that they shall have the right to pursue their usual vocations of hunting, trapping and fishing throughout the tract surrendered as heretofore described."

The right to pursue their "usual vocations" is subject to several qualifications. First, hunting, trapping and fishing are to be subject to "such regulations as may from time to time be made by the government of the country." Second, the right is not deemed to exist on "such tracts as may be required or taken up from time to time for settlement, mining, lumbering, trading or other purposes."

The explicit inclusion of a "trapping" right in the treaty led to an Ontario District Court decision that provincial regulation of commercial traplines does not apply to Treaty No. 9 Indians.[52]

A report written in respect of Treaty No. 9 by Morrison gives indications that the terms of the treaty may not accurately reflect the understanding or intentions of the Aboriginal parties.[53] Morrison indicates that, in his opinion, had the Aboriginal People known that the treaty would permit the province to authorize timber and mineral resource exploitation, as well as non-Aboriginal hunting and fishing on their surrendered lands,

> most of the Albany River bands would probably have refused to participate. On the other hand, the bands on James Bay, as well as those closest to the railway line, might well have signed the treaty anyway – both because they would have felt they had no real alternative, and because...the Commissioners were very successful at promoting the tangible benefits of adherence to the treaty.[54]

Other accounts are consistent on the point that the Aboriginal parties fundamentally misunderstood the implications of the treaty. One eyewitness to the negotiations was recorded as having said that the Aboriginal People at Fort Albany were told that "there will not be any legislation governing trapping, hunting animals and hunting birds and fishing if you are in favour of the Treaty."[55]

Elders of the groups who had knowledge of the treaty and memories of the negotiations at Fort Albany reported that "it is not clear whether the Indians understood that there was a land surrender, they expected that they would share the resources and act as custodian; they would also retain their right to hunt, their way of life and culture."[56]

---

[52] *Cheechoo v. R.* [1981] 3 C.N.L.R. 45 (Ont. Dist. Ct.).

[53] Morrison, J., *Treaty Research Report: Treaty Nine (1905-1906): The James Bay Treaty*, Treaties and Historical Research Centre, Ottawa, 1986.

[54] *Ibid.*, p. 49.

[55] *Ibid.* Interview with James Wesley, p. 53.

[56] Ojibeway-Cree Cultural Centre, *Nishnawbe-Aski Nation: A History of the Cree and Ojibway of Northern Ontario*, Ojibeway-Cree Cultural Centre, Timmins, 1986, quoted in Lonf, J., "No Bases for Argument": The Signing of Treaty 9 in Northern Ontario, 1905-1906 (1989), 5 *Native Studies Review* 2, p. 37.

Long's analysis shows that the actual terms of the treaty do not represent what was actually promised at the negotiations phase. For one thing, in the written treaty, there is surrender of 99 percent of the lands while the oral agreement made at Osnaburg was that hunting grounds were not surrendered. At Fort Hope, the commissioners assured the Aboriginal People that only the useless land was lost, and there is no evidence to suggest that the Aboriginal People consented to a "surrender" of land. Moreover, the written text permits regulation of hunting, trapping and fishing by Canada, but the oral agreement guaranteed that the Crown would not interfere with this right.

As indicated above, the treaty has two exceptions to the right to hunt, trap and fish, one of which is the exclusion of harvesting rights on "tracts taken up" by the Crown. Imai suggests that the "tracts taken up" by the Crown exception is also vulnerable to reinterpretation.[57] Provincial governments have relied on this exception along with the surrender provisions to unilaterally exploit natural resources on the traditional lands of First Nations. Generally, land and resources are exploited without consultation with or compensation of the Aboriginal People concerned. Imai discusses whether or not it is within the federal or the provincial government's realm to "take up" lands and concludes that, if it is indeed within the province's powers to "take up" lands, then in accordance with recent litigation concerning Aboriginal rights, provincial governments should be under the same obligations as the federal government when it comes to interference with, or curtailment of, Aboriginal treaty rights. The provincial governments would thereby be under a fiduciary duty to protect such rights, and also to engage in effective consultation with affected First Nations and to provide compensation where necessary.

R. v. Delgamuukw indicated that the court is open and receptive to oral evidence that sheds light on the Aboriginal understanding as to the meaning of treaty terms. Treaty No. 9 is certainly a candidate for reinterpretation based on the Aboriginal perception of the treaty's implications and given the promises that were made by the Crown at the time of treaty negotiations. It is clear that the court is certainly willing to "read in" oral terms to the written treaty based on guarantees made by the Crown at the time of negotiations; however, the court has not yet gone so far as to say that oral terms are to override the written terms of a treaty. Given that Aboriginal People at the time were rarely literate, it seems that the oral terms would be those that were understood by both parties and there is no certainty that the written words were actually what was intended. On this basis, it is entirely possible that at some stage in the future the court will be willing to override the treaty's text and uphold the validity of the oral undertakings.

---

[57] Imai, S., "Treaty Lands and Crown Obligations: The "Tracts Taken Up" Provision, 27 Queen's *Law Journal* 1.

Williams Treaties of 1923

In 1923 the Government of Canada purchased three parcels of land in the central and southern parts of Ontario. These land transactions, or acquisitions, are collectively referred to as the Williams Treaties. In actual fact there are only two treaties, which concede three separate parcels of land. The first treaty was made on 31 October 1923 between the Chippewa Indians of Christian Island, Georgina Island and Rama and the Crown. The second treaty was concluded between the Mississauga Indians of Rice Lake, Mud Lake, Scugog Lake and Alderville and the Crown on 15 November 1923. The combined land mass surrendered to the Crown in the Williams Treaties amounts to 12.9 million acres of land.

The 1923 treaties contain the standard basket clause whereby the Aboriginal parties agreed to "cede, release, surrender and yield up" any rights and interests that may have existed in the land surrendered by the treaty.

In 1994 the Supreme Court of Canada handed down its decision in *R. v. Howard*,[58] involving an Aboriginal man who was charged with fishing out of season. In his defence, the appellant argued that he had an existing right to fish in the Otonabee River pursuant to the 1923 treaty. The Crown relied on the "basket" clause in the 1923 treaty to argue that the band's rights to fish had effectively been extinguished by surrender. The Supreme Court upheld the finding of the lower courts that there could be no doubt that, by virtue of this treaty term, the 1923 treaty had extinguished the appellant's rights to fish in the area. The court based this conclusion on the fact that the terms of the treaty were not ambiguous and the First Nation parties would have been aware that any special rights to hunt and fish in the Otonabee River area were being surrendered at that time.

Given the court's decision in *R. v. Howard*, it is unlikely that Aboriginal parties to the Williams Treaties would be able to assert and claim any special rights to hunt, fish and trap on the surrendered land. However, the court makes it clear that its decision was contingent upon evidentiary findings that the Aboriginal signatories were aware of the fact that any rights to resources in the ceded land were being given up. The Supreme Court refers to the testimony of an eyewitness to the negotiations and that all of the Aboriginal signatories were literate, and were involved in business or public service.

---

[58] *R. v. Howard*, [1994] 2 S.C.R. 299 (S.C.C.).

Métis Resource Rights

Ontario courts commenced consideration of what Aboriginal rights belong to the Métis people in *R. v. Powley*.[59] The case concerned two Métis men who were charged with hunting moose without a licence under the provincial wildlife legislation. In their defence, the accused raised an Aboriginal right to hunt moose without a licence, protected by section 35 of the *Constitution Act, 1982*. Status Aboriginals in the Sault Ste. Marie area have a recognized treaty right to hunt for food pursuant to the 1850 Robinson-Huron Treaty and are not subject to certain restrictions imposed by the provincial legislation. At the time of treaty negotiations, Robinson refused to deal with the Métis.

The trial judge, Vaillancourt J., found that a section 35 Aboriginal right was established and that the infringement of that right by the Ontario *Game and Fish Act*[60] was an unjust infringement of that right. The Crown argued that no such right to hunt existed, and in the alternative, that any infringement of their right is justified in the name of conservation, equitable sharing of a scarce resources and social and economic benefit. The individuals were acquitted at trial and at the first level of appeal. In an appeal to the Ontario Court of Appeal in 2001, the judiciary upheld the decision of the lower courts, and ruled that the purpose of the inclusion of Métis rights in section 35 was, as for other Aboriginal People in Canada, to recognize their prior use and occupation of the land. The court found that hunting was an integral part of Métis culture at the time the area was "taken over by the European based culture" and was therefore a right that was afforded constitutional protection. This decision has been upheld by the Supreme Court of Canada.[61]

A different test applies to assertions by Métis to hunting and fishing rights. The test for establishing an Aboriginal or treaty right to harvest wildlife is that propounded in the *R. v. Van Der Peet* case. To identify the nature of the Aboriginal right in issue, the court must first identify precisely the nature of the claim being made and then determine whether the claim is based on a practice, custom or tradition that is integral to the distinctive culture of the Aboriginal group claiming the right. To do this, the applicant must prove that the practice dates back prior to European contact. The claimant must also show that there is continuity between the contemporary community's practice and the historic community's practice. The Court of Appeal in *R. v. Powley* stated that a different test must be applied to the Métis. The court determined that the relevant period from which the practice was derived and continued is a time when the Métis was flourishing. In this case, the court settled on the year 1850. It was for Powley to then show that the activity in question had been continually practised since that date.

---

[59] *R. v. Powley* [2001] O.J. No. 607 (Ont. C.A.).
[60] R.S.O. 1990, c.G.1.
[61] *R. v. Powley* [2003] S.C.C. 43.

The court found that the accused had established an Aboriginal right, and infringement of that right by provincial legislation had occurred. The infringement was not justified because the provincial government had not consulted with the Métis prior to the enactment of the legislative regulations. In fact, Ontario has never recognized that the Métis have any special rights to resources at all and the court admonished the provincial government for failing to do so. This was affirmed at the Supreme Court of Canada.

Public Safety and Harvesting Activities

Another issue that has arisen recently and which has been determined in Ontario courts is the ability of regulations enacted for the purpose of "public safety" to impact upon Aboriginal harvestation rights. The courts have already held consistently that safety considerations can justify what would otherwise be a restriction on Aboriginal or treaty rights. Recent decisions appear to be approaching this issue with greater deference to legislation than has previously been the case. Several decisions have supported the proposition that night hunting can in principle be done safely, and that Aboriginal People may undertake this activity.[62] Where an Aboriginal person is found to be hunting recklessly, the courts indicate that they could be charged with an offence such as dangerous hunting. Where recklessness or dangerous behaviour is not present, then the courts have been willing to hold that the elements of the offence are not present and they should not be charged. Several recent decisions appear to indicate that the courts have accepted the proposition that night hunting is inherently dangerous and that prohibition of night hunting is not even infringement of a hunting right on its face, or are willing to accept such limits as justified infringement of the Aboriginal right to hunt.

The Aboriginal appellants successfully argued in *R. v. Fox*[63] that some prohibitions, which are indirectly related to safety, are really designed to enforce a code of "sportsmanlike conduct" and cannot be a justifiable infringement of Aboriginal or treaty rights.[64] Decisions from other jurisdictions indicate that even when the court accepts that night hunting can be undertaken safely under certain circumstances, the court may still rule that the major purpose of the prohibition is safety and that the prohibition infringes on the right as little as possible and is therefore justified.[65] The British Columbia Supreme Court has taken the position as to inquire whether

---

[62] See *R. v. Prince*, [1964] S.C.R. 81, *R. v. Horseman, supra* note 18 in ch. 2 at 104 (S.C.C.), *R. v. Paul*, [1994] 2 C.N.L.R. 167 (N.B.C.A.) and *R. v. Machimity*, [1996] O.J. 4365 (Ont. C.J. Prov. Div.).

[63] *R. v. Fox*, [1994] 3 C.N.L.R. 132 at 137 (Ont. C.A.).

[64] See also a decision from the Nova Scotia Supreme Court that followed this line of argument: *R. v. Bernard* (February 5, 2001), Sydney, S.H. 162638 (N.S.S.C.).

or not the practice of hunting at night with a light is "integral to the distinct culture" of the First Nation in question in order to define the Aboriginal right in the case of *R. v. Seward*.[66] In this case, an application to appeal to the Supreme Court of Canada was refused.[67]

Current Land Claims

Algonquins of Eastern Ontario Land Claim

The Algonquins of eastern Ontario are currently involved in a land claim to an area of 34,000 square kilometres on the Ontario side of the Ottawa River watershed. The Algonquins claim they have never signed or benefited from the treaty, which covers the lands alleged to be their traditional area of occupation, and that they are the rightful owners of the entire Ottawa Valley and its resources. Canada became a party to the negotiations that were already underway between Ontario and the Algonquins in December 1992. Negotiations are continuing monthly on substantial issues that will form the basis of the Agreement In Principle. The Algonquins are seeking financial compensation for their loss of the land and its natural resources, for titled land and for harvesting rights. The settlement is expected to include parcels of titled land, economic development opportunities, and an agreement on harvesting rights including hunting, fishing, trapping and gathering.

Hunting agreements have been negotiated between the Algonquins and the provincial government on a yearly basis for the last 10 years.

---

[65] *R. v. Stump*, [2000] 4 C.N.L.R. 260 (B.C. Prov. Ct.).

[66] *R. v. Seward*, [1999] 3 C.N.L.R. 299 (B.C.C.A.).

[67] *R. v. Seward* (May 9, 2000).

Chapter 6

Newfoundland and Labrador

Prior to 1987, Newfoundland refused to acknowledge that Aboriginal reserve lands existed on the island and rejected any attempt of application of federal jurisdiction under section 91(24) of the *Constitution Act, 1867* to the Conne River Band. The Newfoundland government refused to accept the band's claim of Aboriginal title to traditional lands on the island.

No express mention was made to Aboriginal People or lands reserved for Aboriginal People in the Terms of Union of Newfoundland with Canada. The issue was, in fact, not incorporated so that the matter could be settled by negotiation after Newfoundland had had time to elect a provincial government. In 1954, after a series of reports commissioned by the federal government, Canada entered into several agreements with Newfoundland under which the federal government assumed financial responsibility for Aboriginal and Inuit affairs, although administrative authority remained with the province.

Provincial Legislation

Note that provincial legislation and regulations are deemed to apply to Aboriginal people subject to two conditions:

- provincial legislation cannot apply exclusively to Aboriginal People or to land reserved for their benefit; and
- a provincial law may be declared invalid or inapplicable to Aboriginal People if it infringes upon an established Aboriginal or treaty right that is constitutionally protected.

Where an Aboriginal person has established an Aboriginal or treaty right to hunt or fish, then the provincial legislation cannot interfere with that right[1] unless the limitation can meet the test of justification and is in keeping with

---

[1] *R. v. White and Bob, supra* note 10 in ch. 2; *R. v. Simon, supra* note 2 in ch. 2; and, *R. v. Sioui, supra* note 2 in ch. 2.

the honour of the Crown.[2] A limitation on the exercise of a treaty or Aboriginal right would need to be tested in the courts for clarification. It is clear that sufficient consideration must be given to the Aboriginal interest. Apart from measures implemented by a province to conserve a resource, it is unlikely that any court in Canada would uphold any other provincial legislation that restricts an Aboriginal or treaty right. Recently, provincial laws designed to protect public safety have been permitted to override and limit Aboriginal resource rights.

Under the *Wildlife Act*[3] the Minister of Natural Resources has the management and control of measures for the protection, preservation and propagation of wildlife.[4]

Fishing in Newfoundland and Labrador

Under section 7(1) of the *Wildlife Act*, the Minister can regulate fishing.[5] Under the *Wildlife Regulations,*[6] the Minister requires that every person fishing in an inland fishery in Newfoundland and Labrador for salmon or trout be in possession of an authorizing licence.[7] A person is not permitted to fish for commercial purposes under an angling licence.[8]

Hunting in Newfoundland and Labrador

Under the *Wildlife Act* the Minister has the power to regulate with respect to hunting and trapping.[9] This includes the power to license hunters and trappers. Under the *Wildlife Regulations,* the Minister requires that any person hunting or trapping within the province must obtain an authorizing licence to do so.[10]

These laws and regulations are deemed to apply generally to Aboriginal People to the point that interference with an established right to hunt and trap is unjustified.

---

[2] *R. v. White and Bob, supra* note 10 in ch. 2; *R. v. Simon, supra* note 2 in ch. 2; and, *R. v. Sioui, supra* note 2 in ch. 2; *R. v. Sparrow, supra* note 5 in ch. 1.
[3] Chapter W-8.
[4] *Wildlife Act*, s. 5(1).
[5] *Ibid.* s. 5(1)(a).
[6] Enacted pursuant to the *Wildlife Act*.
[7] *Wildlife Regulations*, s. 3(1).
[8] *Ibid.* s. 9.
[9] *Wildlife Act*, s. 5(1)(a) and (t).
[10] See also the *Furbearing Animals Trapping Order, 2001-2002* Regulation 88/01.

Modern Agreements

Labrador Inuit Land Claims Agreement

On 10 May 1999, nine years after the Framework Agreement was signed, negotiators for the province, the Labrador Inuit Association (LIA) and the federal government initialled the draft Agreement In Principle for a land claims settlement. Commencing in 1977 with the filing of a claim with the Government of Canada entitled "A Statement of Claim to Certain Rights in the Land and Sea-Ice in Northern Labrador," the Labrador Inuit Land Claims Agreement In Principle was initialled by both the Labrador Inuit Association and the Canadian government on 10 May 1999.[11] The Labrador Inuit approved ratification of the Agreement In Principle two months later in July 1999. The Final Agreement creates two areas of land: the Labrador Inuit Settlement Area and Labrador Inuit Lands. The Settlement Area consists of 28,000 square miles of land and 17,000 square miles of adjacent ocean extending out 12 miles (referred to as the Zone). The Settlement Area will include the five Inuit communities of Nain, Hopedale, Makkovik, Postville and Rigolet. In the northern part of the Settlement Area, approximately 3,700 square miles will be set aside for the establishment of the Torngat Mountains National Park Reserve. Inuit will have special rights in all of these areas. Within the Settlement Area, Inuit will own 6,100 square miles of land, referred to as Labrador Inuit Lands. It is in this area where Inuit have the most rights and benefits.[12]

Inuit Land

Minerals

In Labrador Inuit Lands, Inuit will have the exclusive right to carving stone, ownership of 1,525 square miles (3,950 square kilometres) of specified quarry materials and a right to 25 percent of provincial revenues from subsurface resources. Existing mineral rights holders in Labrador Inuit lands will continue to be regulated by the province. Any person wishing to explore for subsurface resources in Labrador Inuit Lands after the Final Agreement will be required to submit a work plan for approval by the government of Newfoundland and Labrador and the Inuit Central Government. Existing surface interests in Labrador Inuit Lands will continue under their current

---

[11] Labrador Inuit Land Claims Agreement In Principle, online:<http://www.gov.nf.ca/laa/claimsaip/liaaip.htm>.

[12] See Newfoundland Government online: <http://www.gov.nf.ca/laa/labradorlandclaims/what.html##Mineral Resources>, as at 19 November 2001.

terms and conditions. Applications for renewal or extensions of such interests must be made to the Inuit Central Government, which may establish additional reasonable terms and conditions. Provincial regulations continue for mining and mineral exploration. Existing mineral rights holders will continue to exercise their rights subject to regulation. The provincial and Inuit governments must approve new exploration permits. All companies must comply with joint exploration and quarrying standards developed by the province and the Inuit government. Impact Benefit Agreements must be negotiated with the Inuit government for all mineral developments. Companies are subject to access conditions and fees required by the Inuit government; the fee schedule will be published and uniformly applied. Inuit will own 1,525 square miles of quarry materials within Inuit Lands. The Inuit government will issue quarry permits in this area, and an Impact Benefit Agreement will be required. With the exception of quarry developments in the 1,525 square miles of quarry materials owned by Inuit, developers are not required to negotiate Impact Benefit Agreements for quarry developments.

Harvesting Rights

If you wish to harvest on Inuit Lands, you will need a permit from the Inuit government. Existing outfitters and sawmill operators will continue under laws of general application. The Inuit Central Government has the exclusive right to authorize new outfitting and sawmill operations in Labrador Inuit Lands.

Everyone can continue to fish in marine waters, including ice fishing. However, you need permission from the Inuit government to fish in inland waters. Existing commercial fishing licenses are not affected. Inuit will be guaranteed a percentage of new or additional commercial fishing licenses for specified species within the Zone and in waters adjacent to the Zone. They will also receive 70 percent of new processing licences. Non-Inuit long-term residents of Inuit communities will be given special consideration for harvesting wildlife, firewood and berries.

The Settlement Area

Minerals

In addition to receiving 25 percent of provincial revenues from subsurface developments in Labrador Inuit Lands, Inuit will receive 50 percent of the first $2 million and 5 percent of any additional provincial revenues from subsurface resources in the settlement area outside of Labrador Inuit Lands. These revenues will be capped when the amount, if distributed equally among all beneficiaries, would result in an average per capita income of beneficiaries that exceeds the average per capita income of all Canadians. The Inuit Central Government will receive 3 percent of provincial revenues from subsurface resources from the Voisey's Bay project. Labrador Inuit land and resource rights that will apply within the Voisey's Bay project area will be negotiated prior to the Final Agreement.

Water Rights

New commercial or industrial developers on Labrador Inuit Lands must acquire a water use permit from the province, which may only be issued if also approved by the Inuit Central Government. Any developer in the settlement area who proposes to use water after the Final Agreement in a way that may substantially affect the quantity, quality and rate of flow of water on Labrador Inuit Lands will be required to first negotiate a compensation agreement with the Inuit Central Government. Any initiatives to establish marine management plans or to develop non-renewable resources in the Zone (ocean area adjacent to the Settlement Area extending out to 12 miles) will require prior consultation with the Inuit Central Government. Inuit Impacts and Benefits Agreements are required for major developments in the Zone.

Harvesting Rights

Outside Inuit Lands, non-Inuit can harvest in accordance with provincial and federal regulations. A co-management board appointed by the province, the Government of Canada and the Inuit Central Government will be established as the primary body for making recommendations to governments on the conservation and management of wildlife and plants in the settlement area. The relevant provincial or federal Minister will retain the overall responsibility for the conservation and management of wildlife and plants in the Settlement Area.

A co-management board appointed by the Government of Canada, the province and the Inuit Central Government will be established as the primary body for making recommendations to governments on the conservation and management of fish in the Settlement Area. The Minister will retain the overall responsibility for the conservation and management of fish in the settlement area. Existing commercial fishing licenses are not affected. Inuit will be guaranteed a percentage of new or additional commercial fishing licenses for specified species within the Zone and in waters adjacent to the Zone.

Inuit can harvest year-round for subsistence[13] purposes according to Inuit regulations. If conservation requires that resource harvesting be limited, Inuit will have priority rights. All harvesting by non-Inuit must be closed before there are any reductions to Inuit harvesting. The Minister will consult with the Inuit government before reducing Inuit harvesting limits. Sawmills in the settlement area are not affected. However, Inuit have the first option to establish new sawmill operations. If hunting, cutting firewood or berry picking is closed to non-Inuit, special consideration will be given to non-Inuit long-term residents of Inuit communities. (Long-term residents must have lived in the Inuit communities since 1980.)

The Final Agreement was not yet in place at the time of writing but is likely to be finalized and set in place in the not too distant future. The finalization of this agreement will signify an important step for the Inuit of Labrador, with whom a treaty or land claim agreement has never been negotiated.

Current Land Claims

In July 1987 Canada and Newfoundland entered into an Agreement recognizing that the lands of the Conne River Band were within federal jurisdiction and affirmed that the lands are reserve lands.

Miawpukek Mi'kamawey Mawi'omi (Conne River Mi'kmaq Band of Newfoundland)

In 1973 an Agreement was concluded between Canada and Newfoundland whereby federal funding was extended to the Miawpukek Mi'kamawey Mawi'omi (Conne River Mi'kmaq Band of Newfoundland). In 1996 the band submitted a comprehensive land claim to south-central Newfoundland. This land claim is still awaiting decision regarding its acceptance or rejection.[14] The reserve upon which the Conne River Mi'kmaq Band currently resides is still subject to federal administration.

Labrador Métis Nation Statement of Claim 1991

The federal government has consistently maintained that the Métis are not within its exclusive legislative jurisdiction held under section 91(24) of the *Constitution Act, 1867*, notwithstanding that the Métis are recognized as one

---

[13] "Subsistence" is defined in the Agreement as the hunting, trapping and gathering of wildlife and plants as the primary, non-commercial, means of providing food and fuel for an individual and his or her immediate household; see Chapter 12.1 of the Agreement, online: < http://www.gov.nf.ca/laa/claimsaip/Aipchp12.htm>.

[14] Comprehensive Claims, Policy and Status of Claims, Indian and Northern Affairs Canada, online: <http://www.ainc-inac.gc.ca/ps/clm/brieff_e.html>.

of the Aboriginal Peoples of Canada. The Supreme Court of Canada has not yet had the opportunity to decide whether Métis people fall within the definition of "Indian,"[15] although a Manitoba Queen's Bench decision determined that they did not.[16] Despite this denial of Métis identity, the *Constitution Act, 1982* incorporates Métis people under the section 35(2) definition of Aboriginal People. The result is that the federal government has consistently denied that the Métis people are a federal responsibility and has maintained that the Métis are primarily a provincial responsibility. The Queen's Bench Court ruling has been upheld by the Supreme Court of Canada.[17]

The Labrador Métis Nation has also submitted a statement of claim to the Canadian government seeking land title to the area of their traditional lands. In particular the First Nation seeks an end to exploitation of their land and resources by outside interests. Up until the middle of this century, governments ignored the Métis people. Unlike many other Aboriginal People in Canada, the Métis have never signed a treaty. Effectively, the Métis of Labrador have *never* ceded their land. The Métis were considered "enfranchised and full citizens of the Province on the day when Newfoundland entered Canada in 1949."[18] Consequently, the Métis have consistently been prosecuted for "illegal" salmon fishing and other activities linked to their continued traditional association with their land.

Naskapi of Quebec (Schefferville) Comprehensive Land Claim

The Naskapi of Quebec (Schefferville) submitted a comprehensive land claim to a large portion of Labrador in 1995. The claim is stalled at present due to incomplete documentation to substantiate certain comprehensive land claims acceptance criteria. The Naskapi are required to provide additional information.

Makivik Claim – Offshore (Nunavut) and Labrador (Onshore and Offshore)

The federal government agreed to negotiate with the Inuit of Northern Quebec, as represented by the Makivik Corporation, with respect to islands along the coast of Quebec and in Nunavut, and also to islands off the coast of Northern Quebec and Labrador, and also an inland area in northern Labrador.

---

[15] This has been settled by the Supreme Court of Canada. See *R. v. Powley, supra* note 61 in ch. 5.

[16] *R. v. Blais,* [1998] 4 C.N.L.R. 130 (Man. Q.B.).

[17] *R. v. Blais,* [2003] S.C.C. 44 File 28645.

[18] Letter to the Solicitor General of Canada, 21/03/1962, *Report of the Royal Commission on Labrador*, Chaired by D. Snowden, Queen's Printer, St. Johns, 1974, volume 6 at 1174-75.

A Framework Agreement was signed in August 1993, and in January 2001, negotiators reached an understanding on the key elements of an Agreement In Principle with respect to the Nunavut portion. The Labrador portion remains unsettled.

Innu Nation Claim

Formal negotiations began with the Innu, Canada and the government of Newfoundland and Labrador in July 1991. All parties signed a Land Claim Framework Agreement on 29 March 1996. Due to disruptions in the negotiation process, progress has been stalled several times. A new land claims proposal was submitted in May 2001. Both governments have agreed that the claim constitutes a reasonable basis for resuming land claim negotiations.

The main cause of disruptions to the negotiation process has been the prospect of a major mining development at Emish. The discovery, along with over 250,000 smaller mineral claims, has increased pressure on the provincial government to develop the region and thus circumvent the negotiation process.

The Innu are extremely concerned about the pace of exploration, and the pressure that is being exerted to develop the Voisey's Bay discovery into a producing mine is impeding a careful assessment of the social, economic and environmental impacts of these activities and is negatively influencing the outcome of land rights negotiations.

Chapter 7

British Columbia

Prior to 1990, British Columbia did not recognize an obligation to treat with Aboriginal Peoples with respect to land title. The government of British Columbia consistently asserted that Aboriginal title to land never existed, and if it did, it was extinguished prior to Confederation. By virtue of a Proclamation made in 1858, the governor of British Columbia was given the power to have Crown lands sold within the colony and was authorized to grant any land belonging to the Crown in the colony. By a later Proclamation of 1859, all lands in British Columbia and all mines and minerals underlying the province were declared to belong to the Crown in fee simple. The British Columbia Terms of Union[1] of 1871 do not expressly require the province to treat with Aboriginal People. This represents a stark contrast to the assurances extracted by the federal government from other provinces during the course of the transfer of ownership and control over public lands. Article 13 of the Terms of Union reads:

> The charge of the Indians, and the trusteeship and management of the lands reserved for their use and benefit, shall be assumed by the Dominion Government, and a policy as liberal as that hitherto pursued by the British Columbia Government shall be continued by the Dominion Government after a Union.

> To carry out such policy, tracts of land of such extent as it has hitherto been the practice of the British Columbia Government to appropriate for that purpose, shall from time to time be conveyed by the Local Government to the Dominion Government in trust for the use and benefit of the Indians on application of the Dominion Government; and in case of disagreement between the two Governments respecting the quantity of such tracts of land to be so granted, the matter shall be referred for the decisions of the Secretary of State for the Colonies.

---

[1] R.S.C. 1985, App. II, No. 10.

While the Terms of Union recognized that land needed to be set aside for Aboriginal People as settlement progressed, the policy that had developed in British Columbia was more restrictive than the policy that had been developed in Ontario and the Prairie provinces. Existing reserves in British Columbia have for the most part been set apart by executive action and not by treaty.

Reserve lands agreed upon under the Mckenna-McBride Agreement[2] were conveyed in 1938 and were made subject to the reservations and conditions generally attached to Crown grants issued under the *Crown Lands Act* to settlers, except that minerals were not reserved. An Order in Council of 1961, declaring itself to be "full and final settlement" of outstanding obligations to provide reserve lands pursuant to Treaty No. 8 in the Peace River Block, conveyed 24,448 acres to Canada, but subject to all the conditions attached to Crown grants issued under the *Crown Lands Act* to settlers. The province ultimately exercised its jurisdiction over public lands and its claim to a reversionary interest in reserve lands to extract conditions upon the establishment of reserves. The conditions are unique to British Columbia.

In the late 1960s, the Nisga'a brought their case before the courts in *Calder v. Attorney General of British Columbia.*[3] In the Supreme Court of Canada in 1973, six judges ruled in *Calder* that Aboriginal title had existed in British Columbia. All judges agreed, with the exception of Justice Pigeon, that Aboriginal title existed at common law and continued to exist unless validly extinguished by the Crown. The court was divided on whether or not the title, which the Nisga'a claimed, was extinguished. This case affirmed that Aboriginal rights to land exist independent of the *Royal Proclamation, 1763* but rather flow from Aboriginal Peoples' traditional use and occupancy of the land, rejecting that the Proclamation was the source of Aboriginal rights as determined in *St. Catherine's Milling and Lumber Co. v. R.*[4] Not long after the decision in the *Calder* case, the federal government, which until then had denied the existence of Aboriginal title, initiated its comprehensive land claims process to settle the issue of Aboriginal title over those tracts of land where Aboriginal title had not been ceded by treaty. The federal government established the Office of Native Claims to negotiate settlements in non-treaty areas, including British Columbia.

In *Delgamuukw v. British Columbia,*[5] the majority opinion of the Supreme Court written by Chief Justice Lamer was whether or not British Columbia had the power to extinguish Aboriginal rights after 1871, either by

2   24/09/1912, approved by Dominion order in council on 27 November1912, quoted in P.C. 208-1930, 03/02/1930 [unpublished].
3   *R. v. Calder, supra* note 11 in ch. 1.
4   *Saint Catherine's Milling and Lumber Co. v. R., supra* note 10 in ch. 1.
5   *Delgamuukw v. British Columbia, supra* note 24 in ch. 1, para. 153.

way of its own jurisdiction or by the application of section 88 of the *Indian Act*.[6] The majority reiterated the fact that the federal government has exclusive jurisdiction to extinguish Aboriginal rights and title by virtue of section 91(24) of the *Constitution Act, 1867*.[7] The court did not explicitly consider whether British Columbia had the authority to do so prior to 1871.

In 1990, the government of British Columbia reversed its decision that Aboriginal rights to land did not exist in British Columbia and, in December 1990, approved the establishment of a task force to advise the Government of Canada, the government of British Columbia and the First Nations Summit on treaty negotiations in British Columbia.

In June 1991, the task force released its report, which made 19 recommendations. One recommendation was the establishment of an impartial, tripartite treaty commission to coordinate the commencement of land claims negotiations in British Columbia. Canada, British Columbia and the First Nations Summit signed the Tripartite Treaty Commission Agreement[8] on 21 September 1992, supporting the establishment of a Treaty Commission. The Commission is the keeper of the process.

The British Columbia Treaty Commissioners were appointed in May 1993. It was also in May 1993 that the *Treaty Commission Act*[9] was passed in the provincial legislature. In December 1993, the Treaty Commission opened its doors to accept Statements of Intent (to negotiate) from British Columbia First Nations. In December 1995, the *British Columbia Treaty Commission Act*[10] was passed by federal Parliament.

Reserves Established on Federal Lands

In 1930, lands along the CPR railway and extending up the Peace River were transferred back to British Columbia. The reserves contained in this transfer were to continue to be under the jurisdiction of the federal government but subject to such terms and conditions as determined by the provincial government. In order to arrive at an agreed form of conveyance for reserve lands elsewhere in the province, the Canadian government agreed to the imposition of terms and conditions. The terms and conditions are the most burdensome imposed on reserves anywhere in Canada. No obligation to treat with Aboriginal People for the surrender of their title was entrenched, nor was the province obliged to meet promises to set aside lands pursuant to

---

[6] *Ibid.* paras. 172-82.

[7] *Ibid.* paras. 173.

[8] Tripartite Treaty Commission Agreement, British Columbia Treaty Commission, online: <http://www.bctreaty.net/files/bctcagreement.html>.

[9] *Treaty Commission Act* [RSBC 1996] Chapter 461.

[10] *British Columbia Treaty Commission Act* [1995, c. 45].

unfulfilled treaties. For bands within the Treaty No. 8 region that were not signatories to the treaty, reserve land was set aside. The Fort Nelson Band, a signatory to Treaty No. 8, ultimately sacrificed its mineral entitlement under the treaty in order to receive some benefits from mineral development on lands set aside as reserve lands.

The McLeod Lake Band was residing within the boundaries of Treaty No. 8 at the time that negotiations were undertaken with other bands within that vicinity. However, the McLeod Lake Indian Band was not visited in 1899 by government negotiators when Treaty No. 8 was negotiated. Historical evidence shows that the band was eligible and entitled to the benefits bestowed by the treaty. After initiating court action in 1982, in 1999 a Final Agreement was reached between the band and the provincial and federal governments. The *McLeod Lake Indian Band Treaty No. 8 Adhesion and Settlement Agreement Act*[11] was enacted in 2000 giving effect to the Final Agreement. The settlement included a transfer of $9.75 million with respect to claims for specified treaty benefits and other claims and 19,810 hectares of land. The McLeod Lake Indian Band is given the capacity to administer forestry standards and will establish a Forest Practice Code that is to meet or beat provincial standards.

Land Set Aside by Executive Action

Most reserve lands in British Columbia were set aside by executive action following agreement between the province and the federal government in 1938. The provincial government withheld wide-ranging powers over the land conveyed to the federal government for the use and benefit of the Aboriginal People. In particular, the province reserved water privileges, and the power "to take from or upon any part of the hereditaments...any gravel, sand, stone, lime, timber, or other material which may be required in the construction, maintenance, or repair of any roads, ferries, bridges, or other public works." Reserve minerals were not expressly referred to in the 1938 form of conveyance. However, British Columbia has successfully secured federal acknowledgement of its ownership of the precious metals and utilized this acknowledgement to gain extraordinary powers over mineral development on reserves. In 1943 the two governments reached an agreement respecting the development of minerals on reserve lands.[12] The agreement vested in the British Columbia government the right to develop all minerals and mineral claims both precious and base in, upon or under reserve lands.

---

[11] [S.B.C. 2000] Chapter 8.
[12] Canada-British Columbia Agreement, S.C. 1943, c. 19, Schedule.

British Columbia Indian Reserves Mineral Resources Act[13]

Natural resources were transferred to British Columbia by Canada in 1930.[14] In 1938, Aboriginal reserves were conveyed to Canada by the province and no mention was made of minerals.[15] In 1943, the *British Columbia Indian Reserves Mineral Resources Agreement* passed jurisdiction over minerals on reserves to the provincial government. The *British Columbia Indian Reserves Mineral Resources Act* is the enabling Act of that Agreement.

The Act gives the provincial government the sole right to develop and exploit minerals – both precious and base – on or under reserve lands. Administration, control and disposal of all minerals and mineral claims, both precious and base, on or under reserve lands is the responsibility of the province, which is to administer and regulate prospecting, staking, recording, developing, leasing, selling, or otherwise disposing of or dealing with all such minerals and mineral claims.

Under the Act, the term "mineral" includes gold, silver and all naturally occurring useful minerals. Not included in that term are: peat, coal, petroleum, natural gas, bitumen, oil shales, limestone, marble, clay, gypsum, or any building stone when mined for building purposes, earth, ash, marl, gravel, sand or any element that forms part of the agricultural surface of the land.

The Department of Mines of British Columbia collects revenue by way of purchase money, rent, recording fees, royalty or otherwise in respect of any sale or other disposition of minerals and mineral claims in or under the reserves, together with all licence, permit or other fees. From the sales, rents or royalties of minerals underlying reserve lands, one-half is payable to the province and the other half is payable to the federal government for the benefit of the Aboriginal People. Notably, the province does not take into account provincial taxes on minerals and metals when undertaking the 50-50 split. This significantly reduces the viability of the Agreement for the Aboriginal Peoples concerned. In effect, the provincial government conferred on the Aboriginal People an interest that is no different from that extended to any settler in the later era of settlement in the province.[16]

As will be discussed below, lands covered by Treaty No. 8 and the Douglas Treaties were conveyed to the federal government subject to certain terms and conditions. In light of 1982 constitutional amendments for the

---

[13] 1943-44, c. 19.

[14] *Canada-British Columbia Natural Resources Transfer Agreement.*

[15] Order in Council, 1036, 1938.

[16] See the *Canada-British Columbia Agreement*, S.C. 1943.

protection of treaty rights, the terms and conditions imposed on the reserves by the 1943 Canada-British Columbia Agreement[17] seem to be an outright violation of the rights conveyed by those treaties.

Fort Nelson Indian Reserve Minerals Revenue Sharing Act[18]

The *Fort Nelson Indian Reserve Minerals Revenue Sharing Act* was enacted to implement an agreement between the provincial government of British Columbia and the federal government respecting revenue sharing from the exploitation of minerals in the Fort Nelson Indian Reserve. The Act applies solely to the Fort Nelson Indian Band.

Under Treaty No. 8, the Fort Nelson Indian Band surrendered all their rights, titles and privileges whatsoever to certain lands in British Columbia to the federal government. Although a promise was made at that time to set aside reserve land for the exclusive use of the band, this was not done until 1961, whereupon lands were conveyed by the province to Canada in trust for the use and benefit of the Fort Nelson Indian Band. This Act was undertaken in accordance with an agreement dated 24 September 1912 between J.A.J. McKenna, special commissioner appointed by Canada, and the then premier of the province of British Columbia. The province reserved to itself all rights to any minerals, precious or base, including coal, petroleum and gas underlying the reserve land. The band then argued that this was contrary to the terms and meaning of the McKenna-McBride Agreement and Treaty No. 8.

Until the enactment of this Act, the band continued to demand that the province convey to Canada, as trustee for the band, the rights to any minerals found underlying the reserve. The Agreement now ensures that Canada and British Columbia enjoy an equal share of the net profit and gross revenue from the disposition of coal, petroleum and any gas or gases, and other minerals underlying the reserve. The minerals on the Fort Nelson Reserve are now treated as though incorporated into the *British Columbia Indian Reserves Mineral Resources Act.*

Ownership and administration of peat, limestone, marble, clay, gypsum, or any building stone when mined for building purposes, earth, ash, marl, gravel, sand or any element that forms part of the agricultural surface of the land in, upon or under the reserve resides with the federal government. All revenues derived from such materials will be put to the use and benefit of the Fort Nelson Band.

---

[17]   Canada-British Columbia Agreement, *supra* note 40 50 in ch. 5.

[18]   1980-81-82-83, c. 38.

Ownership, administration and control of timber and lime reside with the federal government and are to be utilized for the use and benefit of the band. The province nevertheless retains rights to take timber and lime from the reserve in certain circumstances.[19]

British Columbia retains ownership, administration, control and power over the disposition of coal, petroleum and natural gas under the reserve. Revenue from the disposition of such materials is to be collected by the province and the net profit and gross revenue is to be shared equally between Canada for the use and benefit of the band and the province.

Mineral Potential on Indian Reserve Lands in British Columbia[20]

The Mineral Potential of Indian Reserve Lands report compiled by the Department of Indian and Northern Affairs Canada[21] in British Columbia provides overall rating measures of the economic mineral possibilities of each reserve as a whole, on a scale of low/moderate/good. Factors that affect this rating are the size of the reserve, the location with respect to markets, transportation, access, value and type of commodity, social and cultural barriers to mining on certain lands and areas, marketability of a commodity at any given time and other differentials.

The following rating applies in British Columbia:

- 1,194 reserves were given a low rating;
- 356 reserves were given a moderate rating; and
- 56 were given a good rating.

The report indicates that 168 reserves have at least one commodity that has potential for development. At the time of the report, of the total number of reserves, 45 had already surrendered their minerals in some way.

---

[19] Provided under BC O-I-C No. 1036 of 1938 and Dominion PC Order No. 208 of 1930.

[20] See Department of Indian and Northern Affairs Canada, online: <http://www.ainc-inac.gc.ca/ntr/bc_e.html>.

[21] Keep in mind that, although this site was last updated on the 30 April 2001, the report was actually completed in 1991.

Provincial Legislation

Note that provincial legislation and regulations are deemed to apply to Aboriginal People subject to two conditions:

- provincial legislation cannot apply exclusively to Aboriginal People or to land reserved for their benefit; and
- a provincial law may be declared invalid or inapplicable to Aboriginal People if it infringes upon an established Aboriginal or treaty right that is constitutionally protected.

Where an Aboriginal person has established an Aboriginal or treaty right to hunt or fish, then the provincial legislation cannot interfere with that right[22] unless the limitation can meet the test of justification and is in keeping with the honour of the Crown.[23] A limitation on the exercise of a treaty or Aboriginal right would need to be tested in the courts for clarification. It is clear that sufficient consideration must be given to the Aboriginal interest. Apart from measures implemented by a province to conserve a resource, it is unlikely that any court in Canada would uphold any other provincial legislation that restricts an Aboriginal or treaty right. Recently, provincial laws designed to protect public safety have been permitted to override and limit Aboriginal resource rights.

Fishing in British Columbia[24]

The British Columbia *Fisheries Act* provides for licensing and regulatory control of activities associated with commercial fisheries and aquaculture operations in waterways over which the province exerts jurisdiction. The primary concerns are the licensing of: fish processing plants, fish buying establishments, fishers selling their own catch, wild oyster and marine plant harvesting, and aquaculture operations with the province of British Columbia. Any person fishing in British Columbia is required to first obtain a licence from the province to do so.[25] Provincial wildlife legislation exempts Aboriginal People from having to obtain a licence to fish in the province.[26] The commercial harvest of kelp or aquatic plants also requires an authorizing licence from the province.[27]

---

[22] *R. v. White and Bob, supra* note 10 in ch. 2; *R. v. Simon, supra* note 2 in ch. 2; and, *R. v. Sioui, supra* note 2 in ch. 2.

[23] *R. v. White and Bob, supra* note 10 in ch. 2; *R. v. Simon, supra* note 2 in ch. 2; and, *R. v. Sioui, supra* note 2 in ch. 2; *R. v. Sparrow, supra* note 5 in ch. 1.

[24] *Fisheries Act,* R.S.B.C. 1996, Chapter 149.

[25] *Ibid.* ss. 7 and 8; note that an angling licence is required under the British Columbia *Wildlife Act,* [RSBC 1996] Chapter 488, s. 12.

[26] *Ibid.,* s.12(b).

[27] *Ibid.* s. 24.

Under the *British Columbia Fisheries Act Regulations,*[28] the Minister of Agriculture, Food and Fisheries can issue a licence for the harvest and process of marine plants in a defined area and can determine the quantity and type of marine plants that may be harvested. The Minister also regulates marine plant processing establishments under the Regulations. The Regulations also deal with the licensing of oyster harvesting rights on vacant Crown foreshores. Any person who harvests oysters with commercial intent is required to obtain a licence from the province.[29] Any person in the province is, however, lawfully able to gather oysters from Crown land for domestic consumption, so long as the number of oysters harvested does not exceed 15.

Under the *Fish Protection Act,*[30] the province can impose such regulations as necessary to ensure that the provincial fishery resources are sustainable. The Act states at section 2: "For greater certainty, the provisions of this Act are intended to respect Aboriginal and treaty rights in a manner consistent with section 35 of the *Constitution Act, 1982.*" What this means is that where Aboriginal People have established a treaty or Aboriginal right to fish, the Act will be required to meet the justification standard established by *R. v. Sparrow.* As indicated earlier, the province must be able to show that the objective of the legislation or regulations is to conserve the resource, and then show that Aboriginal interests have been given priority over the interests of other groups and interfered with as minimally as possible.

Pursuant to the *Fisheries Renewal Act,*[31] the British Columbia Fisheries Renewal Board (established by the Act) has committed to giving First Nations the opportunity to express their interests in the provincial fisheries. Section 6 reads: "In carrying out its responsibilities, the Board and any committee of the Board must take into account the interests of First Nations and Aboriginal people in the fisheries resource." First Nations can also have the opportunity to have representatives seated on the Board. The mandate of the Board is to deliver programs for the renewal of fisheries and the enhancement of fish, fisheries and fish habitat by agreement with First Nations and other parties with interest in the fisheries industry.[32]

Hunting in British Columbia

Ownership of all wildlife within British Columbia is vested in the provincial government by virtue of the *Wildlife Act.*[33] The Minister's powers include the capacity to enter into and carry out an agreement with a person, association

---

28 B.C. Reg. 281/94.
29 *Fisheries Act Regulations*, s. 9(1)(a).
30 [SBC 1997] Chapter 21.
31 [SBC 1997] Chapter 22.
32 *Fisheries Renewal Act*, s. 12(1).
33 *Supra* note 8, s. 2(1).

or other body for the purpose of accessing or managing the protection of wildlife.[34] The Minister may also designate a species as an endangered species and regulate the habitat and harvest of that species.[35]

The Minister has the power to grant hunting authorizations within British Columbia and can do so by granting licences and permits to eligible applicants.[36] Limited entry hunting licences may have to be obtained for the harvest of certain species in designated areas within the province.[37] Under the *Wildlife Act Hunting Regulations,*[38] the Minister has the capacity to determine quotas and bag limits for harvestable animals, as well as areas within which hunting may take place and when hunting may take place.[39]

Under the Act, it is an offence for any person to take, injure, molest or destroy a bird or its egg or nest except by virtue of the Act and its accompanying Regulations whereby a permit or licence to do so may be obtained.[40]

Aboriginal People residing in British Columbia are not required to obtain a licence to hunt.[41] Under the *Wildlife Designation and Exemption Regulations,*[42] any Aboriginal person residing in British Columbia is exempt from section 41 of the *Wildlife Act* in relation to hunting, provided that such hunting does not occur on occupied land or Crown land that is subject to a right of occupation without consent.[43] Section 41 relates to requirements that licences be obtained for the purposes of hunting and trapping furbearing creatures in the province. Accordingly, an Aboriginal person need not be a registered holder of the trapline for the area in which the animal is harvested.

Where an Aboriginal person in British Columbia can establish an Aboriginal or treaty right to harvest wildlife within the province, then the above legislation and accompanying Regulations are deemed not to apply to him or her unless the province can prove that the restrictions on such rights are justified that the Aboriginal interest has been given priority over all considerations apart from conservation, and that the Aboriginal interest has been interfered with as minimally as possible. Examples of where provincial regulation may be justified are where the purpose of the provision is to

---

[34] *Wildlife Act*, s. 3.
[35] *Ibid.* s. 6.
[36] *Ibid.* s. 14; see also the *Wildlife Act Permit Regulations*, B.C. Reg. 249/2001 and the *Wildlife Act General Regulations*, B.C. Reg. 166/2001.
[37] *Limited Entry Hunting Regulations*, B.C. Reg. 173/2001.
[38] B.C. Reg. 168/2001.
[39] *Wildlife Act Hunting Regulations*, s. 11.
[40] *Ibid.* s. 34.
[41] *Wildlife Act*, s. 11(9).
[42] B.C. Reg. 166/2001.
[43] *Wildlife Designation and Exemption Regulations*, s. 11.1(1).

preserve a resource, or where the provision is designed to promote public safety. Where an Aboriginal person cannot establish right to hunt, an inherent or treaty right, then these Regulations will be applicable.

As indicated earlier, these laws and regulations are deemed to apply generally to Aboriginal people to the point that interference with an established right to hunt and trap is unjustified.

British Columbia Agreements and Treaties

Treaty No. 8[44]

Treaty No. 8, made on 21 June 1899, involved the surrender of vast tracts of land in what is now northern Alberta, northeastern British Columbia, northwestern Saskatchewan and part of the Northwest Territories. In exchange for the land, the Crown made a number of commitments, for example, to provide the bands with reserves, education, annuities, farm equipment, ammunition and relief in times of famine or pestilence. The treaty also purported to accommodate the needs of those bands who wished to continue hunting and fishing.

The text of the treaty has the surrender clause that the Aboriginal signatories to the treaty agree to "cede, release, surrender and yield up to the Government of the Dominion of Canada...all their rights, titles, and privileges whatsoever, to the lands included" within the treaty, and the rest of Canada. The treaty retained the right of the signatory First Nations to

> pursue their usual vocations of hunting, trapping and fishing throughout the tract surrendered as heretofore described, subject to such regulations as may from time to time be made by the Government of the country...and saving and excepting such tracts as may be required or taken up from time to time for settlement, mining, lumbering, trading or other purposes.

The Report of Commissioners for Treaty No. 8, written by Clifford Sifton, the then superintendent-general of Indian Affairs, reveals that the loss of hunting and fishing rights was the primary concern of the Aboriginal People present at the treaty negotiations:

> Evidence from our chief difficulty was the apprehension that the hunting and fishing privileges were to be curtailed. The provision in the treaty under which ammunition and twine is to be furnished went far in the direction of quieting the fears of the Indians, for they admitted that it would be unreasonable to furnish the means of

---

[44] Note that Treaty 8 will also be discussed in the section devoted to treaties of Alberta.

hunting and fishing if laws were to be enacted which would make hunting and fishing so restricted as to render it impossible to make a livelihood by such pursuits. But over and above the provision, we had to solemnly assure them that only such laws as to hunting and fishing as were in the interest of the Indians and were found necessary in order to protect the fish and fur-bearing animals would be made, and that they would be as free to hunt and fish after the treaty as they would be if they never entered into it.

It is extremely clear from the text of the Commissioner's report that the negotiators' intention was to ensure that the Aboriginal People concerned had their traditional rights of hunting and fishing accommodated within the terms of the treaty.

In *R. v. Badger*,[45] the Supreme Court affirmed that Treaty No. 8 guaranteed Aboriginal hunting rights, subject to two limitations. Note that this case was decided on appeal from the Alberta Court of Appeal and therefore the relationship of the treaty with regulations in British Columbia was not expressly discussed. First, there is a limitation with respect to geography – harvesting rights could be exercised throughout the tract surrendered except for those tracts required or taken for the purposes of settlement, mining, lumbering, trading, or other purposes. Second, harvesting rights could be limited by government regulations regarding conservation measures.

Justice Cory for the majority found that it was

...clear that for the Indians the guarantee that hunting, fishing and trapping rights would continue was the essential element, which led to their signing the treaties. The report of the Commissioners who negotiated Treaty No. 8 on behalf of the government underscored the importance to the Indians of the right to hunt, fish and trap. The Commissioners wrote:

There was expressed at every point the fear that the making of the treaty would be followed by the curtailment of the hunting and fishing privileges. . . .

Treaty No. 8 conveys to Aboriginal People in the contained area of British Columbia the constitutionally guaranteed right to hunt and fish on their traditional lands, subject to inconsistent land occupation and use and possibly to conservation legislation.

---

[45] *R. v. Badger, supra* note 19 in ch. 2.

In accordance with the current Supreme Court method of treaty interpretation, the court is to strive to give effect to the "common intention" of the parties in order to give the document its true meaning. In so doing, the court is entitled to consider all contextual evidence, including oral evidence and written evidence relating to the negotiation period. The courts will particularly place emphasis on verbal promises made by the Crown and will read those oral undertakings into the terms of the treaty.

In the 1970s, Daniel and Fumoleau interviewed Elders who were either witnesses to the Treaty No. 8 negotiations or have knowledge of those negotiations on account of stories told to them by ancestors who were.[46] Both authors suggest that the literary content of the treaty was beyond comprehension for the First Nation signatories. Not only does evidence suggest that inadequate interpretation of the treaty terms was given to the Aboriginal People present,[47] but also that, had the terms been translated into the native tongue, experientially speaking those present could not hope to understand the treaty's cultural, economical and political context.[48]

Responses given to Fumoleau by Slavey people who were present at Treaty No. 8 negotiations indicate that among the Aboriginal People there was much confusion as to what was actually going on.[49] One respondent indicated that the Treaty Commissioners "talked nice to us...but nobody understood their language...[and] we have no idea what was written on the paper." Another indicated that the Treaty Commissioners "used long words we couldn't understand," and still others responded that "treaty rights were not much explained to the [Aboriginal] people." Evidence given by witnesses to the treaty signings indicates that the Aboriginal People understood the treaty to be merely a peace and alliance treaty, not a land cession treaty. A government document relating to preparations for the treaty negotiations also lends support to that theory.[50] The document refers to a report written by the superintendent-general of Indian Affairs in 1898 authorizing the appointment of Commissioners to negotiate a treaty with certain Aboriginal societies who were "inclined to be turbulent and were liable to give trouble to isolated parties of miners or traders who might be regarded by the Indians as interfering with what they considered their vested rights."

[46] Daniel, R., "The Spirit and Terms of Treaty Eight" in Price, R. ed., *The Spirit of the Alberta Indian Treaties*, Institute for Research on Public Policy, Toronto, 1979, 47; Fumoleau, R., *As Long as This Land Shall Last*, McClelland and Stewart, Toronto, 1973.

[47] For example, during negotiations with the Dene Tha', Louis Cardinal was the interpreter and supposedly explained Treaty No. 8 to the Dene Tha', yet he spoke only Cree. *The Dene Tha' First Nation, Dene Tha' Traditional Land Use and Occupancy Study*, Arctic Institute of North America, Calgary, 1997, p. 4.

[48] Fumoleau, R., p. 19.

[49] *Ibid.* p. 95-96.

[50] *Order in Council Setting up Commission for Treaty No. 8,* P.C. No. 2749, Indian and Northern Affairs Development, online: <http://www.ainc-inac.gc.ca/pr/trts/trty8/ordr_e.html>, as at 19 November 2001.

Those interviewed by Fumoleau indicated that statements made by the treaty commissioner support the understanding of the Aboriginal People that the treaty was merely to be a peace and friendship agreement: "We are not looking for trouble. It will not change your life. We are just making peace between Whites and Indians...[a]nd we do not want to change your hunting. If Whites should prospect, stake claims, that will not harm anyone. I have come here to issue this money that is all."[51]

This recollection was supported by Aboriginal People who indicated that the Aboriginal man who had spoken on their behalf had told the treaty commissioners that "if nothing would change and the Indians would live as they had in the past, he'd agree to take the money."[52]

As is the case in the lead-up to most treaty negotiations, ample evidence suggests that a main motivation for the Aboriginal signatory tribes in signing Treaty No. 8 was to protect their hunting, fishing and trapping rights.[53] Intrinsically connected to this was a perceived promise by the Crown to protect the Aboriginal signatory parties from misery and starvation. Again, Furmoleau provides evidence to the effect that the people at Fort Chipewyan were under the impression that, by agreeing to the treaty, the Crown had promised that the "Queen will never let your children die from hunger." The Report of the Commissioners for Treaty No. 8[54] also states that "all asked for assistance in season of distress and urged that the old and indigent who were no longer able to hunt and trap and were consequently often in distress should be cared for by the Government." The Commissioners' report goes on to say that "there was expressed at every point the fear that the making of the treaty would be followed by the curtailment of the hunting and fishing privileges." Accordingly, in order to finalize the treaty, the Crown made promises to keep those Aboriginal privileges intact: "We pointed out that the Government could not undertake to maintain Indians in idleness; that the same means of earning a livelihood would continue after the treaty as existed before it, and that the Indians would be expected to make use of them."

The report indicates further that the apprehension of harvestation privilege curtailment was dispelled by promises made under the treaty to provide the Aboriginal signatories with ammunition and twine, "for they admitted it would be unreasonable to furnish the means of hunting and fishing if laws were to be enacted which would make hunting and fishing so restricted as to render it impossible to make a livelihood by such pursuits." Moreover, the report indicates that the Crown affirmed that "the treaty would not lead to any forced interference with their mode of life."

---

[51] Furmoleau, R. p. 90.
[52] Furmoleau, R., p. 93.
[53] See Daniel, R., p. 64; Furmoleau, R., p. 65.
[54] *Report of Commissions for Treaty No. 8*, Morris, A., Winnipeg, Manitoba, Dated 22 September 1899.

The report does indicate that the Crown told the Aboriginal signatories that the government would retain the right to make laws in relation to hunting and fishing under certain circumstances:

> We had to solemnly assure them that only such laws as to hunting and fishing as were in the interest of the Indians and were found necessary in order to protect the fish and furbearing animals would be made, and that they would be as free to hunt and fish after the treaty as they would be if they never entered into it.

The Crown apparently understood that, so long as the resources remained, the "great bulk of the Indians will continue to hunt and to trap." Evidence that was presented in *Re Paulette*[55] was to the effect that the Aboriginal understanding of the treaty was that their way of life would last forever.

Some evidence obtained from Aboriginal People by Daniel suggests that the Aboriginal understanding may have been that they retained ownership of the wildlife.[56]

Treaty No. 8 permitted two types of government limitations: geographical and regulatory. The rights contained in the treaty are "subject to such regulations as may from time to time be made by the Government of the Country"; and those rights could be exercised on the treaty land mass "saving and excepting such tracts as may be required or taken up from time to time for settlement, mining, lumbering, trading or other purposes."

"Government of the Country" has been interpreted to mean the federal government.[57] The types of regulations that would be permitted, as indicated in the Treaty Commissioners' report, would be those that are in the interest of the Aboriginal parties, and ultimately, those laws and regulations that are implemented to conserve natural resources to ensure continued hunting, fishing and trapping.

While hunting, trapping and fishing regulations existed around the time of the treaty negotiations, there were no restrictions on lumbering. It is for this reason that Ross and Sharvit[58] question to what extent the rights to hunt, trap and fish are subject to the taking up by the government of lands for purposes including lumbering:

> It makes little sense to argue that while they were to be free from laws which unnecessarily restricted the exercise of their rights by limiting Aboriginal use of wildlife resources, they would not be

---

[55] [1973] 6 W.W.R. 97 at 121 (N.W.T.S.C.).

[56] Daniela, R., p. 82-83.

[57] *R. v. Batisse*, (1978), 84 D.L.R. (3d) 377 at 383 (Ont. D.C.); *R. v. Napoleon*, [1982] 3 C.N.L.R. 116 at 120 (B.C. Prov. Ct.); *R. v. Horseman*, *supra* note 18 in ch. 2.

[58] Ross, M. and Sharvit, C., "Forest Management in Alberta and Rights to Hunt, Trap and Fish Under Treaty No. 8," (1998) 36 *Alberta Law Review* (No. 3) 645.

protected from legislation allowing the exploitation of forest resources in a manner which interferes with their ability to earn a livelihood from hunting, trapping and fishing. If the government could not directly interfere with these activities neither could it permit third parties to do to.[59]

Ross and Sharvit's discussion of this issue is contained to the operation of the treaty in Alberta. For this reason, the treaty and the possibility for its reinterpretation in relation to forestry will be discussed below.

A 1999 discussion of the implications of Treaty No. 8 can be found in the British Columbia Court of Appeal decision in *Halfway River First Nation v. British Columbia (Ministry of Forests)*.[60] The Ministry of Forests and Canadian Forest Products Limited were appealing an order of the Supreme Court of British Columbia, which quashed the decision of the district manager on 13 September 1996 approving Canfor's application for a cutting permit. The timber harvesting licence held by Canfor was for a wilderness area on Crown land, adjacent to the reserve land granted to the Halfway River First Nation. The issue resolved around the section of Treaty No. 8 that preserved the right of the Treaty Aboriginals to hunt. Under the treaty, the right to hunt is subject to the exception that excluded hunting grounds include "such tracts as may be required or taken up from time to time for settlement, mining, lumbering, trading or other purposes." The Court of Appeal found that the district manager should have been aware of his fiduciary duty as an officer of the Crown with respect to the band's treaty rights. The Court of Appeal upheld the Chambers judge's decision to quash the district manager's approval of the permit application given that the issuance of the cutting permit infringed the band's right to hunt and the Crown had failed to show that the infringement was justified. The Crown did not adduce evidence that the legislative or administrative objectives were of sufficient importance to warrant infringement or that the conduct infringed the treaty right as little as possible. Moreover, the Crown did not show that the effects of the timber licence outweighed the derived benefits, nor that adequate and meaningful consultation had taken place. The district manager was found to have failed to provide a full opportunity to be heard to the Halfway River First Nation, and had thus breached the principles of procedural fairness.

The obligation on the Crown to consult is counterbalanced with a duty on First Nations to respond. *Kelly Lake Cree Nation v. British Columbia (Minister of Energy and Mines)*[61] involved an application by two First Nations groups for judicial review of the decision of the Ministry of Energy and Mines (MEM) and the Ministry of Forests to permit the use and

---

[59] *Ibid.* para. 38.

[60] [1999] 4 C.N.L.R. 1 (B.C.C.A.).

[61] [1999] 3 C.N.L.R. 126 (B.C.S.C.).

occupation of Crown land for gas well development. The Ministry granted a permit to Amoco to develop an exploratory gas well, while the Ministry of Forests granted a cutting permit for the development of an access trail to the well site. The First Nations claimed that the activities would impact on their Aboriginal, treaty and constitutional rights and that the Crown had breached its duty to consult in a meaningful way with the affected First Nations prior to making its decision. The court found that consultation was a reciprocal process and given the failure of the First Nations to participate in the process, non-participation in the process, the government had determined that further consultation would not alter the First Nations' position and its decision to proceed was not unfair. The Crown's obligation to consult was met when the Nation failed to respond to the Crown's letter following discussions with the Crown.

Douglas Treaties: 1850-1854

Between 1850 and 1854, James Douglas, as chief factor of Fort Victoria and governor of the colony, made a series of 14 land purchases from Aboriginal Peoples. The Douglas Treaties cover approximately 358 square miles of land around Victoria, Saanich, Sooke, Nanaimo and Port Hardy, all on Vancouver Island.

The 14 Douglas treaties are similar in approach and content.[62] An area of land was surrendered "entirely and forever" in exchange for cash, clothing, or blankets. The surrendered land was to become "the entire property of the white people forever." The signatories and their descendants retained existing village sites and fields for their continued use and the use of their children and all who might follow after, the "liberty to hunt over unoccupied lands" and the right to "carry on their fisheries as formerly." The language used and the objectives generally attached to the establishment of reserves suggest that the Aboriginal People concerned were to be granted full ownership in the land.

Although the land was transferred to Canada with the same terms and conditions attached as with other reserve lands, the Douglas land purchases have been upheld as treaties by the courts.[63] In *Claxton v. Saanichton Marina*[64] the customary right to fish was upheld by the court, which recognized that members of the band were held to "not unreasonably consider Saanichton Bay their home and their sanctuary."[65]

---

[62] Recorded by the Ministry of Attorney General Treaty Negotiations Office, Government of British Columbia, online: <http://www.aaf.gov.bc.ca/history/dotreaty.stm>.

[63] *R. v. White and Bob, supra* note 10 in ch. 2; *R. v. Bartleman*, B.C. C.A., (Unreported, June 27, 1984); *Claxton v. Saanichton Marina Ltd., supra* note 13 in ch. 2.

[64] *Claxton v. Saanichton Marina Ltd., supra* note 13 in ch. 2.

[65] *Ibid.* at 58.

In 1987 the Tsawout Band successfully obtained a permanent injunction restraining the construction of a marina in Saanichton Bay on the grounds that the proposed facility would interfere with fishing rights promised to them by their 1852 treaty.[66]

One case that has specifically considered the treaty right to hunt on unoccupied private land is *R. v. Bartleman.*[67] There, the accused was charged with using ammunition that was prohibited under the provincial *Wildlife Act.*[68] He had been hunting on uncultivated bush land. No livestock or buildings were present, no fence surrounded the land and no signs had been posted. He claimed that, on the basis of his treaty hunting right, the provincial legislation did not apply to him. His hunting rights were set out in the 1852 North Saanich Indian Treaty, which provided that the Indians "are at liberty to hunt over the unoccupied lands, and to carry on our fisheries as formerly." The British Columbia Court of Appeal held that it was necessary to interpret the right on the basis of what the Aboriginal signatories would have understood in 1852 by the words of the treaty. It held that the treaty right to hunt could be exercised where to do so would not interfere with the actual use being made of the privately owned land. At page 97 this was written: "…the hunting must take place on land that is unoccupied in the sense that the particular form of hunting that is being undertaken does not interfere with the actual use and enjoyment of the land by the owner or occupier."

In this case the Court of Appeal found that hunting was not incompatible with the minimal level of use to which the land was being put. The "visible, incompatible use" approach requires that the particular land use be considered in each case. Interestingly, the court decided that the treaty right to hunt in this case extended beyond the boundaries of the original treaty to traditional lands that were not covered by it.

Since the Supreme Court decision of *Delgamuukw v. R.*,[69] it is suggested that Aboriginal People affected by the Douglas Treaties are in a much stronger position to enforce their treaty rights to ensure that they are in a position to "carry on their fisheries as formerly."[70]

---

[66] *Ibid.*

[67] *R. v. Bartleman* (1984), 55 B.C.L.R. 78 (B.C.C.A.).

[68] *Wildlife Act*, [RSBC 1996] Chapter 488.

[69] *Delgamuukw v. R.*, [1997] 3 S.C.R. 1010.

[70] Morales, R., *James Douglas Meet Delgamuukw: The Implications of the Delgamuukw Decision on the Douglas Treaties*, Delgamuukw / Gidsay'wa National Process, online: <http://www.delgamuukw.org/research/douglastreaties.pdf>.

Modern Agreements and Treaties

More recently the provincial government has sought to treat with the indigenous inhabitants of British Columbia. British Columbia boasts more outstanding comprehensive claims from First Nations than the rest of Canada combined. The treaties signed in British Columbia – Treaty No. 8 and the Douglas Treaties – cover only small areas of the province.

There are presently 44 treaty tables in the British Columbia Treaty Commission process. Forty-one of the 48 Statements of Intent accepted as complete by the Treaty Commission have had the Framework of the Agreement signed. The First Nations organizations participating in the process represent approximately 125 of the 197 bands in British Columbia. The province of British Columbia negotiates in four regions and at one transboundary (British Columbia/Yukon) treaty table. One Agreement In Principle has been signed, as with the Sechelt Indian Band, which is discussed below.

The Nisga'a Final Agreement

The Nisga'a Final Agreement, which came into effect on 11 May 2000,[71] represents British Columbia's first modern-day land claims agreement. The Agreement transferred almost 2,000 square kilometres of Crown land to the Nisga'a Nation.

The estate is transferred in fee simple to the Nisga'a Nation but is not subject to any condition, proviso, restriction, exception, or reservation set out in the *Land Act*,[72] or any comparable limitation under any federal or provincial law. Moreover, no estate or interest in Nisga'a lands can be expropriated except as permitted by, and in accordance with, the Final Agreement.[73] What this means is that the Nisga'a Nation is free to convey any portion of their land in fee simple, or dispose of any other interest in the land, to another person or entity without having to seek the permission of the Canadian or British Columbia governments. Moreover, if a portion of land is conveyed to another party in fee simple, that land remains part of the Nisga'a Nation and therefore continues to be subject to Nisga'a laws and regulations. The land is also exempt from other common law property rules that may detract from the Nisga'a Nation's right to enjoy that land in its entirety. The Agreement specifically states that Nisga'a lands are not to be considered "land reserved for the Indians" for the purposes of the *Constitution Act, 1867.*[74]

---

[71] The Agreement was brought into effect by the *Nisga'a Final Agreement Act*, S.C. 2000, C. 7.

[72] *Land Act*, [RSBC 1996] Chapter 245.

[73] *Nisga'a Final Agreement Act*, Chapter 3, paragraph 3.

[74] *Ibid.* Chapter 2, paragraph 11.

Federal and provincial laws are to continue to apply to the Nisga'a villages, institutions, corporations, citizens and lands, but in the event of an inconsistency or conflict between the Final Agreement and those laws, the Agreement is to prevail to the extent of the inconsistency.[75] This rule also applies to activities on Nisga'a land where any licence, permit or other authorization must be obtained under a federal or provincial law.[76] Importantly, the Agreement purports to be an exhaustive compendium of the treaty rights guaranteed to the Nisga'a Nation by virtue of section 35 of the *Constitution Act, 1982.*[77] The Agreement further provides that, where an Aboriginal right is identifiable outside of the Nisga'a Nation, at the present time, or at any time in the future, the Nisga'a agree to release Canada, British Columbia and all other persons from all such claims, demands, actions, or proceedings of whatever kind.[78] In response to the general rules of treaty interpretation developed by the courts, the Agreement states that its terms are not to be interpreted in favour of one party over another; not, therefore, in favour of the First Nations party concerned.[79]

Land

The Nisga'a own two types of land in fee simple: Nisga'a lands and Nisga'a fee simple lands outside Nisga'a lands. Rights to resources contained in or under such lands depends upon which category it falls into.

Nisga'a Lands

Nisga'a lands consist of 1,992 square kilometres of land located in the lower Nass River area, comprised of 1,930 square kilometres of provincial Crown land and 62 square kilometres of former Nisga'a Indian reserves (56 in number), including the four villages of New Aiyansh (Gitlakdamiks), Canyon City (Gitwinksihlkw), Greenville (Lakalzap) and Kincolith (Gingolx), which cease to be Indian reserves. As indicated above, the Nisga'a Nation may dispose of the whole of its estate in fee simple in any parcel of Nisga'a Lands to any person, and dispose of any lesser estate or interest in its lands without requiring the consent of Canada or British Columbia.[80] Where land is transferred to another party, it remains part of the Nisga'a Lands and is subject to Nisga'a laws.[81] The law of adverse possession and

---

[75] *Ibid.* paragraph 13.
[76] *Ibid.* paragraph 14.
[77] *Ibid.* paragraph 23.
[78] *Ibid.* paragraph 27.
[79] *Ibid.* paragraph 57.
[80] *Ibid.* Chapter 3, paragraph 4.
[81] *Ibid.* paragraph 5.

other common law rules that may result in the diminishing of Nisga'a lands do not apply in respect of such lands.[82]

The Nisga'a Lisims Government is to allow reasonable public access to and onto Nisga'a public lands, but only for temporary non-commercial and recreational uses. Public access is to be provided, however, to satisfy a requirement that "reasonable opportunities" exist for the public to hunt and fish on Nisga'a public lands,[83] as governed by federal and provincial laws of general application and Nisga'a laws.[84] Public access does not include harvesting or extracting resources, unless with the authority of the Nisga'a Lisims Government.[85] Nisga'a Lisims Government can require persons other than Nisga'a citizens to obtain a permit or licence upon payment of a fee.[86] Nisga'a citizens also have a right of reasonable access to and onto Crown lands that are outside of Nisga'a lands, including streams, to allow for the normal use and enjoyment of Nisga'a interests, including the use of resources for purposes incidental to the normal use and enjoyment of those rights or interests, provided that this access does not interfere with other authorized uses or the ability of the Crown to authorize uses or dispose of Crown land.[87] Where the land is already being put to an alternative, inconsistent use, the Crown is under an obligation to ensure that reasonable access to that land is provided.[88]

Nisga'a Fee Simple Lands

The second type of land holdings are Nisga'a fee simple lands outside Nisga'a lands. These lands are divided into two categories. Category A lands consist of 18 Nisga'a Aboriginal reserves. Some of these have been adjusted to include additional Crown land, totalling 12.5 square kilometres. All of these reserves cease to be Aboriginal reserves. The total size of Category A lands is 25 square kilometres. Category B lands consist of 15 parcels of Crown land, totalling 2.5 square kilometres. These lands have been transferred to the Nisga'a government to provide economic development opportunities. Both categories of land are owned by the Nisga'a government, but will be subject to provincial laws.

---

[82]   *Ibid.* paragraph 6.
[83]   *Ibid.* Chapter 6, paragraph 4.
[84]   *Ibid.* paragraph 5.
[85]   *Ibid.* paragraph 2.
[86]   *Ibid.* paragraph 7.
[87]   *Ibid.* paragraph 23.
[88]   *Ibid.* paragraph 24.

Category A Lands. The estate in fee simple to Category A lands is subject to the rights referred to in subparagragh of section 50(1)(a)(iii) of the British Columbia *Land Act*.[89] Section 50(1)(a)(iii) conveys to the fee simple holder a right to "take and occupy water privileges and to have and enjoy the rights of carrying water over, through or under any part of the land granted, as may be reasonably required for mining or agricultural purposes in the vicinity of the land, paying a reasonable compensation to the grantee, the grantee's successors and assigns." However, the land is not subject to any other conditions, provisos, restrictions or reservations contained in section 50 of the *Land Act,* which include rights reserved to the province for mineral extraction and expropriation. The Agreement provides specifically for no estate or interest in Category A lands to be expropriated from the Nisga'a Nation except as permitted by and in accordance with the Agreement.[90] One such exception to this general rule is where British Columbia considers expropriation of such lands to be "justifiable and necessary for a provincial public purpose" or for the use of a "provincial ministry or agent of the provincial Crown."[91] In such circumstances, the Nisga'a Nation need not consent to the expropriation, although "fair compensation" is payable.[92] In circumstances where ownership of mineral rights are also expropriated, the provincial government must provide the same amount of Crown land as a replacement for that expropriated from the Nisga'a Nation.[93]

The Nisga'a Nation owns all mineral resources on or under Category A lands.[94] British Columbia retains ownership of submerged lands within Category A lands.[95] The same rights and restrictions apply to Category B lands.

Mineral Resources

The Nisga'a Nation owns all resources on or under Nisga'a lands.[96] The Agreement enables the Nisga'a Lisims Government to enter into agreements in respect of applying provincial administration to claim staking, recording and inspecting subsurface exploration and development, and, the collection of fees, rents, royalties and other charges on Nisga'a lands by British Columbia on the Nisga'a Lisims Government's behalf.[97]

---

[89] *Land Act*, [RSBC 1996] Chapter 245.
[90] *Nisga'a Final Agreement*, Chapter 3, paragraph 49.
[91] *Ibid.* paragraph 55.
[92] *Ibid.* paragraph 56.
[93] *Ibid.* paragraph 57.
[94] *Ibid.* paragraph 50.
[95] *Ibid.* paragraph 52.
[96] *Ibid.* Chapter 3, paragraph 19.
[97] *Ibid.* paragraph 21.

Forest Resources

The Nisga'a Nation owns all forest resources on Nisga'a lands.[98] The Nisga'a Lisims Government has the exclusive authority to determine, collect and administer any fees, rents, royalties or other charges in respect of both timber and non-timber forest resources on Nisga'a lands. However, full rights to all timber resources on Nisga'a lands are not transferred until the end of a transition period of 5 years.[99] Until 2005, the allowable volume is 165,000 cubic metres, after which time the volume is reduced to 135,000 cubic metres until 2009 and then to 130,000 cubic metres until 2010. Of those volumes, the Nisga'a Lisims Government has the power to authorize harvesting of 10,000 cubic metres in the first three years, 30,000 cubic metres cubed in the fourth year and 40,000 cubic metres cubed in the fifth year.[100] After the fifth year, the Nisga'a Lisims Government is in full control of forest resource harvest, subject only to the volume restrictions imposed on the government until the end of a nine-year period and to the requirement that any such laws meet or exceed the established provincial standard applying to forests on Crown land. The Agreement is clearly designed to slowly introduce the Nisga'a Lisims to the point that it is given full control of forest resources after the transition period. In 2006, full ownership of forest resources will pass to the Nisga'a Nation. Provincial laws will continue to apply to the holders of agreements and licences under the *Forest Act* on Nisga'a lands during the transition period.[101]

Laws enacted by the Nisga'a Lisims Government in respect of timber resource management, but not in relation to existing agreements and licences, and on Nisga'a lands took effect on 13 April 2000.[102] Such laws, however, must include forest standards that meet or exceed forest standards established under forest practices by British Columbia in respect of Crown land,[103] and must be no more intrusive to the environment than the forest standards applicable to such land.[104] The capacity of the Nisga'a Lisims Government extends to harvesting and conservation of non-timber resources on Nisga'a lands.[105]

---

[98] *Ibid.* Chapter 5, paragraph 3.
[99] *Ibid.* paragraph 4.
[100] *Ibid.* paragraph 20.
[101] *Ibid.* paragraph 5.
[102] *Ibid.* paragraph 6.
[103] *Ibid.* paragraph 8.
[104] *Ibid.* paragraph 10.
[105] *Ibid.* paragraph 11.

Until 2006, provincial laws will continue to apply to timber scaling. However, after the transition period, the Nisga'a Lisims Government may make compatible laws.[106] Provincial legislation will continue to apply in relation to timber marks.[107] The Agreement dictates the volume of timber that may be harvested on Nisga'a lands until 2010. To oversee the administration of imposed restrictions on harvestation on Nisga'a lands, under the Agreement, the Nisga'a Nation and British Columbia agreed to establish a Forestry Transition Committee.[108]

Provincial laws in respect of manufacture in British Columbia of timber harvested from Crown lands apply to timber harvested from Nisga'a Lands.[109] Where the Nisga'a Nation wishes to export timber harvested on Nisga'a lands, permission must be obtained from the provincial government.[110] During the transition period, however, federal laws will continue to apply to timber removed from former reserve lands.[111]

Finally, British Columbia agrees in principle to an acquisition by the Nisga'a Nation of a forest tenure or tenures outside of Nisga'a lands, having an aggregate allowable annual cut of up to 150,000 cubic metres.[112] Approval of such an application would be subject to the *Forest Act*[113] and then to a range of factors set out in the Agreement.[114]

Fisheries

Nisga'a citizens have the right to harvest fish and aquatic plants subject to conservation measures and legislation enacted to protect public health and safety.[115] The Nisga'a Nation's fish entitlement is a percentage of the total allowable catch and is not given priority in fishery management decisions concerning recreational and commercial fisheries.[116] Federal and provincial laws governing fish and aquatic plants are not displaced by the Agreement.[117] The Minister remains responsible for the management of fisheries on Nisga'a lands,[118] although the Nisga'a Lisims Government may make laws in respect

---

[106] *Ibid.* paragraph 14.
[107] *Ibid.* paragraph 16.
[108] *Ibid.* paragraph 32.
[109] *Ibid.* paragraph 65.
[110] *Ibid.* paragraph 66.
[111] *Ibid.* paragraph 69.
[112] *Ibid.* paragraph 76.
[113] R.S.B.C. 1996, Chapter 157.
[114] *Ibid.* paragraphs 77 & 78.
[115] *Ibid.* Chapter 8, paragraph 1.
[116] *Ibid.* paragraph 2.
[117] *Ibid.* paragraph 3.
[118] *Ibid.* paragraph 68.

of rights granted to them under the Agreement, with the proviso that such laws are consistent with the Agreement, the Harvest Agreement, and in accordance with the Nisga'a annual fishing allocation.[119]

The fish harvesting entitlement is to be held by the Nisga'a Nation,[120] which cannot lawfully dispose of its fish entitlements,[121] although it can authorize persons other than Nisga'a citizens to access Nisga'a fisheries.[122]

Neither the federal nor provincial government can require Nisga'a entities to have a licence to fish or harvest aquatic plants, or to pay fees, charges and royalties in respect of harvests for domestic purposes.[123] Charges will be applicable to persons who sell fish harvested under the Agreement, such as are applied to commercial harvesters, except where fees and charges are levied by the Nisga'a Lisims Government.[124] Trade and barter between Nisga'a citizens does not invoke this law and will be subject only to Nisga'a laws.[125]

Salmon. The provincial Minister for Agriculture, Food and Fisheries will determine a minimum escapement level for one or more species of Nass salmon where it is considered necessary for conservation.[126] The allocation of salmon to the Nisga'a Nation will be determined annually and will be based on the number of fish returning to Canadian waters.[127] The Agreement allows for a Harvest Agreement to be entered into between the Nisga'a Lisims Government and the federal and provincial governments to govern allowable catch.[128] The Harvest Agreement will be administered by way of issuing licences to the Nisga'a Lisims Government.[129] Fisheries under the Harvest Agreement do not have any priority in fisheries management decisions made by the Minister concerning commercial and recreational fisheries.[130] Fish harvested by the Nisga'a Nation and agents, contractors and licensees authorized to harvest can be sold commercially.[131]

---

[119] *Ibid.* paragraph 69.
[120] *Ibid.* paragraph 4.
[121] *Ibid.* paragraph 5.
[122] *Ibid.* paragraph 6.
[123] *Ibid.* paragraph 7.
[124] *Ibid.* paragraph 8.
[125] *Ibid.* paragraph 9.
[126] *Ibid.* paragraph 11.
[127] *Ibid.* paragraphs 13 – 20.
[128] *Ibid.* paragraphs 21 – 30.
[129] *Ibid.* paragraph 25.
[130] *Ibid.* paragraph 26.
[131] *Ibid.* paragraph 27 & 31 – 33.

Steelhead. Under the Agreement, the Nisga'a fish entitlements of Nass steelhead are for domestic purposes only.[132] Where sale of Nass steelhead, harvested under the Agreement, occurs, this activity will be in accordance with federal and provincial laws of general application, and any applicable Nisga'a law.[133]

Non-Salmon Species and Aquatic Plants. The Nisga'a Nation has the right to harvest non-salmon species and aquatic plants for domestic use.[134] Allocation to such resources will be determined under the Agreement, after taking into consideration a variety of factors.[135]

Oolichan. The Nisga'a Nation, and other persons who have Aboriginal rights to harvest oolichan in the Nass area, have an exclusive harvesting right.[136] Intertidal bivalves may be harvested by the Nisga'a Nation for domestic purposes only, and not for sale.[137]

Wildlife and Migratory Birds. Throughout the Nass Wildlife area, Nisga'a citizens have a right to harvest wildlife subject to measures deemed necessary for conservation and legislation enacted to protect public health and safety.[138] Harvest of wildlife is to be for domestic purposes, in the traditional seasons of the Nisga'a harvest, and cannot interfere with other authorized uses of Crown land.[139] The Crown can, however, authorize uses of or dispose of Crown land affecting harvesting provided that Nisga'a citizens are given a reasonable opportunity to harvest wildlife, and also so that Nisga'a wildlife allocations are not reduced.[140] Nisga'a citizens may further harvest on lands owned in fee simple off Nisga'a lands. Laws of general application will govern such activity.[141] The Agreement states that, although Nisga'a wildlife entitlements are treaty rights, where a wildlife allocation is set out as a percentage of the total allowable harvest, that right will have no priority over recreational and commercial harvest of the total allowable harvest of that species.[142]

Nisga'a citizens will not be required to obtain a licence or to pay any fees, charges or royalties in respect of harvest of wildlife or migratory birds under Nisga'a wildlife entitlements.[143]

---

[132] *Ibid.* paragraph 38.
[133] *Ibid.* paragraph 43.
[134] *Ibid.* paragraph 52.
[135] *Ibid.* paragraphs 52 – 61.
[136] *Ibid.* paragraph 62.
[137] *Ibid.* paragraphs 64 – 66.
[138] *Ibid.* Chapter 9, paragraph 1.
[139] *Ibid.* paragraph 2.
[140] *Ibid.* paragraph 3.
[141] *Ibid.* paragraph 4.
[142] *Ibid.* paragraph 6.
[143] *Ibid.* paragraph 10.

The Minister has designated several wildlife species, the harvesting of which poses a significant risk to a wildlife population. For these species, the Minister will establish a total allowable harvest. Currently, moose, grizzly bear and mountain goat are the initial designated species.[144] Designated species can be added if the Minister considers that protection of the species is warranted. The Agreement contains formulas that will be used to determine what percentage of the total allowable harvest will be available to the Nisga'a Nation.[145]

Subject to the Agreement, the Minister is responsible for wildlife. The Nisga'a Lisims Government can make laws for the management and conservation of wildlife only to the extent that such laws do not conflict with an annual management plan that is to be submitted to the Minister.[146] The Nisga'a Lisims Government is also able to make laws in respect of any sale of wildlife, migratory birds, or the inedible by-products or down of migratory birds that are harvested under the Agreement.[147] The Crown can further authorize use of or dispose of land that may affect harvests of migratory birds, but only insofar as Nisga'a citizens are not denied the reasonable opportunity to harvest migratory birds under Nisga'a wildlife entitlements.[148] Nisga'a citizens have the right to trade or barter any migratory birds, harvested under the Agreement, among themselves, or with other Aboriginal People.[149] Sale and export of migratory birds from British Columbia or Canada must be in accordance with federal and provincial laws of general application.[150] The Agreement grants to Nisga'a citizens the right to sell inedible by-products, including down, of migratory birds harvested under the Agreement.[151]

Nisga'a citizens have the right to trade or barter any wildlife or wildlife parts harvested under the Agreement among themselves or alternatively with other Aboriginal People.[152] Export of wildlife from British Columbia or Canada will be in accordance with federal and provincial laws of general application, as will any sale of wildlife harvested under the Agreement, which will also be in accordance with any Nisga'a law in respect of sale of wildlife.[153] Nisga'a citizens have the right to harvest migratory birds throughout the year for domestic purposes in accordance with conservation

---

[144] *Ibid.* paragraph 15.
[145] *Ibid.* Schedule A.
[146] *Ibid.* paragraphs 35 & 37.
[147] *Ibid.* paragraph 39.
[148] *Ibid.* paragraph 89.
[149] *Ibid.* paragraph 90.
[150] *Ibid.* paragraphs 91 & 92.
[151] *Ibid.* paragraph 93.
[152] *Ibid.* paragraph 68.
[153] *Ibid.* paragraphs 69 & 70.

measures and legislation enacted to protect public health and safety.[154] This right is further restricted in that such harvest cannot interfere with other authorized uses of Crown land.[155]

Upon coming into force, the Agreement transferred registration to the Nisga'a Nation of all unregistered traplines wholly or partially on Nisga'a lands that are not registered to any person.[156] Traplines held by Nisga'a citizens who hold traplines outside of Nisga'a lands continue to hold those traplines in accordance with federal and provincial laws of general application.[157] Where new traplines are to be registered within Nisga'a lands, the Nisga'a Nation must first give its consent.[158] Trapping on Nisga'a lands is regulated in the same manner as trapping is regulated on fee simple land in British Columbia.[159] Federal and provincial laws of general application apply to the sale of furs.[160]

Submerged Lands

Fee simple title to submerged lands is not transferred to the Nisga'a Nation, but remains vested in the government of British Columbia.[161] The provincial government cannot deal with submerged lands so as to adversely affect Nisga'a lands or Nisga'a interests without the consent of the Nisga'a Nation.[162] However, consent is not to be "unreasonably withheld," which means that the Nisga'a Nation's decision to withhold consent will not absolutely restrain the provincial government from using the land in a manner that the Nisga'a Nation may find adverse to its interests, but may be subject to interpretation by the Dispute Resolution Tribunal established by the Agreement of what constitutes "unreasonableness."[163] Conversely, where the Nisga'a Nation seeks the use and occupation of submerged lands, or an interest in or title to such lands, the government of British Columbia may not unreasonably withhold its consent for the Nation to do so.[164]

In addition, the province retains full ownership and regulatory authority over water, and existing water licences are to remain in place. The Nisga'a have a water allocation equal to 1 percent of the annual average flow from the Nass Valley watershed for their domestic, industrial and agricultural needs. The Nisga'a also have a reservation for the purpose of conducting

---

[154] *Ibid.* paragraph 87.
[155] *Ibid.* paragraph 88.
[156] *Ibid.* paragraph 71.
[157] *Ibid.* paragraph 74.
[158] *Ibid.* paragraph 75.
[159] *Ibid.* paragraph 78.
[160] *Ibid.* paragraph 80.
[161] *Ibid.* Chapter 3, paragraph 22.
[162] *Ibid.* paragraph 24.
[163] *Ibid.*
[164] *Ibid.* paragraph 25.

studies to determine the suitability of streams for hydro power purposes. Any hydro development will be subject to provincial approval and regulation.

The British Columbia Supreme Court has since clarified that the Nisga'a Agreement between Canada, British Columbia and the Nisga'a Nation is a treaty and land claims agreement within the meaning of section 25 and 35 of the *Constitution Act, 1982* and is constitutionally valid. Any decision or action that results from the exercise of the treaty is subject to being infringed upon by Parliament and the Legislative Assembly. Both Aboriginal and treaty rights guaranteed by section 35 may be impaired if such interference can be justified and is consistent with the honour of the Crown.[165]

Nisga'a Final Agreement Annual Report 2000-01

Fisheries

Nisga'a Fisheries was established in 1992 to co-manage the fisheries resources. Canada managed the reallocation of salmon to the Nisga'a through a licence retirement program whereby Canada and the commercial salmon fishing industry agreed upon the number and type of licences that would be retired and awarded to the Nisga'a. The Nisga'a Lisims Government established its own application and permit process, and under the new arrangements, 900 applications were received for salmon fishery licences and 450 of those applicants actually participated in commercial salmon fishing. In 2000, 35,000 salmon were harvested by Nisga'a fishers, which represented $900,000 in revenue. The harvest for consumption by the Nisga'a communities reached its harvesting target of 25,000 salmon.

The Nisga'a Lisims Government has also entered into several partnerships outside of government in the 2000-01 period. The Nisga'a entered into an alliance with Canfisco Fishing Company, which provided the Nisga'a with personnel, fish totes and expertise in fish processing.

Wildlife Management

The annual Nass Wildlife Management Plan for 2000-01 focused on three species: moose, grizzly bear and mountain goat. Roughly 1,500 moose were estimated to be living in the Nisga'a area, and of that estimation, an allocation of 120 moose was made to the Nisga'a. An evaluation of the grizzly bear population estimated that 1,000–1,200 grizzly bears were living on Nisga'a lands. The Nisga'a were permitted to harvest 2 bears in 2000-01. No grizzly bears were actually harvested during that period. The mountain goat population was estimated at 4,000 on Nisga'a lands and the Nisga'a were allocated 65 of those. Of that allocation, only 6 mountain goats were actually harvested.

---

[165] *Campbell v. British Columbia (Attorney General)*, [2000] 4 C.N.L.R. 1 (B.C.S.C.).

Forest Management

In 2000, 99,588 cubic metres of timber was harvested from Nisga'a lands. This amount was much lower than the expected harvest amount and was due to a depressed forestry industry. The present non-Aboriginal contractors engaged in harvesting forestry products are gradually being phased out over the 2000-05 period and those contracts are being made available to the Nisga'a people.

Pine mushrooms are the second most valuable resource found in the Nisga'a forests. Pine mushrooms are in high demand in Asia and amounted to a valuable revenue source in 2000-01. The 2000 mushroom harvest was 13,620 kilograms and is estimated to have added $400,000 to the local economy. The Nisga'a Lisims Government is currently attempting to regulate to ensure that the resource is managed to ensure its sustainability. Prior to the conclusion of the Agreement, the Nisga'a had no control over the use and sale of this resource.

Sechelt Agreement In Principle

The *Sechelt Indian Band Self-Government Act*[166] was enacted by the federal legislature to enable the Sechelt Indian Band to assume complete responsibility for administration and control of all Sechelt land. The Act transfers to the Sechelt Indian Band fee simple title in all Sechelt reserve lands. Under section 14(1) of the Act, the Sechelt Indian Band Council is granted legislative powers with respect to the preservation and management of natural resources on Sechelt lands,[167] and the preservation, protection and management of furbearing animals, fish and game on Sechelt lands.[168] However, the fee simple title of the band in the lands transferred[169] is to be subject to the *British Columbia Indian Reserves Mineral Resources Act* and the *Indian Reserves Minerals Resources Act*. The *Self-Government Act* provides for the grant of fee simple title to the band, subject to the rights of the province to minerals, expropriation, water, construction materials and highways, the same conditions and exceptions that are applicable to other reserves in the province.

The transfer of title is subject to any rights or interests under a mortgage, lease, occupation permit, certificate of possession or other grant or authorization in respect of the lands in question.[170] Specifically, the *Sechelt Indian Band Self-Government Act* states that the federal *Indian Oil and Gas Act* and the British Columbia *Indian Reserves Mineral Resources Act* are to apply in respect of Sechelt lands.

[166] *Sechelt Indian Band Self-Government Act*, S.C. 1986, c. 27.
[167] *Ibid.* s. 14(1)(j).
[168] *Ibid.* s. 14(1)(k).
[169] *Ibid.* s. 23(1).
[170] *Sechelt Indian Band Self-Government Act*, S.C.1986, c. 27, s. 24.

The Sechelt Agreement In Principle[171] of 16 April 1999 recognizes that the Sechelt Band has never before entered into any agreement regarding the appropriation and use of their traditional lands with the Canadian government or the government of British Columbia. The province currently holds all interests in subsurface resources in the Sechelt lands. The Agreement recognizes that the only way that interests can be conferred to the Sechelt people is by virtue of negotiations between the provincial government and the Sechelt in the Final Agreement.[172] Where the Sechelt Indian Band can negotiate to take the ownership interest in mineral rights on Sechelt Treaty Land, British Columbia will agree to withdraw from taxation of minerals under the *Mineral Tax Act,*[173] the *Mining Tax Act*[174] and the *Petroleum and Natural Gas Act.*[175] In the Taxation Agreement, Sechelt will be exempt from the *Mineral Land Tax Act*[176] on Sechelt Treaty Land.[177]

Notwithstanding any successful negotiations, federal and provincial laws with respect to the ownership, development, production, handling, possession of or use of atomic energy or any of the prescribed substances that may be used in its formulation will apply on Sechelt Treaty Land.[178] The Sechelt will have the authority to set fees, royalties, rents and other charges for subsurface resources development and extraction on Sechelt Treaty Land.[179]

Fisheries

Under Chapter 7 of the Agreement, the Minister maintains authority for managing and conserving fish and fish habitat and marine plants on Sechelt lands. A Sechelt fish licence may authorize harvesting of allocations under the Agreement, which will permit harvesting and use for domestic use, but not for sale. The right to harvest fish and marine plants is not an interest that can be sold by the Sechelt. Canada agrees, however, subject to the Final Agreement, that commercial fishing licences will be issued "to assist Sechelt's participation in the commercial fishery."[180] The Agreement In Principle proposes to transfer 11 commercial fishing licences to the value of $1.5 million. Further, the Agreement sets out certain allocations of salmon to which the Sechelt are entitled. Although the Sechelt people are entitled to

---

[171] See Ministry of Attorney General Treaty Negotiations Office, Government of British Columbia, online: <http://www.aaf.gov.bc.ca/nations/sechelt/secheltaip199.stm#CHAPTER4-SUBSURFACE>.

[172] *Sechelt Agreement In Principle,* April 16, 1999, ss. 4.1.1 and 3.4.2.

[173] *Mineral Tax Act,* R.S.B.C. 1996, c.290.

[174] *Ibid.* c.295.

[175] *Petroleum and Natural Gas Act,* R.S.B.C. 1996, c.361.

[176] *Mineral Land Tax Act,* R.S.B.C. 1996, c.291.

[177] *Sechelt Agreement In Principle,* April 16, 1999, s.17.5.6 and 17.5.7.

[178] *Ibid.* s. 4.2.1.

[179] *Ibid.* s. 4.2.2.

[180] *Ibid.* s. 7.8.1.

a certain proportion of salmon within their prescribed area of land, depending upon the season and the volume of salmon available,[181] what happens to the surplus is entirely at the discretion of the Minister.

Fishing and Wildlife Harvest

Federal and provincial wildlife laws are to apply to Sechelt lands. The Sechelt Indian Band is given the right to harvest wildlife throughout the Wildlife Harvest Area in accordance with the Final Agreement, subject to measures that are necessary for conservation and legislation enacted for the purposes of public health or public safety. This right to harvest can only take place in the traditional harvesting season and for domestic purposes.[182] The harvesting of Sechelt's wildlife entitlements will be authorized by a licence, based on the Sechelt annual harvest plan issued by the Minister as provided for in the Final Agreement,[183] and will not be a transferable interest.[184]

Harvest of migratory birds, again, will be solely for domestic use and subject to terms and conditions laid out in the Final Agreement.[185]

Forest Resources

The Sechelt Indian Band has the authority to manage forest resources on Sechelt Treaty Land and is responsible for their protection under the Final Agreement.[186] The band will also have the authority to determine, collect and administer all fees, rents, royalties and other charges relating to forest resources on Sechelt Treaty Land.[187]

The Sechelt do not have exclusive use of the resources pertaining to their land; even fishing, hunting and recreation. Under the Agreement, the public retains the right to access Sechelt land for the purpose of fishing, hunting and recreation. Non-Aboriginal persons remain subject to federal and provincial laws.

Caselaw in British Columbia

Van der Peet, a member of the Sto:lo, was convicted of selling fish caught under an Aboriginal food fishing licence contrary to section 27(5) of the

---

[181] *Sechelt Agreement In Principle,* April 16, 1999, s. 7.3.0.

[182] *Ibid.* s. 8.2.2 and 8.2.3.

[183] *Ibid.* s. 8.2.6.

[184] *Ibid.* s.8.2.5.

[185] *Ibid.* chap. 9.

[186] *Ibid.* s. 10.1.1.

[187] *Ibid.* s. 10.1.4.

federal *Fishery Regulations*.[188] She argued that she was exercising an Aboriginal right to sell fish and therefore that her conviction was in violation of section 35(1) of the *Constitution Act, 1982*. The first step for the court was to characterize the Aboriginal right claimed. In this case the court characterized the right as "an Aboriginal right to exchange fish for money or for other goods." The size of the sale was not substantial enough that the transaction could be characterized as "commercial fishing." The court then addressed a second question: "Was the practice of exchanging fish for money or other goods an integral part of the specific distinctive culture of the Sto:lo prior to contact with Europeans?"[189] In this case the court found that fishing for food and ceremonial purposes was integral to the culture, but the exchange of fish was merely incidental and therefore not a right that was protected by section 35(1). Van der Peet's conviction was thereby upheld.

In *R. v. N.T.C. Smokehouse*,[190] the NTC, a food processing plant, had bought fish caught by members of the Sheshaht and Opetchesaht Indian Bands and resold it. The NTC was subsequently charged under the B.C. *Fishery (General) Regulations*, which prohibited the sale, barter or purchase of any fish caught pursuant to an Aboriginal food fishing licence for purchasing and selling fish caught without a commercial fishing licence. The NTC then argued that the Regulations were of no force and effect because they were in violation of the Aboriginal rights recognized by the *Constitution Act, 1982*.

Chief Justice Lamer characterized the claimed right as a "large scale commercial activity" – more than 119,000 pounds of salmon had been purchased and resold by the NTC. The court found that the exchange of fish for money was not an integral part of the distinctive cultures of the two bands prior to contact with Europeans. Sales of fish were sporadic and insufficient as evidence that there was an Aboriginal right to exchange fish for money or other goods on this scale. Exchanges of fish at ceremonial occasions did not have the significance required to constitute an Aboriginal right. Accordingly, there were not sufficient facts to support a claim to fish commercially.

The Heiltsuk occupy the central coast of British Columbia and have traditionally regulated the use and allocation of resources within their traditional territories.[191] In 1988 Donald and William Gladstone, members of the Heiltsuk First Nation, were charged with attempting to sell over 4,000 pounds of herring spawn on kelp that had been harvested under an Aboriginal

---

[188] *R. v. Van der Peet, supra* note 2 in ch. 1.

[189] *Ibid.* p. 563.

[190] [1996] 4 C.N.L.R. 130 (S.C.C.).

[191] See Harris, D., "Territoriality, Aboriginal Rights, and the Heiltsuk Spawn-on-Kelp Fishery" (2000) 34 *University of British Columbia Law Review* 195.

food fishing licence.[192] The Department of Fisheries and Oceans regulates the herring spawn on kelp fishery under its "J-licence" scheme: only those with J-licences can harvest and sell spawn on kelp, and then only in limited amounts. They subsequently argued that they had an Aboriginal right to engage in commercial fishing. The Supreme Court found that the "exchange of herring spawn on kelp for money or other goods was a central, significant and defining feature of the culture of the Heiltsuk prior to contact."[193] Moreover, the court held that this exchange had occurred on a scale that would be considered a large commercial scale today. While this commercial Aboriginal right had been regulated over time, it had not been extinguished and the *Fisheries Act* infringed upon this right by limiting the amount of herring spawn on kelp that could be harvested by the Heiltsuk. No evidence was submitted to indicate whether there was justification for the *Fisheries Act* limitation and the matter was sent back to trial on that issue. Whether or not the government had taken adequate account of its special trust relationship with Aboriginal people and given sufficient priority to the Heiltsuk fishery when it allocated herring licences remains to be answered. The Crown did not pursue the issue and dropped the charges.

The Heiltsuk Tribal Council has held nine herring spawn on kelp harvesting licences since 1998 – three for closed pond operations and six for open ponds.[194] Operations are directed by the council's Spawn on Kelp Management Board. The crew involved in each operation receives a share of any profits and the council keeps 40 percent of all profits to put towards community projects. The council has tended to use their percentage of profits to put towards the fish processing plant. A licence quota is pooled by the council into a Heiltsuk allocation, and any member of the First Nation with equipment can fish towards the open-pond allocation upon the payment of a $10 fee to the council. Those engaging in harvest in the open pond are required to follow harvesting and packing regulations specified in the Heiltsuk Commercial Aboriginal Right Management and Operations Plan. Participants may fish until the allocation is filled and are then paid according to their contribution. Where the fish is harvested after the allocation is filled, this product is then distributed among community members for food, or is sold in an unofficial market. Such commercial activity is contrary to federal fishery regulations. However, if challenged, the Heiltsuk practice that has continued for centuries would undoubtedly be upheld in the courts as an Aboriginal right.[195] Harris is one commentator who has argued that the Heiltsuk regulation and use of the resource is sufficient to challenge Crown regulation of the resource off the British Columbia coastline. Accordingly, the

---

[192] *R. v. Gladstone, supra* note 22 in ch. 1.

[193] *Ibid.*, para. 26.

[194] Harris, D., *supra* note 172, para. 70.

[195] *Ibid.* para. 71.

Heiltsuk ought to enjoy the right to control and benefit from the human use of that resource within their territory.[196]

In an earlier case, that of *Reid v. Canada*,[197] the Heiltsuk had argued Harris' line of reasoning that they had an Aboriginal right both to the resource and to govern the use of that resource. A remarkable array of Heiltsuk testimony and expert opinion was submitted in evidence. However, the trial judge dismissed their claim. This case preceded *R. v. Gladstone,* and while the Heiltsuk filed an appeal of the trial judge's decision, they have not pursued it. The Heiltsuk are apparently setting aside 5 percent of all profits taken by the council for herring spawn on kelp to support future litigation against the Crown and this may be an avenue that is pursued by the First Nation in the future.[198]

In *R. v. Nikal,*[199] a member of the Moricetown First Nation was charged with fishing without a licence on the Buckley River, which flowed through his reserve. Nikal argued that he had the right to fish on the river pursuant to a bylaw that had been passed by the First Nation that authorized unrestricted fishing in the river and other water bodies located upon or within the boundaries of the reserve by members of the band. Nikal argued that the common law presumption of *ad medium filum aquae* (that water surrounded by land was the property of the owner of the land up to the middle of the water body) applied. Additionally, he argued that his rights under section 35(1) of the *Constitution Act, 1982* were violated by the licensing scheme.

The conviction was set aside, but the court found that the bylaw did not apply to the river. Actions by the Crown before and after Confederation and by the Reserve Commissioner who dealt with the band made it clear that there was never any intention to allot an exclusive fishery to the band. Moreover, the river did not form a part of the reserve, even where it flowed through the reserve land and the common law presumption could not apply to it. In addition, the court found that the requirement of obtaining a licence to fish did not infringe upon the appellant's Aboriginal rights because such rights are limited by the need to preserve fishery resources and the licence requirement was therefore reasonable. In this case, however, Nikal's constitutional rights were infringed by the conditions of the licence, which dictated when the fisher could fish and to whom the fish may be given. Although the Crown argued that these conditions were never enforced, the court found that these conditions were not justified by the Crown as having a valid legislative objective and were unconstitutional. The licence was

---

[196] *Ibid.*
[197] [1993] F.C.J. No. 178 (Q.L.) (T.D.).
[198] Harris, D., *supra* note 178, para. 73.
[199] [1996] 5 W.W.R. 305 (S.C.C.).

therefore invalid and there could not be an offence created of fishing without a licence.

As mentioned earlier, in *R. v. Seward,*[200] the British Columbia Court of Appeal found that there was no evidence to support the accused's claim that hunting at night, an activity prohibited by the provincial *Wildlife Act*, was an Aboriginal right. The fact that the accused had hunted for the purpose of obtaining fresh meat for food and for a burning ceremony was irrelevant. In the later case of *R. v. Stump,*[201] the British Columbia Provincial Court found that the Chilcotin Band did have an Aboriginal right to hunt at night, but that safety concerns provided sufficient justification for the infringement.

In *R. v. Alphonse*[202] the accused had shot a deer on unoccupied, unfenced and uncultivated private land, contrary to the provincial *Wildlife Act*. The court found that the right had not been extinguished and that the *Wildlife Act* constituted an infringement of that right and was therefore unconstitutional.

The British Columbia Supreme Court held in *R. v. Pike*[203] that Aboriginal rights to fish are not exercisable by anyone outside of the collective that holds that right. An Aboriginal person has no right to assign a right to fish to another person. In a separate case,[204] the accused was charged with fishing without a licence while with his Aboriginal wife who held a legitimate licence. The court found that the man was entitled to help his wife exercise her constitutional right as he was there to assist her to minimize her exposure to danger.

---

[200] *Supra* note 55 in ch. 5.
[201] [1999] B.C.J. No. 2577 (B.C. Prov. Ct.).
[202] [1993] 5 W.W.R. 401.
[203] (1993), [1994] 1 C.N.L.R. 160 (B.C. S.C.).
[204] *R. v. Cunningham*, [1990] 2 C.N.L.R. 110 (B.C. Prov. Ct.).

Chapter 8

Yukon and the
Northwest Territories

The Yukon and the Northwest Territories are federal lands. The Yukon and the Northwest Territories were admitted into Canada in 1870 by imperial order in council that imposed an obligation to treat with the Aboriginal Peoples for compensation for their traditional lands of occupation. The lands within the Yukon and Northwest Territories boundaries are subject to administration by the federal government.

Section 19 of the *Yukon Act*[1] and section 18 of the *Northwest Territories Act*[2] enable the territorial legislatures to make laws regarding the preservation of game in the territories and such laws are applicable to and in respect of Aboriginal and Inuit Peoples. However, such laws cannot restrict or prohibit Aboriginal or Inuit Peoples from hunting for food on unoccupied Crown land unless the game has been declared by the federal government as game that is in danger of becoming extinct. Further, sections 48-51 of the *Yukon Act* and sections 45-48 of the *Northwest Territories Act* authorize the federal Minister to enter into agreements with Indian and Inuit Peoples for the herding, control, management, administration, sale, slaughter and protection of reindeer in the territories.

Mineral Potential on Indian Reserve Lands in the Yukon[3]

The Mineral Potential of Indian Reserve Lands report compiled by the Department of Indian and Northern Affairs Canada[4] in the Yukon provides overall rating measures of the economic mineral possibilities of each reserve

---

[1] *Yukon Act*, R.S.C. 1985, C. Y-2.
[2] *Northwest Territories Act*, R.S.C. 1985, c. N-27.
[3] See Department of Indian and Northern Affairs Canada, online: <http://www.ainc-inac.gc.ca/ntr/bc_e.html>.
[4] Keep in mind that although this site was last updated on the 30 April 2001, the report was actually completed in 1991.

as a whole, on a scale of low/moderate/good. Factors that affect this rating are the size of the reserve, the location with respect to markets, transportation, access, value and type of commodity, social and cultural barriers to mining on certain lands and areas, marketability of a commodity at any given time and other differentials.

The following rating applies in the Yukon:

- 15 reserves were given a low rating;
- 5 reserves were given a moderate rating; and
- 4 reserves were given a good rating.

No reserves in the Yukon were found to have at least one commodity that could be developed. None of the 24 reserves had surrendered their minerals in any way at the time of the completion of the report.

Mineral Potential on Indian Reserve Lands in the Northwest Territories[5]

The Mineral Potential of Indian Reserve Lands report compiled by the Department of Indian and Northern Affairs Canada[6] in the Northwest Territories provides overall rating measures of the economic mineral possibilities of each reserve as a whole, on a scale of low/moderate/good. Factors that affect this rating are the size of the reserve, the location with respect to markets, transportation, access, value and type of commodity, social and cultural barriers to mining on certain lands and areas, marketability of a commodity at any given time and other differentials.

The following rating applies in the Northwest Territories:

- 1 reserve was given a low rating;
- 1 reserve was given a moderate rating; and
- 0 reserves were given a good rating.

No reserves in the Northwest Territories were found to have any commodities that could be developed. None of the reserves had surrendered their minerals in any way at the time of the completion of the report.

---

[5] See Department of Indian and Northern Affairs Canada, online: <http://www.ainc-inac.gc.ca/ntr/bc_e.html>.

[6] Keep in mind that although this site was last updated on the 30 April 2001, the report was actually completed in 1991.

Territorial Legislation

Fishing in the Yukon

To fish in the Yukon, the individual must be the holder of a valid licence issued under the *Yukon Territory Fishery Regulations*,[7] the *Fishery (General) Regulations* or the *Aboriginal Communal Fishing Licences Regulations*. However, there are variances on this requirement.

- If the individual is a beneficiary of a Yukon First Nation with a Final Agreement (with the government), then he or she has a right to hunt and fish for food inside the traditional territory of that First Nation. Any species may be harvested at any time of the year. Catch limits do not apply, but may be regulated by the individual First Nation. A fishing licence is not required. Where this individual wishes to fish outside of the traditional territory, a valid licence must be obtained and laws of general application in the territory will apply. Alternatively, the Aboriginal person may obtain the written consent of a First Nation with a Final Agreement to hunt or fish for food within its traditional territory.

- If the individual is a beneficiary of a Yukon First Nation without a Final Agreement, then he or she has a right to fish for food outside of the traditional territories. Any species may be caught and catch limits do not apply. Inside the traditional territory of a First Nation with a Final Agreement, a valid fishing licence must be obtained and the laws of general application in the territory must be observed. Alternatively, the permission of the First Nation affected may be obtained prior to entry.

- A member of a non-Yukon First Nation can fish for food outside the traditional territories of First Nations with Final Agreements without a licence. Any species can be harvested at any time of the year and no catch limits apply. A valid licence must be obtained in order to fish inside the traditional territories of a First Nation with a Final Agreement. A licensed guide may be required.

- Additional rights apply to beneficiaries of the Inuvialuit Final Agreement or the Gwich'in Comprehensive Claim. These appear in their respective Agreements.

- Fishing for purposes other than obtaining food will attract a requirement to follow all laws of general application.

- Trade of edible parts of a fish can occur with another beneficiary, or with anyone else where the fish by-product is non-edible and was harvested for personal use.[8]

---

[7] *Yukon Territory Fishery Regulations*, C.R.C., c. 854, s. 4(1). The enabling Act is the federal *Fisheries Act*.

[8] *Ibid*. s. 5.1(2).

Hunting in the Yukon

To hunt in the Yukon, the individual must be the holder of a valid licence. However, there are variances on this requirement.

- A beneficiary of a Yukon First Nation with a Final Agreement can hunt for food inside the traditional territory of his or her First Nation. In this area any species, male or female, may be hunted, at any time of year, with no catch limits applicable. Such a right is subject only to regulation by that individual's First Nation. A hunting licence to exercise that right is not required. Outside of the individual's traditional territory, a hunting licence must be obtained and the laws of general application observed; or, the permission of the affected First Nation must be obtained in order to hunt within that First Nation's traditional lands.

- An Aboriginal person who is not a member of a First Nation with a Final Agreement can hunt outside of the traditional territories of such and a hunting licence is not required and harvest of any species, male or female, at any time of the year can occur. No catch limits will apply. Where hunting takes place on the traditional territory of a First Nation with a Final Agreement, consent must be obtained prior to hunting within that tract of land.

- An Aboriginal member of a non-Yukon First Nation can hunt for food outside the traditional territories of First Nations with Final Agreements without a hunting licence. In these areas any species can be harvested, male or female, at any time of year, with no applicable bag limits or catch limits. If an Aboriginal individual wants to hunt or fish inside the traditional territory of a First Nation with a Final Agreement, a valid hunting licence must be obtained and laws of general application observed. A licensed guide may be required.

- Beneficiaries of the Inuvialuit Final Agreement or the Gwich'in Comprehensive Claim have additional rights that are laid out in their agreements.

- Conservation laws continue to apply. At the present time it is unlawful to hunt bison or elk anywhere in the Yukon. Deer may not be hunted inside the traditional territories of First Nations without Final Agreements, and muskox may not be hunted on the Yukon North Slope.

- Where hunting is taking place for a purpose other than for obtaining food, then laws of general application in the Territory will apply.

- The non-edible of the animal hunted for food can be used to make traditional handicrafts for sale. This right is incidental to the right to hunt for food. Meat can be traded, bartered or sold to other First Nation people for traditional sharing purposes. However, trade cannot take place with non-Aboriginal people.

Fishing in the Northwest Territories

Under the *Northwest Territories Fishery Regulations,*[9] no person is permitted to fish within the territory unless holding a licence issued under the Regulations or under the *Aboriginal Communal Fishing Licences Regulations.*[10] The Regulations do, however, recognize that "Indian, Inuk or person of mixed blood" may fish without a licence by angling or by way of gill nets, set lines, spears, snares or dip nets, for food for him or herself, his or her family and dogs.[11] Fish caught under the authority of this section cannot be given to another person, unless that person is an "Indian, Inuk or person of mixed blood."[12] Within the Inuvialuit Settlement Region, beneficiaries under agreements and treaties are also permitted to fish for subsistence usage without a licence.[13] Such persons are permitted to sell, trade or barter fish and fish products with other beneficiaries.[14] Non-edible by-products of fish taken from the Inuvialuit Settlement Region for personal use may be sold, traded or bartered with any person.

Hunting in the Northwest Territories

Under the Northwest Territories Hunting Regulations[15] a licence is required to hunt game within the Northwest Territories. However, as indicated explicitly in the *Canada Wildlife Act*, the Act itself and the accompanying Regulations cannot derogate from any Aboriginal and treaty rights.[16]

These laws and regulations are deemed to apply generally to Aboriginal people to the point that interference with an established right to hunt and trap is unjustified.

Yukon and Northwest Territories Treaties

Treaty No. 8

See analysis in Chapter 7, "British Columbia."

---

[9]   C.R.C., c. 847.
[10] *Northwest Territories Fishery Regulations*, s. 5(1). The enabling act is the federal *Fisheries Act.*
[11] *Ibid.* s. 22(1).
[12] *Ibid.* s. 22(2).
[13] *Ibid.* s. 22.1(1).
[14] *Ibid.* s. 22.1(2).
[15] *Consolidation Of Big Game Hunting Regulations*, R01992; *Consolidation Of Small Game Hunting Regulations,* R02292; *Consolidation Of Wildlife General Regulations*, R02692; *Consolidation Of Wildlife Licences And Permits Regulations*, R02792. Enacted pursuant to the federal *Canada Wildlife Act*, R.S., 1985, c. W-9.
[16] *Canada Wildlife Act*, 2(1).

Treaty No. 11

Treaty No. 11 largely covers land incorporated into the Northwest Territories. The treaty covers a small area of the Yukon Territory. Treaty No. 11 was signed on 27 July 1921 to which there was an adhesion on 17 July 1922. The Commissioners' Report, written by D.C. Scott, reveals that the treaty negotiators dealt with certain concerns raised by the Aboriginal People involved with the negotiations.

> The Indians seemed afraid, for one thing, that their liberty to hunt, trap and fish would be taken away or curtailed, but were assured by me that this would not be the case, and the Government will expect them to support themselves in their own way, and, in fact, that more twine for nets and more ammunition were given under the terms of this treaty than under any of the preceding ones; this went a long way to calm their fears. I also pointed out that any game laws made were to their advantage, and, whether they took treaty or not, they were subject to the laws of the Dominion.[17]

The Aboriginal People present at Treaty No. 11 negotiations were assured of their continued right to hunt, trap and fish – it was on the negotiator's guarantees alone that these rights would continue that the treaty was accepted. This spoken guarantee would seem to limit the type of harvesting regulations that could be enacted by the Crown. Judging by the fact that the court has permitted conservation legislation to override treaty rights, an even higher standard may need to be applied to the interpretation of Treaty No. 11. Upon a strict interpretation, this promise by the Crown would indicate that only regulations that promote the Aboriginal treaty right to harvest would be permitted.

- In 1973, Mr. Justice Morrow of the Northwest Territorial Supreme Court declared that there was sufficient doubt as to whether Treaties Nos. 8 and 11 had extinguished Aboriginal title in the Northwest Territories to entitle the Aboriginal People to file a caveat to protect their interest in the land.[18]
- Subject to more recent land claim agreements in the Northwest Territories, under section 35 of the *Constitution Act, 1982* the Aboriginal People of these areas retain traditional land use rights to the land mass contained within both Treaty No. 8 and Treaty No. 11.

---

[17] Scott, D., *Report of the Commissioner for Treaty No. 11*, Department of Indian and Northern Affairs, online: <http://www.ainc-inac.gc.ca/pr/trts/trty11_e.html>.

[18] *Re Paulette and Registrar of Titles (No. 2)*, [1973] 6 W.W.R. 97 (N.W.T.S.C.).

- The recent case of *Liidlii Kue First Nation v. Canada*[19] confirmed that there is a constitutional duty imposed on the Crown to consult with those exercising Treaty No. 11 rights to hunt, trap and fish on unoccupied Crown lands. In this case the Nation alleged that the Crown had breached its fiduciary obligation to consult the First Nation prior to issuing a land use permit for test drilling. The declaratory relief was denied, but the duty to consult with affected Treaty No. 11 Aboriginal groups was affirmed.

Modern Agreements

Umbrella Final Agreement

After lengthy negotiations, on 29 May 1993 the Council for Yukon Indians, representing 14 Yukon First Nations, signed an Umbrella Final Agreement with the federal government and the Yukon territorial government. The Agreement establishes a framework, which will be used by each of the 14 Yukon First Nations to conclude a final land claim settlement agreement to address the specific circumstances of each Yukon First Nation. Final agreements and self-government agreements have been reached with 7 Yukon First Nations: the Vuntut Gwitch'in First Nation; the First Nation of the Nacho Nyak Dun; the Champagne and Aishihik First Nations; the Teslin Tlingit Council; the Little Salmon/Carmacks First Nation; the Selkirk First Nation; and the Tróndëk Hwëch'in (formerly known as the Dawson First Nation).

The settlement and self-government legislation was introduced into Parliament on 31 May 1994 and received Royal Assent on 7 July 1994.[20] Royal Assent was given to the surface rights legislation on 15 December 1994. All three Acts came into force on 14 February 1995.

The land claims agreements give Yukon First Nations the ability to self-govern, jurisdiction over settlement lands and shared jurisdiction on non-settlements lands, the right to generate tax revenue and the jurisdiction to create laws. Schedule III to the *Yukon First Nations Self-Government Act* sets out the areas in which the Yukon First Nations are to have legislative capacity. Included in that list is the power to legislate for:

1. use, management, administration, control and protection of settlement land;
2. allocation or disposition of rights and interests in and to settlement land, including expropriation by the First Nation for the purposes of the First Nation;

---

[19] [2000] 4 C.N.L.R. 123 (F.C.T.D.).
[20] *Yukon First Nations Self-Government Act*, S.C. 1994, c. 35, as am. SOR/97-451; SOR/97-456; SOR/98-425; 1999, c. 26, s. 35; 1999, c. 31, s. 226.

3. use, management, administration and protection of natural resources under the ownership, control or jurisdiction of the First Nation;

4. gathering, hunting, trapping and fishing and the protection of fish, wildlife and their habitat;

......

20. control or prevention of pollution and protection of the environment.

The Agreement designates land, which is to be divided amongst the Yukon First Nations, whereupon a Final Agreement is reached with each Nation. A total of 41,439 square kilometres has been set aside, which includes 25,900 square kilometres of Category A land, and a remainder which is classified as Category B land.

Rights to Minerals

Category A Land

The 25,900 square kilometres of land falling within the Category A classification is conveyed to a Yukon First Nation in fee simple. Title to that land extends to fee simple title in the mines and minerals and the right to work the mines and minerals pertaining to it.[21] "Minerals" as defined in the Agreement includes "precious and base metals and other non-living, naturally occurring substances, whether solid, liquid or gaseous, and includes coal, Petroleum and Specified Substances."[22]

Category B Land

15,539 square kilometres fall within the definition of Category B land. Title in Category B land amounts to fee simple ownership. The mines and minerals and the right to work the mines and minerals are excluded.[23] However, title does extend to the mines and minerals, and the right to work the mines and minerals of "specified substances."[24] "Specified substances" are defined in the agreement as: "any of carving stone, flint, limestone, marble, gypsum, shale, slate, clay, sand, gravel, construction stone, sodium chloride, volcanic ash, earth, soil, diatomaceous earth, ochre, marl and peat."[25]

---

[21] *Umbrella Final Agreement*, s. 5.4.1.
[22] *Ibid.* Chapter 1 "Definitions."
[23] *Ibid.* s. 5.4.1.2.
[24] *Ibid.* s. 5.4.1.3.
[25] *Ibid.* Chapter 1 "Definitions."

The rights to mines and minerals are subject to some exceptions, namely, that any right, title or interest existing in the land prior to the finalization of agreements is an encumbrance on the Yukon First Nations rights in that land. This exception includes any licence, permit or other right to access and exploit resources on the land existing at the date the land became subject to ownership by the Yukon First Nation. Moreover, the land must remain accessible by the general public for wildlife harvesting.

The Yukon First Nations are to receive full rental revenues from surface leases and royalties for the development of non-renewable resources, and are to have full ownership of mines and minerals on their designated lands.

Harvesting Rights – Fish and Wildlife[26]

The Umbrella Final Agreement conveys rights to harvest wildlife for subsistence purposes throughout the traditional territory. On Category A land, the Yukon First Nation is given exclusive harvesting rights. Under section 16.4.2, the Yukon Indian People have the right to harvest for subsistence purposes within their traditional territory, with the consent of another Yukon First Nation in that nation's traditional territory, all species of fish and wildlife for themselves and their families in all seasons and in any numbers on designated lands and also Crown land to which they have a right of access. Under the Agreement, harvesting and fishing can be undertaken on Crown land so long as it is for non-commercial purposes and access is for a reasonable length of time.[27] Any person is, furthermore, permitted to access the land of the Yukon First Nation and stay on undeveloped settlement land for a reasonable period of time for all non-commercial recreational purposes.[28]

The Yukon Aboriginal People are not restricted to traditional implements and methods of harvesting, but are able to employ current methods of and equipment for harvesting.[29] Edible fish and wildlife products harvested by a Yukon Aboriginal person can be sold to another Yukon Aboriginal person for domestic purposes only, and not for commercial purposes.[30] Aboriginal People of the Yukon do, however, have the right to sell, to any person, non-edible by-products of fish and wildlife that is obtained from the harvesting of the fur bearers, or is incidental to permitted subsistence harvesting.[31]

---

[26] *Ibid.* Chapter 16 "Fish and Wildlife."
[27] *Ibid.* s. 6.2.1.
[28] Ibid. s. 6.3.2.
[29] Ibid. s. 6.4.3.
[30] Ibid. s. 6.4.4.
[31] Ibid. s. 6.4.5.

Approximately 70 percent of the traplines are allocated to Yukon Aboriginal People in the traditional territory. Preferential harvesting of some species is also conveyed where undertaken in the traditional territory. Under the direction of the Fish and Wildlife Management Board, a $3 million joint government-Yukon First Nation trust will be established to restore and enhance wildlife populations and habitat in the Yukon.

The land of the Yukon Nations remains open to access or stay by any person on undeveloped Category B land without the consent of the affected Yukon First Nation for the purpose of non-commercial harvesting if permitted by, and in accordance with, laws applicable to lands under the administration and control of the Commissioner.[32]

The exercise of rights under the fish and wildlife-harvesting chapter of the Agreement are subject to limitations provided in legislation enacted for purposes of conservation, public health or public safety.[33]

Water Rights[34]

The right of Yukon First Nations people to use water on, or flowing through, the settlement lands is subject to a number of restrictions, most importantly, public navigation and passage on water, and any hunting, trapping or fishing by the public.[35] Notwithstanding a Yukon First Nation's ownership of certain beds of water bodies, the government has the right to protect and manage water and beds of water bodies, and to use water incidental to that right throughout the Yukon, for

- management, protection and research in respect of fish and wildlife and their habitats;
- protection and management of navigation and transportation, establishment of navigation aids and devices, and dredging of the beds of navigable waters;
- protection of water supplies from contamination and degradation;
- emergency purposes, including fighting fires, and flood and icing control;
- research and sampling of water quality and quantity; and
- other such government public purposes.

---

[32] Ibid. s. 16.12.3.
[33] Ibid.s. 16.3.3.
[34] Ibid. Chapter 14 "Water Management."
[35] Ibid. s. 14.5.6.

Forest Resources[36]

Subject only to its Final Settlement Agreement, each Yukon First Nation is entrusted with the right to own, manage, allocate and protect the forest resources on its settlement land.[37] Yukon Aboriginal People have the right to harvest forest resources on Crown lands also, but only for purposes incidental to the exercise of their traditional pursuits of hunting, fishing, trapping and gathering.[38] Rights also exist to harvest trees on Crown land to a maximum of 500 cubic metres per year to provide for non-commercial community purposes.[39] Furthermore, Yukon Aboriginal People have the right to harvest forest resources on Crown land at any time, incidental to the practice of their traditional customs, culture and religion or for the traditional production of handicrafts and implements.[40] Rights to Crown land forest resources are, however, subject to legislation enacted for the purpose of managing forest resources, land management, conservation, protection of the environment, and for public health and safety.[41] Where Yukon Aboriginal People are permitted to sell items manufactured from Crown forest resources, trade can only take place between those Yukon Nations subject to the Umbrella Agreement and other Aboriginal People.[42]

Over half of the First Nations concerned have finalized their self-government agreements. There is no variance as to resource access and exploitation. The only difference is in respect to the amount of land that was transferred.

Five-Year Review of the Umbrella Final Agreement Implementation Plan and Yukon First Nation Final Agreement Implementation Plans for the First Four Yukon First Nations (1995–2000)

The report notes that during the five-year period covered, there have been enormous changes in the Yukon. Two significant changes have been the "partnership approaches" that are emerging as a method of addressing various management and regulatory issues and the moves of Yukon First Nations towards implementing self-government agreements.

---

[36] Ibid. Chapter 17 "Water Resources."
[37] Ibid. s. 17.2.1.
[38] Ibid. s. 13.3.1.1.
[39] Ibid. s. 17.3.1.2.
[40] Ibid. s. 17.3.1.3.
[41] Ibid. s. 17.3.2.
[42] Ibid. s. 17.3.5.

The "successes" of the Final Agreement identified by the Implementation Review Working Group include:

- The first four Yukon First Nations have established departments to manage and administer land and resources in connection with resource and harvest management activities as well as heritage resources in the settlement lands.
- The land survey program run by Natural Resources Canada, Legal Surveys Divisions, has been highly successful. The Surveys Division has also been active in helping Yukon First Nations to seize economic opportunities resulting from the survey program. Of the $14 million set aside for the survey program, $2.83 million has gone to the direct benefit of First Nation companies or individuals.
- All boards, councils, commissions and committees have been established as per the terms of the Agreement. The general opinion is that these bodies are doing a good job, in particular the Fish and Wildlife Management Board and the local Renewable Resources Councils.
- The report shows that the development of forest management plans in the Champagne and Aishihik First Nations and the Teslin Tlingit Council Traditional Territories has been initiated, and that these First Nations, the Department of Indian Affairs and Northern Development, Yukon and the local Renewable Resource Councils have signed protocol agreements to complete those plans. Significant growth in the First Nations forest management capacity has resulted from a co-operative effort between the First Nation of the Nacho Nyak Dun and the Department of Indian Affairs and Northern Development.
- Control and administration of the Yukon onshore oil and gas resources was transferred from Canada to the Yukon government in 1998. The 14 Yukon First Nations gave their full support to the passing of the *Oil and Gas Act*. Ongoing Crown royalty-sharing arrangements are still under discussion with Yukon First Nations.

The following are some of the issues and recommendations that came out of the report:

- The pace of implementation has been much slower than the parties envisioned when the implementation plan activity sheets and annexes were drafted. In particular, concerns were expressed about the pace of the progress towards forestry and land use planning. With respect to forestry, an ongoing concern expressed by the Renewable Resources Councils and Yukon First Nations is that the government is not living up to its obligations under section 17.22 of the Agreement. Section 17.22 places a duty to consult with the affected Renewable Resources Councils both prior to establishing a new policy likely to significantly affect forest resources management, allocation or forestry practices and prior to recommending legislation concerning forest resources in the Yukon. This measure was introduced to ensure that there was local input into the management of forest resources in the Yukon, especially as it is a matter of intense local interest.

- The Renewable Resources Councils are critical of the lacklustre consultation efforts by the Department of Indian Affairs and Northern Development Yukon Region and have complained that building a meaningful working relationship with the Forestry division has been extremely difficult. The main problem, articulated by the Councils, is that although the Forestry division has kept them informed of its decisions and changes, the Renewable Resources Councils have not been given any opportunity to input meaningfully into those decisions and future planning. Moreover, the Yukon First Nations were not consulted, as ordered by section 17.5.3 of the Agreement, prior to the commencement or changes to forest resources management planning for their traditional territories.

- Generally speaking, the Yukon First Nations have expressed concerns that the government is not always living up to the consultation requirements of the Agreements. Under the Agreements, the duty to "consult" means to provide

  a) to the party to be consulted, notice of a matter to be decided in sufficient form and detail to allow that party to prepare its views on the matter;

  b) a reasonable period of time in which the party to be consulted may prepare its views on the matter, and an opportunity to present such views to the party obliged to consult; and

  c) full and fair consideration by the party obliged to consult of any views presented.

The Working Group First Nation representatives have expressed concerns that

- attempts to consult are often inappropriate, for example, by contacting the wrong people in the First Nation, or consulting with informal contacts;

- public consultation initiatives are being relied upon that do not meet the consultation test set out in the Agreements;

- insufficient information has been provided to the First Nations to allow them to make informed decisions and opinions; and

- there has often been insufficient time allocated for First Nation governments to undertake internal discussions and deliberations.

The Yukon Fish and Wildlife Management Board has reported that it is frequently informed of amendments to legislation or new legislation being developed by the federal government only after the Bill has been introduced to Parliament and is at the second reading stage, which does not permit meaningful input by the Board.

Canada and the Yukon have also expressed concerns that an enormous amount of resources are going into the consultation process while often Yukon First Nation governments do not respond to these efforts.

Gwich'in Comprehensive Land Claim Agreement

Representatives of the Dene Indians living in the Mackenzie Valley, Arctic Red River and Fort McPherson were signatories to Treaty No. 11. A provision in the treaty promised, among other things, to provide reserves for the signatory Aboriginal Peoples. No reserves had ever been established under Treaty No. 11, and only one was established in the Northwest Territories under Treaty No. 8. In the mid-1970s, the federal government accepted that the Mackenzie Valley treaties had been abortive. In 1976 and 1977, Canada agreed to negotiate comprehensive land claims with the Dene Nation and the Métis Association of the Northwest Territories with respect to the Mackenzie Valley in the western Northwest Territories. Negotiations with the Gwich'in began in November 1990. Negotiators of the Gwich'in and the federal and territorial governments initialled an agreement to settle the Gwich'in claim on 13 July 1991. The Agreement gained the force of law on 22 December 1992.[43]

The Agreement granted the Gwich'in fee simple or private ownership of the surface of 22,422 square kilometres of land in the Northwest Territories, which includes 6,158 square kilometres of land where the Gwich'in also own the subsurface resources, and the surface of 1,554 square kilometres of land in the Yukon. The Gwich'in also receive a tax-free payment of $75 million (1990 dollars) payable over 15 years. Furthermore, the Agreement guarantees to the Gwich'in a share of resource royalties in the western Arctic. The Gwich'in are also conveyed exclusive license to conduct commercial wildlife activities in Gwich'in lands and preferential rights in the settlement area.

Wildlife Harvesting and Management

The purpose of the Agreement is to confer harvesting rights and not to confer rights of ownership in wildlife to the Gwich'in people.[44]

---

[43] *Gwich'in Land Claim Settlement Act*, 1992, c. 53.
[44] *Ibid*. s. 12.3.3.

Personal Harvest

The Agreement confers exclusive wildlife harvesting rights on the Gwich'in within Gwich'in lands at all seasons of the year subject only to certain provisions of the Agreement.[45] The right to harvest wildlife is an exclusive right, except as to fish or migratory game birds, which may be harvested by non-Gwich'in persons pursuant to the Agreement.[46] In some instances, persons who are not participants to the Agreement may not have access to certain lands to harvest specified wildlife where such harvesting may interfere with the Gwich'in people's right to harvest particular species.[47] Non-participants to the Agreement are permitted to harvest moose in designated areas for a certain period of time per year,[48] and also wolves, wolverines and coyotes outside the Gwich'in lands in the settlement area.[49] However, the Gwich'in retain the exclusive right to harvest fur bearers throughout the settlement area.[50] The harvesting right includes an ancillary right to travel and establish and maintain hunting, trapping and fishing camps.[51] This includes a right to use plants and trees for such purposes.[52]

The right to harvest wildlife does not extend to migratory non-game birds and migratory insectivorous birds as defined in the *Migratory Birds Convention Act*,[53] and no right to buy, sell or offer for sale any migratory game bird, or parts thereof, or a migratory game bird's egg is conveyed by the Agreement.[54]

Pursuant to this Agreement the Gwich'in have the right to trade edible products of wildlife harvested by them among themselves and with other Aboriginal persons (defined as those who reside in and are eligible to harvest wildlife in the Northwest Territories and those who are members of a Yukon First Nation and who reside in the Yukon).[55] This right is designed to maintain traditional sharing among Aboriginal individuals and communities and is not to be exercised in a manner that would be considered "commercial."[56] Whether such activities amount to "commercial" activities is left to the determination of the Renewable Resources Board (established pursuant to the

---

[45] *Gwichin Comprehensive Land Claim Agreement*, s. 12.4.1 and s. 12.4.3.
[46] *Ibid.* s. 12.4.3(b).
[47] *Ibid.* s. 12.4.4.
[48] *Ibid.*
[49] *Ibid.* s. 12.4.5(b).
[50] *Ibid.* s. 12.4.5(a).
[51] *Ibid.* s. 12.4.11(a).
[52] *Ibid.* s. 12.4.11(c).
[53] *Migratory Birds Convention Act*, R.S. 1985, c.M-7.
[54] *Gwich'in Comprehensive Land Claim Agreement*, ss. 12.3.4 and 12.3.5.
[55] *Ibid.* s. 12.4.16(a).
[56] *Ibid.* s. 12.4.16(d).

Agreement), which is to regulate such trade. The Gwich'in are guaranteed the right to trade with any person any non-edible products of wildlife that are obtained from the harvest of fur bearers, or incidentally from harvesting wildlife for personal use.[57]

Commercial Harvest

The Renewable Resources Board is vested with the power to determine whether commercial harvesting is to be permitted. The Board can determine for which species commercial harvesting is permitted and in which particular areas it is to be permitted. The Board can determine the terms and conditions under which such species are harvested.[58] The right of first refusal to any new licence for the commercial harvest of wildlife resides with the Gwich'in Tribal Council.[59]

The government (which includes the federal government and the government of the Northwest Territories) is restricted as to the issuance of commercial fisheries licences in the waters overlying Gwich'in lands. The governments cannot issue a commercial licence for a fishery in such waters to a person who is not a participant to the Agreement, except where a valid licence was held by such a person at the date of settlement legislation, and such an entity continues to apply for a re-issuance annually.[60] The Gwich'in Tribal Council has the right of first refusal, for each fishery, to one-half of any new licences that are issued.[61] After that percentage of licences have been offered to the Gwich'in Tribal Council, licences are then offered to all applicants, whether Gwich'in residents or not, on an equal basis.[62]

Similar provisions apply to commercial naturalist activities and to commercial guiding and outfitting activities in respect of hunting and sport fishing.[63]

The Gwich'in Tribal Council is to have the first right of refusal with respect to licences for proposed commercial activities for the propagation, cultivation or husbandry of a species of wildlife indigenous to the settlement area.[64]

The Gwich'in Tribal Council has the exclusive right to be licensed to commercially harvest muskox and the exclusive right to be licensed to

---

[57] *Ibid.* s. 12.4.17.
[58] *Ibid.* s. 12.7.1(a).
[59] *Ibid.* s. 12.7.2.
[60] *Ibid.* s. 12.7.3.
[61] *Ibid.*
[62] *Ibid.*
[63] *Ibid.* ss. 12.7.4 – 12.7.6.
[64] *Ibid.* s. 12.7.8.

provide guiding services and harvesting opportunities with respect to this species.[65]

The Gwich'in shall have the exclusive right to be licensed to conduct commercial wildlife activities on Gwich'in lands and to permit others to do so.[66] The Renewable Resources Board has certain powers. The Board can establish policies in respect of

- harvesting of wildlife, including the class of persons that may harvest;
- commercial harvesting of wildlife, including
  - commercial activities in relation to harvesting, propagation, cultivation and husbandry of fur bearers and other species;
  - commercial processing, marketing and sale of wildlife and wildlife products;
  - guiding and outfitting services;
  - hunting, fishing and naturalist camps and lodges;
  - approval and review of plans for the management and protection of particular wildlife populations and habitats.[67]

Forestry

The Gwich'in have the right to harvest trees throughout the settlement area at all seasons of the year, for certain purposes. The harvested wood can be put to the following purposes:

- firewood for person use only;
- construction of camps for hunting, trapping and fishing for personal use;
- handicrafts and traditional, cultural and medicinal uses;
- construction of boats and rafts for personal uses; and
- house building for personal use.[68]

The Gwich'in people may dispose of harvested trees with other Gwich'in, by way of trade, who intend to use the timber for the above purposes.[69]

The right to harvest trees (including dead trees) within the settlement area remains subject to federal legislation and provincial laws of general application in respect of forest management, land management within local government boundaries, conservation, public health, public safety and protection of the environment from significant damage.[70]

---

[65] *Ibid.* s. 12.7.9.
[66] *Ibid.* s. 12.7.10.
[67] *Ibid.* s. 12.8.23.
[68] *Ibid.* s. 13.1.2.
[69] *Ibid.* s. 13.1.5.
[70] *Ibid.* s. 13.1.3.

The right to harvest trees for commercial purposes remains subject to legislation.[71] No new licence for the commercial harvesting of trees is to be granted by any level of government without the consent of the affected Renewable Resources Council where such harvesting would significantly affect the harvesting of wildlife by the Gwich'in.[72] The Renewable Resources Board holds the final say as to whether or not a commercial licence can be issued and can override a decision of a council.[73] The council is to be consulted prior to any change in the area of operation of an existing licence.[74]

The Agreement explicitly indicates that it in no way confers any rights of ownership of trees except those situated on Gwich'in lands. There is no guarantee as to the supply of trees. Non-participants are not restricted from harvesting trees on lands other than Gwich'in lands (subject to legislation), and the Gwich'in people are not entitled to any compensation for damage to or loss of trees or harvesting opportunities on lands other than Gwich'in lands.[75] The Board retains the right to regulate who may harvest trees; commercial harvesting of trees including cutting rates, yields, reforestation measures and Gwich'in employment and training; and for devising forest conservation and management plans.[76]

Plants

The Gwich'in may gather plant material for food, medicine, cultural and other personal purposes and for purposes required in the exercise of wildlife harvesting rights within the settlement area. Such a right is subject to legislation in respect of conservation, land management within local government boundaries, public health and safety and protection of the environment from significant damage.[77] The cultural purposes referred to here include the trade of plant material gathered by the Gwich'in with other Aboriginal persons for their personal consumption.[78]

Where the government seeks to regulate or prohibit plant gathering, it is to consult with the Gwich'in Tribal Council.[79] Legislation that regulates the gathering of plants is to provide a preferential right of gathering by the Gwich'in for food, medicine, cultural and other personal uses and for purposes required in the exercise of wildlife harvesting rights.[80]

---

[71] *Ibid.* s. 13.1.6.
[72] *Ibid.* s. 13.1.7(a).
[73] *Ibid.* s. 13.1.7(c).
[74] *Ibid.* s. 13.1.7(b).
[75] *Ibid.* s. 13.1.8.
[76] *Ibid.* s. 13.1.10.
[77] *Ibid.* s. 14.1.1.
[78] *Ibid.* s. 14.1.5(a).
[79] *Ibid.* s. 14.1.3.
[80] *Ibid.* s. 14.1.4.

The Agreement does not purport to confer rights of ownership to plants, except those situated on Gwich'in lands, or guarantee the supply of any plants. The Agreement further does not preclude non-participants from gathering plants on lands other than Gwich'in lands and does not commit anything by way of compensation to the Gwich'in for damage to or loss of plants or gathering opportunities on lands other than Gwich'in lands.[81]

Gwich'in Lands

The Agreement conveyed title to settlement lands as follows:

a) 16,264 square kilometres of land was conveyed in fee simple, with the mines and minerals (whether solid, liquid or gaseous) reserved by the provincial government. All pre-existing rights, titles or interests in the lands existing at the date of settlement also burden the Gwich'in title to that land. The Gwich'in retain a right to exploit specified substances on this land.[82] These are: "carving stone, clay, construction stone, diatomaceous earth, earth, flint, gravel, gypsum, limestone, marble, marl, ochre, peat, sand, shale, slate, sodium chloride, soil and volcanic ash."

   The right to exploit specified substances is subject to existing rights to exploit such materials. However, the Agreement is clear on the point that such rights and interests belonging to a non-Gwich'in person or entity may not be renewed.[83]

   The Gwich'in are under an obligation to provide supplies of sand, gravel, clay and other construction materials to the provincial government on their lands if no alternative source of supply is determined to exist in the surrounding area[84] and must be paid compensation.[85]

b) 4,299 square kilometres of lands in fee simple including mines and minerals, subject only to existing rights, titles or interests in the lands.

c) A further 1,766 square kilometres of lands in fee simple was conveyed to the Gwich'in including the mines and minerals and a further 93 square kilometres of land was conveyed whereby the mines and minerals underlying such lands were conveyed, but rights to the surface of that land were not conveyed. This portion of the Gwich'in land mass is referred to as the Aklavik lands.[86]

---

[81] *Ibid.* s. 14.1.6.
[82] *Ibid.* s. 18.2.1.
[83] *Ibid.* s. 18.2.2.
[84] *Ibid.* s. 18.2.3(a).
[85] *Ibid.* s. 18.2.3(b).
[86] *Ibid.* s. 18.1.2.

Title extends to those portions of the beds of lakes, rivers and other water bodies contained within the boundaries of the Gwich'in lands. However, title does not include title to the bed of any lake, river or other water body where any body of water forms part of the boundary of Gwich'in lands.[87]

Title to Gwich'in lands vests in the Gwich'in Tribal Council.[88] Management and control of Gwich'in lands belongs to the Gwich'in people. This includes the purposes of development and administration of land management programs and policies, and also charging rent or other fees for the use and occupation of the land.[89]

Settlement lands are not to be subject to seizure or sale under court order, writ of execution or any other process.[90] Furthermore, such lands cannot be mortgaged, charged or given as security.[91] No person can acquire an estate or interest in settlement lands except by prescription.[92]

Water Rights and Management

The Gwich'in have the exclusive right to use waters that are on or flow through Gwich'in lands when such waters are on or flowing through Gwich'in lands.[93] Such use is, however, subject to legislation in respect of water use[94] and also to the existing rights of those who are not participants to the Agreement.[95]

The provincial government retains the right to protect and manage water and beds of water bodies, and to use water in connection with such rights throughout the settlement area for certain purposes relating to wildlife management, navigation, community water supplies, fire fighting, flood control and research.[96] Gwich'in water use cannot interfere with the rights of the government to access the water and use it for certain periods, and furthermore, the Gwich'in cannot use the water to impede any right of access associated with a right to fish or to hunt migratory game birds.[97]

Nothing in the Agreement is intended to grant the Gwich'in property rights in respect of water.[98] However, the Gwich'in have a right to have their

---

[87] *Ibid.* s. 18.1.3.
[88] *Ibid.* s. 18.1.4.
[89] *Ibid.* s. 18.1.6.
[90] *Ibid.* s. 18.1.7.
[91] *Ibid.* s. 18.1.8.
[92] *Ibid.* s. 18.1.9.
[93] *Ibid.* s. 19.1.3(a).
[94] *Ibid.* s. 19.1.3(b).
[95] *Ibid.* s. 19.1.4.
[96] *Ibid.* s. 19.1.5.
[97] *Ibid.* s. 19.1.6.
[98] *Ibid.* s. 19.1.7(a).

waters remain substantially unaltered as to quality, quantity and rate of flow when such waters are on or flow through or are adjacent to their lands.[99] Any disturbance to the quality or quantity of such water is therefore actionable against any person.[100]

The Gwich'in are granted a right to use water without a licence or permit for trapping and non-commercial harvesting of wildlife, including for transportation in relation to such activities and also for traditional heritage, cultural and spiritual purposes.[101]

A Land and Water Board was established under the Agreement and enabling Act to regulate and manage the use of water on Gwich'in lands.

Access

Pursuant to the Agreement, persons who are not participants to the Agreement are not permitted to enter, cross or stay on Gwich'in lands and waters overlying such lands without the permission or agreement of the Gwich'in Tribal Council.[102] Members of the public have the right to use water bodies for navigational purposes but cannot harvest wildlife, engage in any commercial activity or establish a permanent or seasonal camp on Gwich'in lands.[103]

Members of the public are permitted to fish in certain waters identified in the Agreement and may also hunt migratory game birds in navigable waters overlying certain areas of Gwich'in lands.[104] This right does not, however, include a right to engage in any commercial activity or to establish any permanent or seasonal camp or structure on such lands.[105]

The government retains a right to enter, cross and stay on Gwich'in lands and waters and to use natural resources incidental to such access to deliver and manage government programs and services, to carry out inspections pursuant to law and to enforce laws.[106] Gwich'in land may also be used for military purposes by the Department of National Defence and the Canadian Armed Forces.[107]

---

[99] *Ibid.* s. 19.1.8.
[100] *Ibid.* s. 19.1.9.
[101] *Ibid.* s. 19.1.13.
[102] *Ibid.* s. 20.1.2.
[103] *Ibid.* s. 20.2.1.
[104] *Ibid.* s. 20.2.2.
[105] *Ibid.*
[106] *Ibid.* s. 20.3.1.
[107] *Ibid.* s. 20.3.3.

Rights of commercial access to Gwich'in land is deemed to continue regardless of this Agreement and it is at the discretion of the governmental body concerned whether or not to renew that permit, licence or other rights of access.[108] Prior notice of access to Gwich'in lands must be given by such persons to the Gwich'in Tribal Council and no permanent or seasonal camp or structure may be established on lands to which such rights apply. Also no significant alteration or damage must occur to Gwich'in land during the course of carrying out such activities.

Subsurface Resources

Prior to opening any lands within the settlement area for oil and gas exploration, the government is to notify the Gwich'in Tribal Council and provide it with an opportunity to present its views on the matter.[109] A number of issues must be discussed with the Gwich'in Tribal Council prior to the exercise of a developer's rights to develop or produce, including the environmental impact of the activity and the impact on wildlife harvesting, and mitigative measures.[110] Such conditions also apply to any person who proposes to explore for, or develop, minerals other than oil and gas and who requires a land use permit or water licence.[111] A duty to consult also applies to the government in relation to any proposed legislation that affects subsurface exploratory and exploitation rights.[112]

Land and Water Regulation

There is to be an integrated system of land and water management in the Mackenzie Valley, within which the regulation of land and water will be co-ordinated. The government of British Columbia is to retain the ultimate jurisdiction for the regulation of land and water.[113] A single Land and Water Board is established under the Agreement and enabling Act to regulate land and water use throughout the settlement area, including Gwich'in lands.[114] The objective of the Board is to provide for conservation, development and utilization of the land and water resources of the settlement area in a manner that will provide the optimum benefit for the present and future residents of the settlement area and the Mackenzie Valley and for all Canadians.[115]

---

[108] *Ibid.* s. 20.4.1.
[109] *Ibid.* s. 21.1.2.
[110] *Ibid.* s. 21.1.3.
[111] *Ibid.* s. 21.1.4 & 5.
[112] *Ibid.* s. 21.1.7.
[113] *Ibid.* s. 24.1.1.
[114] *Ibid.* s. 24.4.1.
[115] *Ibid.* s. 24.4.2(a).

Various powers are vested in the Land and Water Board. The Board is authorized to issue, amend or renew licences and permits and to devise terms and conditions for all uses of land and water. It is also to oversee compliance with its decisions and enforce or secure such compliance by suspending or cancelling licences and permits. The Board is also authorized to hold public consultations and hearings in communities in relation to matters within its jurisdiction, and is also in a position to propose changes to legislation in respect of land or water use to the Minister.[116]

Land Surface Regulation

Pursuant to the Agreement, a Surface Rights Board is established as a statutory body to be governed by legislation and will be funded by the federal government. The Board has jurisdiction over matters relating to surface entry and payable compensation for access.[117] The Board is to have jurisdiction to hear and determine matters relating to

- dispute resolution of conflicts between holders of surface or subsurface interests;
- granting right-of-entry orders whether or not compensation for entry has been determined;
- attaching conditions to right-of-entry orders;
- determining compensation for the use of the surface;
- determining compensation for unforeseen damage resulting from entry;
- prescribing rules and procedures for negotiations required by this agreement;
- reviewing and or terminating any right-of-entry order; and
- awarding costs.[118]

Sahtu/Dene/Métis Agreement 1993

The Sahtu Dene and Métis Land Claim Agreement was signed on 6 September 1993.[119] Under the Agreement, a compensation package of $75 million (1990) payable over 15 years as well as a share of resource royalties in the western Arctic was promised to the Sahtu Dene and Métis people concerned. The package included 41,000 square kilometres of land, of which 1,813 square kilometres included subsurface mineral rights that were handed over to the Sahtu Dene and Métis people.

---

[116] *Ibid.* s. 24.4.5(a).

[117] *Ibid.* s. 26.1.1.

[118] *Ibid.* s. 26.2.1.

[119] Given the force of law by the *Sahtu Dene and Métis Land Claim Settlement Act*, S.C. 1994, C. 27.

Harvesting Rights[120]

Participants to the Agreement have the right to harvest all species of wildlife within the settlement area at any time,[121] subject to limitations outlined in the Agreement. No person who is not a participant to the Agreement may harvest wildlife, other than fish or migratory game birds as may be harvestable under the Agreement, on or in waters on Sahtu lands.[122] Special harvesting areas are set aside by the Agreement[123] for the Sahtu and Métis people where non-participants to the Agreement are not allowed to harvest or where such harvesting would be inconsistent with the special harvesting rights granted to participants to the Agreement.[124] Moose may, however, be harvested by non-participants subject to certain time and legislative restrictions.[125]

Participants to the Agreement have the exclusive right to harvest fur bearers throughout the settlement area.[126] Harvesting rights are not restricted to traditional equipment and/or methods but extend to any methods of harvesting and use of any equipment for that purpose.[127]

Participants have the right to trade among themselves and with other Aboriginal persons, for personal consumption, edible products of wildlife harvested by the participants.[128] Trade for commercial purposes is not permitted. Trade with any person of any non-edible by-products of wildlife that are obtained incidentally from the harvest of fur bearers or incidentally from the harvest of wildlife for personal use, however, is permitted.[129]

The Renewable Resource Board established under the Agreement and the associated Act has the ability to limit the number of species that may be harvested in accordance with a procedure defined in the Agreement.[130] Limits on the allowable harvest level are permissible only to the extent necessary to achieve conservation.[131]

The right to harvest wildlife does not extend to migratory non-game birds and migratory insectivorous birds as defined in the *Migratory Birds Convention Act*.[132] The Sahtu Métis people under this Agreement are

---

[120] *Sahtu/Dene/Métis Agreement 1993*, Chapter 13 "Wildlife Harvesting and Management."
[121] Ibid. s. 13.4.3(a).
[122] *Sahtu/Dene/Métis Agreement 1993*, s. 13.4.3(b).
[123] *Ibid*. Schedules V, VI and VII, appendix E.
[124] *Ibid*. s. 13.4.4(a) and (b).
[125] *Ibid*. s. 13.4.4(c).
[126] *Ibid*. s. 13.4.5(a).
[127] *Ibid*. s. 13.4.14.
[128] *Ibid*. s. 13.4.16(a).
[129] *Ibid*. s. 13.4.17.
[130] *Ibid*. s. 13.5.
[131] *Ibid*. s. 13.5.2.
[132] *Migratory Birds Convention Act*, R.S. 1985, c. M-7.

permitted to harvest migratory game birds in accordance with total allowable harvest figures established by the Renewable Resources Board.[133]

Participants to the Agreement have the exclusive right to be licensed to conduct commercial wildlife activities on Sahtu lands and to permit others to do so, subject only to rights that were held by anyone at the date of settlement legislation.[134] The commercial wildlife activities referred to in the Agreement, however, are to be conducted in accordance with legislation affecting such activities. As such, a licence fee may be required to engage in such activities.[135] It is for the Renewable Resources Board to determine whether commercial harvesting is to be permitted in a particular area for a particular species or population and may prescribe terms and conditions for such harvesting.[136]

The government may only issue a licence for a commercial fishery in waters on Sahtu lands to a person who is a participant, except where the licence existed at the date of settlement legislation and that person has applied for a renewal of that licence.[137]

Licences may also be obtained to undertake commercial naturalist activities and commercial guiding and outfitting activities in respect of hunting and sport fishing.[138]

The Sahtu Tribal Council holds the right to refuse a new licence for such activities in return for promising that a portion of such licences for guiding and outfitting for barren-ground caribou be reserved for residents who are not participants.[139] The Sahtu Tribal Council has the exclusive right to be licensed to commercially harvest free-roaming muskox and the exclusive right to be licensed to provide guiding services and harvesting opportunities with respect to the species.[140]

Forestry[141]

Participants to the Agreement are entitled to harvest trees, including dead trees, throughout the settlement area at all seasons of the year for:

- firewood for personal use;
- the construction of camps for hunting, trapping and fishing for personal use;

---

[133] *Sahtu/Dene/Métis Agreement 1993*, s. 13.5.14.
[134] *Ibid.* s. 13.7.10.
[135] *Ibid.* s. 13.7.12.
[136] *Ibid.* s. 13.7.1.
[137] *Ibid.* s. 13.7.3.
[138] *Ibid.* s. 13.7.4.
[139] *Ibid.* s. 13.7.5.
[140] *Ibid.* s. 13.7.9.
[141] *Ibid.* Chapter 14 "Forestry."

- handicrafts and traditional, cultural and medicinal uses;
- the construction of boats and rafts for personal uses; and
- house building for personal use.[142]

The right to harvest for these purposes is not exclusive, but is subject to legislation in respect of forest management, land management protocols within local government boundaries, conservation, public health and safety and protection of the environment from significant damage.[143] Further, this right does not apply to land held in fee simple, or subject to a lease, on Crown lands where the land is being used for a conflicting purpose, and in national parks.[144]

Commercial harvesting of trees throughout the settlement area is subject to legislation.[145] The Renewable Resources Council has the final say in consenting to a new licence for the commercial harvesting of trees where such harvesting would significantly affect the harvesting of wildlife by participants.[146] The Renewable Resources Board has the power to establish policies and propose regulations in respect of commercial harvests, forest conservation and management.[147]

Plants[148]

Participants to the Agreement are entitled to gather plant material for food, medicine, cultural and other personal purposes and for purposes required in the exercise of wildlife harvesting rights within the settlement area, subject to legislation in respect of conservation, land management within local government boundaries, public health and safety and protection of the environment from significant damage.[149] Again, plant removal is subject to the land restrictions applicable to forest harvesting.[150] Any legislation regulating (but not prohibiting) the gathering of plants is to provide a preferential right of gathering by participants for food, medicine, cultural and other personal uses and for purposes required in the exercise of wildlife harvesting rights and may describe on which lands and under what conditions the preferential right is to apply.[151]

---

[142] *Ibid.* s. 14.1.2.
[143] *Ibid.* s. 14.1.3.
[144] *Ibid.* s. 14.1.4.
[145] *Ibid.* s. 14.1.6.
[146] *Ibid.* s. 14.1.7(a).
[147] *Ibid.* s. 14.1.9.
[148] *Ibid.* Chapter 15 "Plants."
[149] *Ibid.* s. 15.1.1.
[150] *Ibid.* s. 15.1.2.
[151] *Ibid.* s. 15.1.4.

Sahtu Lands[152]

The Agreement conveys title to 39,624 square kilometres of lands in fee simple, from which rights to mines and minerals, whether solid, liquid or gaseous that may be found on or under the land are reserved.[153] Despite the fact that the province has reserved mines and minerals in Sahtu lands, Sahtu title does include the right to exploit "specified substances" and the right to work with such substances. "Specified substances" are defined in the Agreement as: "carving stone, clay, construction stone, diatomaceous earth, earth, flint, gravel, gypsum, limestone, marble, marl, ochre, peat, sand, shale, slate, sodium chloride, soil and volcanic ash."[154] Even though the Sahtu have rights to "specified substances," they may be required to provide supplies of, and permit access to, such materials if, in the opinion of the Land and Water Board, no alternative supply is reasonably available in the surrounding area.[155]

A further 1,813 square kilometres were conveyed in fee simple, including the mines and minerals existing on or under the lands, subject to any rights, titles or interests in the lands existing at the date of settlement.[156] Sahtu title extends to beds of lakes, rivers and other water bodies contained within the described boundaries of Sahtu lands. However, title does not include the bed of any lake, river or other water body where any lake, river or water body is described as a boundary of Sahtu lands.[157]

Water Rights and Management[158]

The First Nation participants to this Agreement have the exclusive right to use waters that are on or flow through Sahtu lands at the point that such water is geographically situated on the land.[159] The federal government does, however, retain the right to regulate water and waterbeds situated on First Nations land for "public purposes," including

- the management and research in respect of wildlife, and aquatic habitat;
- the protection and management of navigation and transportation;
- protection of water supplies including community water supplies from contamination and degradation;

---

[152] *Ibid.* Chapter 19 "Sahtu Lands."
[153] *Ibid.* s. 19.1.2.
[154] *Ibid.* s. 19.1.1.
[155] *Ibid.* s. 19.2.3(a).
[156] *Ibid.* s. 19.1.2.
[157] *Ibid.* s. 19.1.3.
[158] *Ibid.* Chapter 20 "Water Rights and Management."
[159] *Ibid.* s. 20.1.3.

- fighting fires;
- flood control; and
- research and sampling with respect to water quality and water quantity.[160]

Another limitation on water use by the First Nation participants is that the right to use water shall not interfere with or detract from any right of access associated with a right to fish or to hunt migratory game birds.[161] Although water flowing through or adjacent to Sahtu lands can be used, by virtue of this Act, the water cannot be used so as to substantially alter the quality, quantity and rate of flow of the water.[162]

The right to use water for trapping and non-commercial harvesting of wildlife exists without the First Nations concerned having to obtain a licence or permit.[163] However, the Land and Water Board reserves the right to authorize water use that will interfere with the rights of the First Nations where the Board can find no alternative which could reasonably satisfy the requirements of the applicant, and that there are no reasonable measures that could be implemented to avoid interference.[164]

Subsurface Resources[165]

With respect to settlement lands, the First Nation participants to the Agreement have little say with respect to subsurface resource exploitation. The government is merely required to notify the Sahtu Tribal Council prior to opening any lands within the settlement area for subsurface resource exploration. At such time, the council will be given the opportunity to present its views on the matter and make suggestions as to terms and conditions to be attached to the issued right.[166] Consultation is also to take place between the person proposing to explore and the Sahtu Tribal Council on issues such as impact on the environment and wildlife, including mitigative measures, and any other matters of importance to the parties.[167] Such consultations do not, however, give rise to any sort of statutory obligations upon the party proposing resource exploitation. The government is also required to consult with the Sahtu Tribal Council whereupon proposed legislation affects subsurface resource exploitation on lands concerning them.[168]

---

[160] *Ibid.* s. 20.1.5.
[161] *Ibid.* s. 20.1.6.
[162] *Ibid.* s. 20.1.8.
[163] *Ibid.* s. 20.1.13.
[164] *Ibid.* s. 20.1.14.
[165] *Ibid.* Chapter 22 "Subsurface Resources."
[166] *Ibid.* ss. 22.1.2 & 22.1.4.
[167] *Ibid.* ss. 22.1.3. & 22.1.5.
[168] *Ibid.* s. 22.1.7.

Inuvialuit Final Agreement[169]

The Inuvialuit Final Agreement was signed by the federal government and the Committee for Original People's Entitlement representing the 2,500 Inuvialuit of the western Arctic on 5 June 1984. Under the Agreement, the Inuvialuit gave up any claim to the lands in the western Arctic[170] in exchange for legal title to selected lands, financial compensation and a variety of other rights. The Agreement was given the force of law by the *Western Arctic (Inuvialuit) Claims Settlement Act*.[171]

Inuvialuit Lands

The settlement provided the Inuvialuit with 91,000 square kilometres of land. Of that land, 8,000 square kilometres was granted "more or less, in fee simple absolute."[172] Title to this land includes all minerals, whether solid, liquid or gaseous and all granular materials. A further 48,000 square kilometres of land was granted minus rights to oil, gas, related hydrocarbons, coal and sulphur.[173] Title to Inuvialuit land cannot be conveyed, except to Inuvialuit individuals or corporations controlled by the Inuvialuit or to the federal government.[174]

The Inuvialuit are granted title in fee simple absolute to the beds of all water bodies found on their lands,[175] although the Crown retains "ownership" of all waters in the Inuvialuit settlement region[176] and title remains subject to existing easements, servitudes and rights of way.[177] Notwithstanding Inuvialuit ownership of beds of rivers, lakes and other water bodies, Canada retains the right to manage and control such water bodies to regulate

- fisheries; and
- migratory and non-migratory game birds, and insectivorous birds and their habitat.[178]

Laws of general application applicable to private lands continue to be applicable to Inuvialuit lands.[179] Where the Inuvialuit dispose of new rights respecting oil, gas, coal, minerals, sand, gravel and rock on Inuvialuit lands,

---

[169] Published in: Department of Indian Affairs and Northern Affairs, *The Western Arctic Claim: The Inuvialuit Final Agreement*, Ottawa, 1984.

[170] *The Inuvialuit Final Agreement*, ss. 3(4) and (5).

[171] 1984, c. 24.

[172] *The Inuvialuit Final Agreement*, s. 7(1)(a)(i).

[173] *Ibid*. s. 7(1)(b).

[174] *Ibid*. ss. 7(43) and (44).

[175] *Ibid*. s. 7(2).

[176] *Ibid*. s. 7(3).

[17] *Ibid*. s. 7(4).

[178] *Ibid*. s. 7(85).

[179] *Ibid*. s. 7(97).

the Inuvialuit Land Administration may set terms and conditions with respect to the environment and safety that equal or exceed the standards provided under laws of general application.[180]

Access to Inuvialuit Lands

Canada reserves a right of access to Inuvialuit lands; however, this right is limited to use of water bodies for travel, recreation or emergency purposes only and does not permit any person to engage in any development or wildlife harvesting activities.[181] The public is entitled to access unoccupied Inuvialuit lands for emergency purposes, and to access adjacent land for recreation[182] provided that no damage or significant interference with the Inuvialuit use of the land occurs.[183]

Any person fishing in waters situated on Inuvialuit lands that are granted in fee simple absolute is required to register with the appropriate Hunters and Trappers Committee.[184] Entry across Inuvialuit lands to which title is granted absolute for the purpose of fishing will be granted solely at the discretion of the Inuvialuit.[185] On all other Inuvialuit lands, the Inuvialuit agree to allow the public to enter such lands for the purpose of sport and commercial fishing where such persons are licensed or registered with the appropriate person or body.[186]

Sand and Gravel

The Agreement states that the Inuvialuit are to reserve supplies of sand and gravel of appropriate quality and within reasonable transport distances on Inuivialuit lands in order to meet public community needs in the Western Arctic Region and in Inuvik.[187] As a second priority, the Inuivialuit are required to reserve adequate supplies of sand and gravel of appropriate quality on Inuvialuit lands for the direct private and corporate needs of the Inuvialuit, but not for sale.[188] Third, sand and gravel must be made available for any project approved by an appropriate governmental agency.[189] The removal of sand and gravel is subject to the issuance of a licence or concession from the Inuvialuit Land Administration.[190]

---

[180] *Ibid.* s. 7(99).
[181] *Ibid.* s. 7(13).
[182] *Ibid.* s. 7(14).
[183] *Ibid.* s. 7(15).
[184] *Ibid.* s. 7(22).
[185] *Ibid.* s. 7(23).
[186] *Ibid.* s. 7(24).
[187] *Ibid.* s. 7(27).
[188] *Ibid.* s. 7(28).
[189] *Ibid.* s. 7(29).
[190] *Ibid.* s. 7(32).

Harvesting Rights

Western Arctic Region

Exercise of the Inuvialuit right to harvest within the western Arctic region is subject to laws of general application respecting public safety and conservation. The Agreement is not intended to give the Inuvialuit a proprietary interest in any wildlife.[191] Inuvialuit harvesting rights include:

- the preferential right to harvest all species of wildlife except migratory non-game birds and migratory insectivorous birds for subsistence usage;
- the exclusive right to harvest fur bearers, including black and grizzly bears;
- the exclusive right to harvest polar bear and muskox; and
- the exclusive right to harvest game on Inuvialuit lands.[192]

The Inuvialuit are entitled to sell the non-edible products of legally harvested game,[193] and may sell, trade and barter game among Inuvialuit beneficiaries.[194]

The Wildlife Management Advisory Council[195] and the Fisheries Joint Management Committee[196] serve as bodies that distribute the harvest allocations for subsistence purposes among all the Native Peoples living in the vicinity of the Inuvialuit settlement region.[197] Harvesting means are not limited to traditional methods, and the right to harvest includes the right to travel and establish camps as necessary to exercise that right.[198]

Ownership of water bodies on Inuvialuit lands does not convey a proprietary interest in fish or give the Inuvialuit an exclusive right to harvest fish.[199] The Inuvialuit are entitled, however, to sell, trade or barter fish and marine mammal products acquired in subsistence fisheries to other Inuvialuit without restriction.[200] Subject to the *Fisheries Act* and any Regulations enacted pursuant to that Act, the right to harvest fish and marine mammals includes the right to sell the non-edible products of legally harvested fish and marine mammals.[201] The Inuvialuit are granted a preferential right within the

---

[191] *Ibid.* s. 14(6).
[192] *Ibid.*
[193] *Ibid.* s. 14(11).
[194] *Ibid.* s. 14(12).
[195] *Ibid.*, established by s. 14(45).
[196] *Ibid.* established by s. 14(65).
[197] *Ibid.* s. 14(19).
[198] *Ibid.* s. 14(23).
[199] *Ibid.* s. 7(90).
[200] *Ibid.* s. 14(24).
[201] *Ibid.* s. 14(27).

Inuvialuit settlement region to harvest fish for subsistence usage, including trade, barter and sale to other Inuvialuit.[202]

The Inuvialuit are granted the first priority for the harvest of marine mammals, including first priority of access to all harvestable quotas for marine mammals within the Inuvialuit settlement region and the right to harvest a subsistence quota, which is to be set jointly by the Inuvialuit and the government.[203] Harvesting of both fish and marine mammals is to be subject to conservation principles.[204]

The Inuvialuit are issued non-transferable licences to harvest under the commercial quota for any waters within the Inuvialuit settlement region, including the offshore, in the amount of the total weight of fish per species equal to the weight of the largest annual commercial harvest of that species from those waters taken by the Inuvialuit in the preceding three years.[205] Where the Inuvialuit desire to commercially harvest fish in excess of such an amount, they will be treated on the same basis as other commercial fishery applicants.[206] These provisions apply to the entire Inuvialuit settlement region.[207]

The Inuvialuit are to have the first priority in the western Arctic region for any authorized commercial activities related to wildlife.[208]

The Agreement established several bodies to administer these provisions. The Wildlife Management Advisory Council is to determine the total allowable harvest for game according to conservation criteria. That information is then passed to the governments having responsibility for wildlife management who will determine harvesting quotas.

The Fisheries Joint Management Committee is also established under the Agreement, which is to assist Canada and the Inuvialuit in administering the rights and obligations relating to Inuvialuit fisheries, and to provide advice and assistance to the Minister of Fisheries and Oceans of Canada.[209] Among other things, the Fisheries Joint Management Committee will determine fishery volumes and allocate subsistence quotas among communities and make recommendations to the Minister of Fisheries and Oceans on subsistence quotas for fish, harvestable quotas for marine mammals, Inuvialuit commercial fishing and allocation of preferential fishing licences.

---

[202] *Ibid.* s. 14(31).

[203] *Ibid.* s. 14(29).

[204] *Ibid.* ss. 14(29) and (30).

[205] *Ibid.* s. 14(32).

[206] *Ibid.* s. 14(33).

[207] *Ibid.* s. 14(35).

[208] *Ibid.* s. 14(42).

[209] *Ibid.* s. 14(61).

The Agreement also establishes the Inuvialuit Game Council.[210] The council is to represent the collective Inuvialuit interest in wildlife.[211] Again, the purpose of the council is more as an advisory body to the government on policy, legislation, regulation and administration respecting wildlife, conservation, research, management and enforcement. The council is also responsible for assigning community hunting and trapping areas within the Inuvialuit settlement region for the purposes of Inuvialuit wildlife harvesting where appropriate.[212]

The Inuvialuit Hunters and Trappers Committees established under section 14(75) of the Agreement are designed to advise the Inuvialuit Game Council on local matters concerning hunting and trapping.

Yukon North Slope

The Yukon North Slope is subject to a special conservation regime that has as its dominant purpose the conservation of wildlife, habitat and traditional Native use.[213] The Inuvialuit right to harvest on the Yukon North Slope, including the preferential right to harvest all species of wildlife, except migratory non-game birds and migratory insectivorous birds for subsistence usage, is subject to conservation and public safety laws of general application.[214] The harvestation right in this area includes an exclusive right to harvest fur bearers and polar bear, and the exclusive right to harvest game within the national park, the territorial park and adjacent islands.[215] Sport fishing continues to be permitted throughout the Yukon North Slope, including both parks.[216] The Inuvialuit are entitled to trade and barter game products with other Inuvialuit beneficiaries in the Yukon North Slope.[217] Subject to the *Migratory Birds Convention Act* and its Regulations, the Inuvialuit may sell game products to other Inuvialuit beneficiaries in the national park for subsistence usage.[218] Non-edible products of legally harvested game may be sold.[219] The right to harvest game includes the right to travel and establish camps as necessary to exercise that right.[220]

The North Slope Wildlife Management Advisory Council is to determine the total allowable harvest for game according to conservation criteria, which

---

[210] *Ibid.* s. 14(73).
[211] *Ibid.* s. 14(74).
[212] *Ibid.*
[213] *Ibid.* s. 12(2).
[214] *Ibid.* s. 12(24).
[215] *Ibid.*
[216] *Ibid.* s. 12(26).
[217] *Ibid.* s. 12(31).
[218] *Ibid.* s. 12(32).
[219] *Ibid.* s. 12(35).
[220] *Ibid.* s. 12(37).

is then passed on to the relevant Minister.[221] The governments having jurisdiction over species and the Inuvialuit are to establish subsistence quotas for wildlife harvest.

Dogrib Agreement In Principle

The traditional territory of the Dogrib First Nation is primarily around the area commonly known as the North Slave region of the Northwest Territories. Approximately 3,000 Dogrib live mainly in the communities of Behcho Ko (Rae-Edzo), Wha Ti (Lac La Martre), Gameti (Rae Lakes) and Wekweti (Snare Lake) in this area. Negotiations for a comprehensive land claim commenced in 1994. This Agreement is the third of the Mackenzie Valley Dene and Métis claims.

The Dogrib Agreement In Principle was signed by representatives of the Dogrib Treaty 11 Council, the government of the Northwest Territories and the Government of Canada at Behcho Ko (Rae-Edzo) on 7 January 2000. Under the Agreement In Principle, the Dogrib First Nation Government would receive $90 million (1997 dollars), which would be paid over a period of years. As well, they will receive a share of resource royalties received by government annually from the Mackenzie Valley. Negotiations concluded and a Final Agreement was signed in the summer of 2003 at Behcho Ko. The Final Agreement contained all of the elements already agreed to under this Agreement. (This Agreement was concluded after the writing of this book; therefore, we refer to the Agreement In Principle and have made updates for changes.)

Nothing in the Dogrib Agreement would be construed to affect, recognize or provide any rights under section 35 of the *Constitution Act, 1982* for any Aboriginal Peoples other than the Dogrib First Nation.[222] In accordance with overlap agreements with Aboriginal groups in adjacent regions, Dogrib would continue to have the right to harvest wildlife within those areas of the Northwest Territories and Nunavut that they have traditionally used and continue to use for that purpose. Aboriginal groups in adjacent regions would have similar rights in the settlement area and the Agreement In Principle acknowledges that discussions between the First Nations concerned will be necessary prior to finalizing negotiations.[223] All laws of general application would continue to apply to Dogrib citizens and the Dogrib First Nation Government.[224] However, in the event of any inconsistency between the provincial or federal legislation and the settlement Agreement or enacting legislation, the Final Agreement or enacting

---

[221] *Ibid.* s. 12(41).
[222] *Dogrib Agreement in Principle, 2000,* s. 2.8.1.; see Final Agreement, online: <www.dogrib.ca>.
[223] *Ibid.* ss. 2.8.2 – 2.8.9.
[224] *Ibid.* s. 2.9.4.

legislation is to override to the extent of the inconsistency.[225] Generally, a person would be eligible to be enrolled as a "Dogrib citizen" if that person is a Dogrib and a Canadian citizen.

Under the Agreement, lands that were previously categorized as "lands reserved for Indians" under the *Constitution Act, 1867*[226] are removed from federal jurisdiction; therefore, the *Indian Act* is no longer applicable to such lands.[227] The Agreement does continue to endorse Treaty No. 11, which is not affected by the Dogrib Agreement and must continue to be respected and recognized as a historically and culturally important document.[228]

Settlement Area

The traditional territory of the Dogrib First Nation is that area of the Northwest Territories commonly known as the North Slave region. The "settlement area" is the area in which most of the rights and benefits under a Dogrib Agreement would apply. Its boundaries have not yet been defined.

Dogrib Primary Use Area

Exclusive or priority rights for the Dogrib First Nation would not be provided throughout the whole of a Dogrib settlement area because the Dogrib share the use of that area with the Yellowknives Dene First Nation. The Dogrib Agreement would propose a solution to this problem, namely, certain exclusive or priority rights could be recognized for the Dogrib in that part of their traditional territory in which they have "primary" use.

Dogrib Lands[229]

The Dogrib First Nation Government is vested with title to a tract of land of approximately 38,850 square kilometres, subject to rights and interests existing at the conclusion of the Final Agreement.[230] Title includes rights to the mines and minerals that may be found to exist on or under such lands.[231] Title to the land does not, however, extend to water in or under the lands.[232] Title does extend to waterbeds, including to the portion of the bed of the water body where the boundary of Dogrib lands crosses a lake, river or other water body, but does not extend to the bed of any lake, river or other water body where the water body is a boundary of Dogrib lands.[233]

---

[225] *Ibid*. s. 2.9.5.
[226] *Constitution Act*, 1867, s. 91(24).
[227] *Dogrib Agreement In Principle, 2000*, s. 2.4.1.
[228] *Ibid*. s. 2.6.1.
[229] *Ibid*. Chapter 18 "Dogrib Lands."
[230] *Ibid*. s. 18.6.
[231] *Ibid*. s. 18.1.1.
[232] *Ibid*. s. 18.1.2.
[233] *Ibid*. s. 18.1.3.

The Dogrib First Nation Government is not prevented from granting leases or licences to any person for the use and occupancy of Dogrib lands, or for granting any person the right to remove natural resources, including minerals, and to own such resources upon removal.[234]

The government is obliged to continue administering the rights and interests of parties with pre-existing rights to lands. Any renewals or replacements of interests in land will continue as if the lands had not become Dogrib lands. The government is also entitled to make discretionary decisions respecting a pre-existing right or interest and to any renewals or replacements granted by the government on the basis of the government's resource management policy, including those respecting rents, royalties and other charges.[235] This right is fettered only by an obligation on the government to consult with the Dogrib First Nation prior to enacting such legislative changes.[236]

Mackenzie Valley Resource Management Act

The land and water regulation and environmental assessment provisions of the *Mackenzie Valley Resource Management Act* would apply to all development activities in the settlement area, including those on Dogrib lands.

At least one member of the Environmental Impact Review Board established under the *Mackenzie Valley Resource Management Act* would be a nominee of the Dogrib First Nation Government. A North Slave Land and Water Board would be established, on the effective date, by legislation, as an institution of public government, to regulate land use and water use in the North Slave region.

Under the *Mackenzie Valley Resource Management Act*, certain decisions of the North Slave Land and Water Board would be subject to policy directions from the Minister. The *Mackenzie Valley Resource Management Act* would also provide that, in relation to land use on Dogrib lands, the decisions of the Board would also be subject to policy directions from the Dogrib First Nation Government.

Part IV of the *Mackenzie Valley Resource Management Act* requires that a Land and Water Board be established for the whole of the Mackenzie Valley. At least one member of the Mackenzie Valley Board is an appointee of the Dogrib First Nation Government. The North Slave Land and Water Board would be a regional panel of the Mackenzie Valley Board.

---

[234] *Ibid.* s. 18.1.6.
[235] *Ibid.* s. 18.6.2.
[236] *Ibid.* s. 18.6.4.

Government, the Dogrib First Nation Government and the Dogrib community governments could agree to establish a land use planning body and a mechanism for the preparation, approval and implementation of a land use plan for all of the settlement area, other than established national parks. Upon the approval of such a plan, government, the Dogrib First Nation Government and the Dogrib community governments and their departments and agencies, including the North Slave Land and Water Board, would exercise their powers in accordance with the plan.

Subsurface Resource Rights[237]

The Dogrib First Nation Government's right to regulate and manage mining and minerals is restricted to input as a consultant only. Under the Agreement In Principle, before any hard rock mining exploration, development or production activities that require a land use permit or water licence occur in the settlement area, the government is to notify the Dogrib First Nation Government and provide it with an opportunity to present its opinion on the matter.[238] The same rule applies for oil and gas explorations.[239] The government is under a similar obligation to consult with the Dogrib First Nation Government in relation to any proposed legislation in relation to mining activities that will have effect in the Dogrib settlement area.[240] The Dogrib First Nation Government will, however, continue to receive a share of the resource royalties that the government receives each year from the Mackenzie Valley.

The government also retains rights of access to Dogrib lands and waters and to use natural resources where doing so is incidental to delivering and managing government programs and services, where carrying out inspections authorized by legislation and in emergency situations.[241] There is no obligation to seek the consent of the Dogrib First Nations Government or to provide them with notice of access where it is not reasonable to do so.[242] This right is extended to any person authorized to provide electrical power or other similar utilities to the public with the added condition that consultation occur with the Dogrib First Nation Government first.[243]

Where materials are required for construction the Dogrib must permit access to sand, gravel, clay and other construction materials on Dogrib lands if the materials are to be used on Dogrib lands.[244] Where the materials are not

---

[237] *Ibid.* Chapter 23 "Subsurface Resources."
[238] *Ibid.* s. 23.2.
[239] *Ibid.* s. 23.3.
[240] *Ibid.* s. 23.6.
[241] *Ibid.* s. 19.5.1.
[242] *Ibid.*
[243] *Ibid.* s. 19.5.6.
[244] *Ibid.* ss. 19.7.1 and 19.7.2.

to be used for construction on Dogrib lands, they must be ceded, nevertheless, where there is no alternative source of supply reasonably available in an area closer to those other lands.[245] Compensation for materials removed from Dogrib lands for this purpose will only be payable in extremely narrow circumstances.[246]

Wildlife Harvesting[247]

Dogrib citizens will have the right to harvest all species of wildlife, including fish, mammals, birds and bird eggs, throughout the settlement area at all times of the year.[248] However, the right to harvest wildlife does not extend to migratory non-game birds or to migratory insectivorous birds as defined in the *Migratory Birds Convention Act*.[249] The Agreement does not confer any rights of ownership over wildlife, nor does it guarantee the supply of wildlife.[250]

Dogrib citizens also have the exclusive right to harvest fur bearers throughout the Dogrib primary use area.[251] Persons who are not Dogrib citizens can hunt, but not trap, wolves and coyotes on lands other than Dogrib lands in the Dogrib primary use area.[252] A person who resides in the Northwest Territories and who held a General Hunting Licence and harvested fur bearers in the Dogrib primary use area in the 10-year period prior to the date of the Agreement In Principle are permitted to continue to exercise the right to harvest fur bearers in the Dogrib primary use area (excluding Dogrib lands).[253] Any person can also harvest fur bearers on Dogrib lands with the consent of the Dogrib First Nation Government.[254]

The Agreement acknowledges that any method of harvestation of wildlife may be used, as may any equipment for that purpose.[255]

A Dogrib citizen has the right to trade with or give to other Dogrib citizens and Aboriginal People edible parts of wildlife harvested, including bird eggs, for their own consumption.[256] Where parts of wildlife harvested are non-edible (including down and other feathers), however, a Dogrib citizen has the right to trade with or give those parts or products to any person.[257]

---

[245] *Ibid.*
[246] *Ibid.* s. 19.7.3.
[247] *Ibid.* Chapter 10 "Wildlife Harvesting Rights."
[248] *Ibid.* s. 10.1.1(a).
[249] *Ibid.* s. 10.1.2.
[250] *Ibid.* s. 10.1.4.
[251] *Ibid.* s. 10.1.1(b).
[252] *Ibid.* s. 10.1.3.
[253] *Ibid.* s. 10.1.5(a).
[254] *Ibid.* s. 10.1.5(b).
[255] *Ibid.* s. 10.2.1.
[256] *Ibid.* s. 10.3.2.
[257] *Ibid.* s. 10.3.3.

A Dogrib citizen has the right to access all the lands within the settlement area for the purpose of harvesting wildlife.[258] Included in this right is the ability to

- establish and maintain hunting, trapping and fishing camps established primarily for use by Dogrib citizens; and
- use plants and trees for purposes ancillary to wildlife harvesting, except trees, where the use of trees conflicts with any activity carried out under an authorization or permit granted by government.[259]

Access does not extend, however, to land being used for military or national security purposes, or land that is being used for certain other legitimate conflicting purposes.[260]

A right of access to lands owned in fee simple or subject to an agreement for sale or surface lands exists, provided that no significant damage is caused to the lands, mischief is not committed on the lands, the occupier's use and enjoyment of the lands is not significantly interfered with and no construction of a seasonal camp or use of wood (other than dead wood) occur without the consent of the owner or occupier.[261] In land put to use for community purposes, the right of access will be restricted further by laws in place to maintain health and safety.[262] A dispute mechanism exists for resolution of alleged interference with land and conflicts that may arise out of authorized use of land and harvesting activities.[263]

Any person has a right of access to Dogrib lands and waters overlying Dogrib lands.[264] This right does not extend to engaging in commercial activities or establishing any permanent or seasonal camp or structure,[265] although a person may harvest wildlife and trees in accordance with Dogrib laws.[266]

The Dogrib have the exclusive right to conduct commercial wildlife activities on Dogrib lands. In particular, the Dogrib First Nation Government has the exclusive right to be licensed to commercially harvest free-roaming muskox or bison in the Dogrib primary use area and the exclusive right to be licensed to provide guiding services and harvesting opportunities with respect to these species in the primary use area.[267]

---

[258] *Ibid.* s. 10.5.
[259] *Ibid.* s. 10.5.2.
[260] *Ibid.* s. 10.5.3.
[261] *Ibid.* s. 10.5.4.
[262] *Ibid.* s. 10.5.6.
[263] *Ibid.* s. 10.6.
[264] *Ibid.* s. 19.2.1.
[265] *Ibid.* s. 19.2.2.
[266] *Ibid.* s. 19.2.3.
[267] *Ibid.* s. 10.8.8.

The Dogrib will have the exclusive right to be licensed to conduct commercial wildlife activities on Dogrib lands. A developer would be liable for any losses or damage suffered by a Dogrib citizen as a result of that developer's activities.

In the settlement area and outside the Dogrib primary use area, the Dogrib First Nation Government is to be treated on the same basis as other licence applicants.[268] The Dogrib First Nation Government has the exclusive right to be licensed to conduct commercial wildlife activities, other than harvesting, on Dogrib lands and to assign any rights under such licences to any other person or entity.[269] Where the government authorizes the commercial harvesting of a species of wildlife in the settlement area, the Dogrib First Nation Government has the power to authorize commercial harvesting of that species on Dogrib lands. No person may harvest wildlife on Dogrib lands, for commercial purposes, without the authorization of the Dogrib First Nation Government.[270]

To oversee the implementation of wildlife regulations, the Agreement In Principle sets up a North Slave Renewable Resources Board.[271] The Board does not have authority respecting wildlife and habitat in a national park within Dogrib lands, or fish or fish habitat in the Great Slave Lake.[272]

The Board has the power to manage wildlife, including commercial wildlife activities, forestry, plants and protected areas.[273] The Board is responsible for making a final determination regarding a total allowable harvest level and for allocating portions of any total allowable harvest levels to groups of persons for specified purposes.[274] This responsibility also extends to harvest quotas for wildlife, limits as to location, methods, or seasons of harvesting wildlife and to prepare a wildlife management plan.[275] Any determination of the Board must be consistent with any international or domestic intergovernmental agreement in relation to a population or stock that migrates in or out of the settlement area.[276] Any recommendation regarding methods of harvesting must also be consistent with any international agreement in relation to humane trapping standards.[277]

---

[268] *Ibid.* s. 10.8.10.
[269] *Ibid.* s. 10.9.1.
[270] *Ibid.* s. 10.9.2.
[271] *Ibid.* s. 12.1.1.
[272] *Ibid.* s. 12.1.2.
[273] *Ibid.* s. 12.4.
[274] *Ibid.* s. 12.5.5.
[275] *Ibid.* s. 12.5.6.
[276] *Ibid.* s. 12.5.9.
[277] *Ibid.* s. 12.5.10.

Fishing Rights[278]

There is to be no harvesting of fish for commercial purposes in the Dogrib primary use area.[279] For licensing of commercial harvesting of fish within the settlement area, a Dogrib citizen, the Dogrib First Nation Government or its designate will be dealt with on the same basis as other licence applicants.[280]

Trees and Forest Management[281]

The Agreement places some exclusions on trees and forests situated on Dogrib lands.[282] A Dogrib citizen is entitled to harvest trees, including dead trees, throughout the settlement area at all times of the year for certain purposes.[283] Those purposes are:

- for firewood that is to be used for either personal or for community purposes;
- in order to construct or maintain camps used primarily by Dogrib citizens for the purposes of hunting, trapping and fishing;
- for making handicrafts;
- for use connected to traditional, cultural or medicinal activities;
- for the construction of boats and rafts, which will be used primarily by Dogrib citizens; and
- for the construction of houses for occupancy by Dogrib citizens and of buildings in a Dogrib community for community purposes.

The general right to harvest trees does not apply to timber grown on lands held in fee simple, or timber that is subject to an agreement for sale or surface lease, on lands being used for military purposes, or where treefelling would conflict with any activity carried out under an authorization or permit granted by government, such as a timber licence or permit, a forest management agreement or a land use permit.[284]

Commercial timber harvesting throughout the settlement area is subject to legislation.[285] Where commercial harvesting would significantly affect the harvesting of wildlife by Dogrib citizens, timber harvesting cannot be authorized without the consent of the Dogrib First Nation Government.[286] The North Slave Renewable Resources Board will have the final say as to

---

[278] *Ibid.* s. 10.7.
[279] *Ibid.* s. 10.7.1.
[280] *Ibid.* s. 10.7.2.
[281] *Ibid.* Chapter 13 "Trees and Forest Management."
[282] *Ibid.* s. 13.1.1.
[283] *Ibid.* s. 13.2.1.
[284] *Ibid.* s. 13.2.2.
[285] *Ibid.* s. 13.1.4.
[286] *Ibid.* s. 13.3.1.

whether consent is granted or not, where it is initially withheld.[287] If there is to be any change in the area of commercial harvesting in the settlement area, the Dogrib First Nation Government is to be consulted beforehand.[288]

The North Slave Renewable Resources Board may, in relation to the settlement area (but not in relation to a national park), make recommendations as to

- policies and rules relating to tree harvesting; and
- plans and policies for forest management that may include
  - o determination of areas of commercial harvesting of trees;
  - o the terms and conditions under which trees may be harvested;
  - o harvesting methods;
  - o allowable harvest rates; and
  - o reforestation measures; and
- provisions for management agreements with commercial harvesters and land owners.[289]

The government may consult the Board on any matter that affects forest management, but must consult the Board on new legislation respecting forest management, changes to land use policies or legislation where forest management may be impacted upon and on the development of policies respecting forest management research.[290]

Plants[291]

The Dogrib First Nation has the right to harvest plants throughout the settlement area at all seasons of the year for a limited range of purposes and subject to measures taken for conservation, land management within a community boundary, environmental protection and for public health and safety reasons.[292] The right to harvest plants applies to Dogrib citizens for the following activities:

- making handicrafts;
- use or consumption for food, medicinal or cultural purposes;
- for purposes ancillary to wildlife harvesting; and
- for trade or for giving to other Aboriginal persons for their own use or consumption.[293]

---

[287] *Ibid.* s. 13.3.3.
[288] *Ibid.* s. 13.3.2.
[289] *Ibid.* s. 13.4.1.
[290] *Ibid.* s. 13.4.2.
[291] *Ibid.* Chapter 14 "Plants."
[292] *Ibid.* s. 14.2.1.
[293] *Ibid.*

This right is further limited in its application to specific categories of land. The right to harvest plants does not apply to lands held in fee simple or subject to an agreement for sale or surface lease; where harvesting would conflict with any activity carried out under an authorization or permit granted by government, such as a timber licence or permit, a forest management agreement or land use permit; and lands reserved for military purposes.[294]

Similar to the timber harvesting provisions, no commercial harvest of plants in the Dogrib primary use area can be granted to any person without the consent of the Dogrib First Nation Government where such activity would significantly affect the harvest of plants by Dogrib citizens.[295] The North Slave Renewable Resources Board will have the final say as to whether consent is granted or not, where it is initially withheld.[296]

The Board is able to make recommendations respecting the management of plants in the settlement area (but not in relation to a national park) with respect to

- policies and rules relating to plant harvest; and
- plans and policies for plant management that may include
  - o determination of areas for commercial plant harvest;
  - o terms and conditions under which plant harvesting can occur; and
  - o provisions for management agreements with commercial harvesters and land owners.[297]

The territorial government may consult the Board on any matter that affects plant management, but must consult the Board on new legislation respecting plant management, changes to land use policies or legislation where plant forest management may be impacted upon and on the development of policies respecting plant management research.[298] The government can prohibit and regulate plant harvest in the settlement area, but must first consult with the Dogrib First Nation Government.[299] Any legislation that has the effect of regulating, but not prohibiting, plant harvesting in the settlement area must provide a preferential right of harvest in the primary use area to the Dogrib First Nation for the reasonable livelihood and societal needs of Dogrib citizens, particularly in relation to plant harvest for food, medicinal and cultural purposes and for purposes ancillary to wildlife harvesting.[300]

---

[294] *Ibid.* s. 14.2.2.

[295] *Ibid.* s. 14.3.2.

[296] *Ibid.* s. 14.3.3.

[297] *Ibid.* s. 14.4.1.

[298] *Ibid.* s. 14.4.2.

[299] *Ibid.* s. 14.5.1.

[300] *Ibid.* s. 14.5.2.

Water Rights[301]

The Dogrib First Nation has the exclusive right to use waters that are on or flow through Dogrib lands.[302] The Dogrib have the right to expect that the water quality, quantity and rate of flow will remain substantially unaltered, subject only to any authorized water use issued by the North Slave Land and Water Board, or any other competent water authority.[303] Legislation of general application and Dogrib laws will continue to regulate the right to use water in the settlement area, although no Dogrib citizen will be required to obtain a licence or permit for harvesting wildlife, or for heritage, cultural or spiritual purposes.[304] The federal government retains the right to use such water for fighting fires and for other conservation and research purposes.[305]

The right of the Dogrib First Nations to water on Dogrib lands cannot impede a right to use the water for commercial navigational purposes. Any person engaged in commercial activities is permitted to navigate upon any water that runs through Dogrib lands or waterfront provided that such navigation is incidental to commercial activities.[306] Notice is to be given to the Dogrib First Nation Government, although consent need not be obtained.[307]

Akaitcho Dene First Nations Framework Agreement

The Akaitcho Dene First Nations Framework Agreement was signed on 25 July 2000 as a result of longstanding complaints by the First Nations that Treaty No. 8 obligations had not been fulfilled. The federal and Northwest Territories governments agreed to resolve outstanding land, resource and governance issues through negotiations. The Northwest Territories government merely has observer status at negotiations. The Framework Agreement sets out the substance of the issues that are to be negotiated by the Akaitcho Dene and the federal government.

Among the issues to be negotiated are

- resource revenue sharing (including royalties);
- lands and waters;
- hunting, fishing, trapping and gathering;
- renewable and non-renewable resources; and
- treaty and Aboriginal rights.

---

[301] *Ibid.* Chapter 21 "Water Rights and Management."
[302] *Ibid.* s. 21.2.1.
[303] *Ibid.* s. 21.2.2.
[304] *Ibid.* s. 21.2.3.
[305] *Ibid.* s. 21.3.2.
[306] *Ibid.* s. 19.4.1.
[307] *Ibid.* s. 19.4.6.

The Akaitcho Dene First Nations incorporates the Dettah, Ndilo, Lutsel K'e and Deninu Kue people.

Deh Cho First Nations Framework Agreement

The federal government and the Deh Cho First Nations have entered into formal discussions concerning a settlement involving land, resources and a self-government agreement. The Framework Agreement and the Deh Cho Interim Measures Agreement were both signed on 23 May 2001. The Framework Agreement sets out the basis for negotiating a Final Agreement that will address a wide range of issues involving

- resource revenue sharing (including royalties);
- lands and waters;
- hunting, fishing, trapping and gathering;
- renewable and non-renewable resources; and
- treaty and Aboriginal rights.

It also encompasses the parties' objectives of establishing a Deh Cho Government, topics for negotiations, and the negotiation procedures and timetables.

Caselaw in the Yukon and Northwest Territories

In a 1991 case,[308] angling and fishing licence requirements imposed on members of the Han Owitch'in people by section 4 of the *Yukon Territory Fishery Regulations* infringed upon their constitutionally protected Aboriginal rights. The infringement was found by the court to be unjustifiable and of no force and effect in relation to Aboriginal People who fish for food.

---

[308] *R. v. Joseph*, [1991] N.Q.T.R. 263 (Y. Terr. Ct.).

Chapter 9

Alberta, Saskatchewan and Manitoba

The lands in Alberta, Saskatchewan and Manitoba were admitted into Canada in 1870 by imperial order in council that imposed an obligation to treat with the Aboriginal People in occupation with respect to compensation for their traditional lands.

The public lands in the provinces were not transferred to the administration of the provinces until 1930. Before then, the federal government entered into treaties for the surrender of Aboriginal title throughout the region and had begun setting apart reserves in fulfilment of the treaty promises. Prior to 1930, Aboriginal title to lands in the Prairie provinces was purportedly surrendered by the numbered treaties that were signed, apart from minor adhesions, between 1871 and 1908. Over 4.3 million acres were originally set aside for the purpose of reserving land for the Aboriginal parties to the treaties on the prairies pursuant to the numbered treaties. Not all such promises were fulfilled by 1930, and accordingly, conditions that sought to ensure their subsequent fulfilment were attached to the transfer of administration to the provinces.

In 1930, the Natural Resources Transfer Agreements came into force. The provinces of Manitoba, Alberta and Saskatchewan originally had no control over Crown lands and natural resources, which were retained by the federal government and administered for the benefit of Canada. The position of the Prairie provinces was, therefore, unlike that of the other provinces, which had enjoyed access to and the ability to exploit natural resources since Confederation. The Natural Resources Transfer Agreements, signed in 1929 and 1930, were designed to place the Prairie provinces in the same position as the other provinces in this respect. Those Agreements were subsequently confirmed by legislation and therefore form part of the Canadian Constitution. Provision was made in the Natural Resources Transfer Agreements to allow the obligations of Canada to the Aboriginal Peoples in the Prairie provinces to be met.

Paragraph 11 of the Manitoba agreement and paragraph 10 of the Alberta and Saskatchewan Agreements provide that the provinces shall set aside, out of unoccupied Crown lands, such areas for reserves as are necessary to enable Canada to fulfil its treaty obligations to the Aboriginal People of Canada. With regard to Aboriginal hunting, trapping and fishing, paragraph 13 of the Manitoba Agreement and paragraph 12 of the Alberta and Saskatchewan Agreements reads:

> In order to secure to the Indians of the Province the continuance of the supply of game and fish for their support and subsistence, Canada agrees that the laws respecting game in force in the Province from time to time shall apply to the Indians within the boundaries thereof, provided, however, that the said Indians shall have the right, which the Province hereby assures to them, of hunting, trapping and fishing game and fish for food at all seasons of the year on all unoccupied Crown lands and on any other lands to which the said Indians may have a right of access.[1]

The wildlife harvesting paragraph is recognition by Canada and the Prairie provinces that Aboriginal People are dependent on game and fish for food and thereby have special hunting, trapping and fishing rights. While it seeks to preserve those sources of food by making provincial game laws applicable to Aboriginal People who are not hunting, trapping or fishing for food or who are not carrying on those activities on unoccupied Crown lands or other lands to which they have a right to access,[2] it reaffirms that Aboriginal People are otherwise free to exercise their treaty rights to hunt, trap and fish at all seasons of the year. A primary purpose of the provision was to ensure that Aboriginal People had an ample supply of game for their subsistence by subjecting them to provincial gaming laws and by guaranteeing them the right to hunt and trap game for food during all seasons on lands to which they had a right of access.[3] Aboriginal People remain subject to federal legislation respecting migratory birds and sea-coast and inland fisheries, notwithstanding the game laws paragraph. Federal laws are not affected by this provision. This means that, while the paragraph purports to guarantee the right of Aboriginal People to fish for food, that guarantee is largely illusory because fisheries lie primarily within federal jurisdiction.

Some recent case law assists in understanding the practical implications of the Natural Resources Transfer Agreements. It is clear that provincial legislation cannot limit the Aboriginal right to hunt for food to particular seasons in the three provinces.[4] Moreover, a province may not attempt to circumvent its *Natural Resources Act*[5] by deeming certain land "occupied Crown lands" if such lands are open to hunting at any time during the year.[6]

---

[1] *Constitution Act, 1930* n.49.

[2] See *Cardinal v. A.G. Alta. per* Martland J. at p. 213.

[3] *R. v. Wesley*, 5 C.N.L.C. 540 at 547 (Alta. C.A.); *R. v. Sutherland, supra* note 10 in ch. 3 at 78.

[4] *R. v. Moosehunter*, [1981] 1 S.C.R. 282, 123 D.L.R. (3d) 95, 9 Sask. R. 149.

[5] *Alberta Natural Resources Act*, S.C. 1930, c. 3; *Saskatchewan Natural Resources Act*, S.C. 1930, c. 41; *Manitoba Natural Resources Act*, S.C. 1930, c. 29.

[6] *R. v. Sutherland, supra* note 10 in ch. 3.

Also the right to game and fish is for subsistence purposes or "for food" only. This is a notable restriction on Aboriginal hunting and fishing rights. Those Aboriginal People who by treaty, namely Treaties No. 6 and 8, had a right to fish and hunt for commercial purposes had that right restricted by the gaming provision. Treaties 6 and 8 granted hunting rights to Aboriginal People that entailed commercial aspects. However, the Natural Resources Transfer Acts restricted Aboriginal rights to sustenance hunting rights that can only be exercised on unoccupied Crown land.[7]

Consideration of the conflict between the treaty right to fish and hunt commercially, and the subsequent restriction of that right under the Natural Resources Transfer Agreements commenced with the case of *R. v. Horseman*.[8] The Supreme Court of Canada held in that case that the right of an Aboriginal man from Alberta to fish and hunt for commercial purposes had been "merged and consolidated" in paragraph 12 of the Alberta Natural Resources Transfer Agreement. Therefore, the treaty Indian commercial hunting and fishing rights were limited to the extent specified by the Agreement and had been partially extinguished by the Agreement (to which they were not a party). The court has considered the potential conflict between section 35 of the *Constitution Act, 1982* protecting Aboriginal treaty rights, and determined that it had no effect on the application of the provision in the Agreements.[9] The wildlife Acts in the Prairie provinces restricting Aboriginal People from selling game are, according to the courts, constitutional, notwithstanding the treaty guarantee of commercial dealings in game.

The theory of "merger and consolidation," formulated by Canadian courts, is problematic. As noted by Mr. Justice Kerans in the Alberta Court of Appeal in *R. v. Badger*,[10] the theory of consolidating treaty rights under the Natural Resources Transfer Agreements was reached without the participation of First Nations in the negotiation process. However, the "modified treaty right" principle was upheld in the Supreme Court.[11] Justices LaForest, L'Heureux-Dubé, Gonthier, Cory and Lacobucci held that the right guaranteed under Treaty No. 8 (the right to pursue their usual vocations of hunting, trapping and fishing) was subject to two limitations: a geographic limitation and the right of the government to make regulations for the purpose of conservation of natural resources. The court indicated that the effect of the Natural Resources Transfer Agreement in Alberta was not to extinguish and replace the right to hunt for food, but was merely intended to eliminate the

---

[7] Note that unoccupied Crown land is very hard to find south of the boundaries of Treaty 6.

[8] *R. v. Horseman, supra* note 18 in ch. 2.

[9] *R. v. Potts*, [1992] 3 C.N.L.R. 100 (Alta. Q.B.); *R. v. Little Wolf*, [1992] 3 C.N.L.R. 100 (Alta. Q.B.).

[10] (1993) 8 Alta L.R. (3rd) 354 (C.A.).

[11] *R. v. Badger, supra* note 19 in ch. 2.

treaty right to hunt for commercial purposes. Chief Justice Lamer and Mr. Justice Sopinka agreed with the majority of the court and stated further that, where the right to hunt for food is asserted, it is now solely derived from the relevant Natural Resources Transfer Agreement. The treaty can be relied upon only for the purpose of assisting in the interpretation of the Natural Resources Transfer Agreements. Otherwise, the treaty itself has no other legal significance.

The geographical limitation on the existing Aboriginal hunting right has been discussed in several cases. In Alberta in *R. v. Alexson,*[12] a grazing lease was held to constitute occupied lands under the *Public Lands Act.*[13] Other decisions indicate that Aboriginal People cannot exercise their right to hunt on unposted private land.[14] The Alberta Provincial Court has held that Treaty No. 8 conveys a right to hunt in national parks.[15] Moreover, the court has said that hunting on occupied lands is permitted where consent has been given, or if no objection has been made to hunting on such lands.[16]

In *R. v. Badger,* the court indicated that the geographical limitation on hunting should be based upon a concept of *visible* incompatible land use and must be a matter of fact that is to be considered on a case-by-case basis. The right to hunt did therefore not apply on lands that are settled, subject to mining or lumbering activities or other purposes. Additionally, the court held that the right to hunt for food was still subject to justifiable regulation. The provincial government's regulatory authority under the treaty and the Natural Resources Transfer Agreement did not extend beyond a capacity to legislate for the conservation of natural resources. In that case it was found that the public safety regulations that formed the first stage in a two-part licensing scheme did not infringe any Aboriginal or treaty rights. The regulations in question require hunters to take gun safety courses and pass certain tests designed to assess the individuals' hunting competency. The safety requirements under the legislation in question were designed to protect the welfare of all hunters, not just Aboriginal hunters, and was therefore not beyond the regulatory capacity of the provincial government. The court did hold, however, that the second step of the licensing scheme was a *prima facie* infringement of the Aboriginal right to hunt for food. The provincial government could not impose restrictions on the method, timing or extent of the use of that right. Licence conditions restricting hunting method, the kind and numbers of game, and determining a hunting season are and were inapplicable to Aboriginal hunters.

---

12   [1991] 4 C.N.L.R. 35.
13   *Public Lands Act,* c.P-30.
14   *R. v. Ominayak* (1989), A.R. 1 (Q.B.)
15   *R. v. Norn,* [1991] 3 C.N.L.R. 135 (Alta. Prov. Ct.).
16   *R. v. Little Bear,* [1985] 25 W.W.R. 577, 37 Alta. L.R. (2d) 223 (C.A.); *R. v. Bird,* [1984] 1 C.N.L.R. 114 (Sask. Q.B.).

The Natural Resources Transfer Agreements transferred all rights of fishery to the provinces, thus giving Manitoba, Saskatchewan and Alberta the same legislative control over proprietary interests in publicly owned fisheries as the other provinces. The Prairie provinces have all enacted legislation relating to the processing and marketing of fish. Those statutes apply to Aboriginal People insofar as they do not interfere with the right to fish for food. In several cases the courts have held that, although treaty Indians have a right to fish for food with a net, they must still get a licence from the relevant authority. The courts found in both instances that requiring licences was a valid conservation measure that regulated but did not extinguish the treaty right to fish and was therefore a reasonable limit on that right.[17]

If the provincial legislation is not covered by the paragraph in the Natural Resources Transfer Agreement, then its application to Aboriginal People would have to be determined on the basis of section 88 of the *Indian Act,* which makes provincial laws applicable to Aboriginal citizens, subject, *inter alia,* to the terms of any treaty. If the conclusion was drawn that commercial fishing rights of Aboriginal People were protected by the treaties, on this approach an argument can be made that the provincial fisheries legislation does not apply to Aboriginal Peoples to the extent that it conflicts with those rights.

In *R. v. Badger,* the court affirmed that the effect of the Natural Resources Transfer Agreement was to extend the right of Aboriginal People to hunt and fish for food. In the *R. v. Frank* case, an Aboriginal living on reserve land, created pursuant to land surrender under Treaty No. 6, was charged under the Alberta *Wildlife Act*[18] with killing a moose on land within the reserve. The Supreme Court held that the effect of the wildlife harvesting paragraph was to extend the area in which Aboriginal People could hunt and fish from their treaty area to the entire province. According to the Supreme Court, that right was not limited to Aboriginal People living in Alberta, but extended to all "Indians" within the boundaries of Alberta.[19]

In *R. v. Horseman,* the court held that the right to hunt and fish for food entails the right to hunt and fish for nourishment. In the case of *R. v. Strongquill,*[20] the accused was acquitted because he was hunting for food for his family of six adults and a number of grandchildren. Whether this principle can be extended to encompass other members of the band, or even the entire band, remains to be litigated for clarification.

---

[17] *R. v. Matchatis; R. v. Martin* (1990), 104 A.R. 33 (Q.B.), affm'd. 117 A.R. 281 (C.A.).
[18] R.S.A. 1970, c. 391.
[19] p. 298.
[20] [1953] 2 D.L.R. 264 (Sask. C.A.), 8 W.W.R. 247, 5 C.N.L.C. 567 (Sask. C.A.).

Treaties in the Prairie Provinces

Treaties No. 1 and 2

Treaties No. 1 and 2 were negotiated to permit settlers to move in and take possession of land around the Winnipeg region and to the west. Both treaties provided for land to be set aside as reserves for the First Nations in occupation of the land sought for surrender. The treaties covered most of southern Manitoba and the southeastern corner of Saskatchewan.

Treaty No. 1 was concluded on 3 August 1871 between the Crown and chiefs as representatives of the Chippewa and Swampy Cree First Nations. Although no mention is made of the continuing right of the Aboriginal People to hunt and fish on their traditional lands, among the items promised to the First Nations are "traps or twine," indicating that the treaty was concluded with the expectation that Aboriginal hunting and trapping rights would continue undisturbed.

Treaty No. 2 was concluded with the same ambiguous terms as Treaty No. 1 on 21 August 1871 between the Crown and the Chippewa First Nations in occupation of the area sought for surrender. Again, nowhere does the treaty refer to the Aboriginal right to hunt and fish on their traditional lands, and the only indication that both parties intended that that right continue was the Crown's promise to provide "traps or twine" in consideration for the surrender of traditional lands. It does appear from records of oral transactions during the course of the treaty negotiations that the Aboriginal right to hunt, fish and trap was intended to be preserved for the First Nation signatories on their traditional lands.[21] Another record shows that the Aboriginal People "wished to have two-thirds of the Province [Manitoba] as a reserve" and that "they have been led to suppose that large tracts of ground were to be set aside for them as hunting grounds, including timber lands of which they might sell the wood as if they were proprietors of the soil."[22]

Principles of treaty interpretation indicate that these assurances are as much a part of the treaty as the written articles.[23] The explicit assertions made by both Lieutenant-Governor Archibald and Commissioner Simpson prior to the signing of Treaty No. 1 are articulate and would certainly be interpreted as guaranteeing, not only fishing and hunting rights to the First Nations concerned, but possibly rights to take timber from a large portion of the surrendered territory. One statement indicates that the Aboriginal signatories

---

[21] See Morris, A., *supra* note 132 in ch. 4, p. 29; and *The Manitoban*, August 12, 1871, cited in McNeil, K., *Indian Hunting, Trapping and Fishing Rights in the Prairie Provinces of Canada*, University of Saskatchewan Native Law Centre, 1983.

[22] *Ibid.* at 33.

[23] *R. v. Taylor and Williams*, *supra* note 4 in ch. 2.

understood the treaty to mean that they would have exclusive rights to game in the surrendered land. Agent F. Ogletree (Agent of the Yellow Quill Band), in a report written to Inspector E. McCall in 1885, wrote in relation to Treaty No. 1 that, "when they agreed to let the Government have the land, they did not give them the Game."[24]

Chief Asham on behalf of the St. Peters Band expressed the same understanding in a letter to the superintendent-general of Indian Affairs in 1892:

> According to stipulations made at the Stone Fort [the location where Treaty No. 1 was signed]..., in the year 1871 although not written in the agreement, [it] was understood thoroughly and distinctly, in regard about game that no Indian was to be prohibited from killing or catching for his own purpose any kind of game all the year round.[25]

There is also evidence to suggest that the negotiators, in the right of the Crown, intended signatories of Treaty No. 2 to maintain similar rights. In a report to the secretary of state for the provinces, Treaty Commissioner Simpson wrote in reference to the treaty negotiations that "it was evident that the Indians of this part had no special demands to make, but having a knowledge of the former treaty, desired to be dealt with in the same manner and on the same terms as those adopted by the Indians of the Province of Manitoba (parties to Treaty No. 1)."[26]

McNeil (see note 21) suggests that the fact that the terms and conditions of Treaty No. 1 would have passed to First Nations affected by Treaty No. 2 by word of mouth, rather than by them having viewed a literary reproduction of the treaty. For that reason, it makes sense to take the view that the parties to Treaty No. 2 would have been aware of the oral assurances preserving their traditional use of the surrendered land, and would have concluded the treaty on that basis.

Rights to hunt, fish and trap are now exclusively dealt with by the Natural Resources Transfer Agreements. Treaty No. 1 and 2 Indians may have a claim to timber harvest on areas of the surrendered lands and also to *exclusive* hunting rights on that land.

---

[24] Public Archives of Canada, Indian Affairs, RG10 Black, Vol. 3692, File 14069.
[25] *Ibid.*
[26] Reproduced in Morris, A., *supra* note 132 in ch. 4, p. 41.

Treaty No. 3 – Between Her Majesty the Queen and the Salteaux Tribe of the Ojibeway Indians at the Northwest Angle on the Lake of the Woods with Adhesions

See discussion of this treaty in the section devoted to treaties in Ontario on page 89.

Treaty No. 4, No. 135 Qu'Appelle

Treaty No. 4, or the Qu'appelle Treaty, was signed by the Crown and the Cree and Saulteaux Tribes in September 1874. According to Moris's report, "[a]fter long and animated discussions the Indians, asked to be granted the same terms as were accorded to the Indians of Treaty Number Three." The Treaty Commissioners agreed to this request and the treaty was signed accordingly.

Treaty No. 4 unambiguously recognizes and protects the Aboriginal right to continue not only hunting and fishing but also trapping.

The case of *R. v. Lerat*[27] considered whether or not the treaty right to "pursue their avocations of hunting, fishing and trapping" entailed a right of treaty Indians to sell fish. The accused was charged with selling fish without a licence contrary to the *Saskatchewan Fishery Regulations* made pursuant to the *Fisheries Act* and contended that the treaty right to fish for food included the sale of fish or alternatively that he had a treaty right to fish commercially. The court held that it could not be concluded from a review of the evidence that the sale of fish was an integral part of the culture of the treaty Indians at the time that the treaty was concluded. Fishing for food was a common activity. However, selling fish to others was not. Therefore, the court determined that what was meant by "avocations" at the time of the treaty negotiations was the right to fish for food alone. The court indicated that selling fish to buy food or fishing supplies is not part of a logical extension of the treaty right. Moreover, a treaty right to sell fish does not mean that fish may be sold without a licence.[28] Government regulations motivated by public health and safety concerns will necessarily constrain the right to sell fish.

As discussed elsewhere, the Supreme Court has indicated that, although several of the numbered treaties, including Treaty No. 4, protected the right of the treaty Indians to hunt commercially, that right was subsequently removed by the Natural Resources Transfer Agreements in 1930.[29]

---

27 [1994] 2 C.N.L.R. 126 (Sask. Prov. Ct.).

28 *R. v. Sundown, supra* note 7 in ch. 2.

29 *R. v. Horseman, supra* note 18 in ch. 2; see also the Alberta Queen's Bench decision in *R. v. Littlewolf*, [1992] 3 C.N.L.R. 100 (Alta. Q.B.).

Treaty No. 5, No. 149A-F Lake Winnipeg

Treaty No. 5, or the Winnipeg Treaty, was signed in September 1875. The treaty was concluded by the Crown's representatives and the Saulteaux and the Swampy Cree Aboriginal societies.

In return for the surrender of all rights in the treaty land, the Crown promised to the treaty Indians that they

> [should have the] right to pursue their avocations of hunting and fishing throughout the tract surrendered...subject to such regulations as may from time to time be made by Her Government of Her Dominion of Canada, and saving and excepting such tracts as may from time to time be required or taken up for settlement, mining, lumbering or other purposes, by Her said Government of the Dominion of Canada, or by any of the subjects thereof duly authorized therefore by the said Government.

As mentioned above, although the courts recognize that this provision protected the right of the treaty Aboriginals to hunt, they have also indicated that this right is superseded by the Natural Resources Transfer Agreements, which abrogate that right. In this instance, records of discussions from the negotiation period reveal that the Treaty Commissioners had indicated to the Indians that their right to hunt commercially would be protected also.[30] If the Natural Resources Transfer Agreements were found to be unconstitutional (as we believe they should be), then this fact would be of importance to the Treaty No. 5 Indians who would then be in a position to assert a right to hunt and fish commercially on their traditional lands.

---

[30] See official letter from Lieutenant Governor Morris dated 11 October 1875 to the Honourable Minister of the Interior. Morris reports that "the Christian Chief stated that as they could no longer count on employment in boating for the Hudson's Bay Company, owing to the introduction of steam navigation, he and a portion of his band wished to migrate to Lake Winnipeg, where they could obtain a livelihood by farming and fishing. We explained why we could not grant them a reserve for that purpose at the Grassy Narrows as they wished, owing to the proposed Icelandic settlement there, but offered to allot them a reserve at Fisher River, about forty miles north of the Narrows, and this they accepted."

Many cases concerning Treaty No. 5 hunting rights and control by federal or provincial governments of hunting have ensued in the last decade.[31] Courts have consistently held that federal laws are held to be valid while the province cannot unilaterally extinguish treaty rights. In one case that is worth mentioning, that of *R. v. Flett*,[32] the Manitoba Queen's Bench held that the *Migratory Birds Act* was not a Regulation that could infringe upon treaty rights, but was actually a prohibition of Treaty No. 5 rights. The court subsequently found that Treaty No. 5 Aboriginals are not subject to the Act. The court cited a case that was argued under Treaty No. 6[33] to conclude that Aboriginal food hunting rights cannot be unilaterally extinguished. This case pre-dates *R. v. Sparrow* and is probably not a strong precedent. Two recent Manitoba cases – *R. v. Muswagon*[34] and *R. v. Daniels*[35] – also restrict application of the Regulations under the *Migratory Birds Convention Act*.

Treaty No. 6, No. 157A-H Fort Carlton, Fort Pitt

Treaty No. 6 was concluded between the Crown's representatives and the Plain and Wood Cree people in 1876 at Fort Carlton, Fort Pitt and Battle River.

In return for the surrender of all rights in the treaty land, the Crown promised to the treaty Indians that they

[should have the] right to pursue their avocations of hunting and fishing throughout the tract surrendered as hereinbefore described, subject to such regulations as may from time to time be made by Her Government of Her Dominion of Canada, and saving and excepting

---

[31] See for example *R. v. McGillivary*, [1990] 1 C.N.L.R. 124 (Sask. Q.B.), reversed [1991] 3 C.N.L.R. 130 (C.A.) that regulation of hunting is permitted by the wording of Treaty No. 5; *R. v. Daniels*, [1990] 1 C.N.L.R. 108 (Man. Prov. Ct.) where the court held that an Aboriginal had exceeded the limits of the "hunt for food" provision and that no historical evidence existed to suggest that he could justify the number of birds he had harvested and that therefore the *Migratory Birds Act* that specified a daily limit was not an unreasonable conservation measure; *R. v. Muswagon*, [1992] 4 C.N.L.R. 159 (Man. Q.B.) in this case the court relied on *R. v. Flett* in which case it was held that the *Migratory Birds Convention Act* did not actually regulate the Aboriginal right to hunt, but rather extinguished that right and was therefore unconstitutional. Note that *Flett* and *Muswagon* predate the decision in *Sparrow* which lays out the circumstances under which the Crown can infringe upon Aboriginal rights and is therefore not strong precedent. This case also supports inherent rights for the Métis of the Prairie provinces; *R. v. McPherson*, [1992] 4 C.N.L.R. 144 (Man. Prov. Ct.) involving the rights of the Métis to hunt moose. The court held that the legislation prohibiting moose hunting out of season was an infringement on their right to do so and that the Crown must consult with the Aboriginal and Métis people prior to the enactment of such regulations and give proper priority to their needs in setting season dates.

[32] [1989] 4 C.N.L.R. 128, [1989] 6 W.W.R. 166 (Man. Q.B.) leave to appeal to the C.A. refused [1991] 1 C.N.L.R. 140.

[33] *R. v. Arcand*, [1989] 3 W.W.R. 635, 65 Alta. L.R. (2d) 326, [1989] 2 C.N.L.R. 110 (Q.B.).

[34] [1992] 4 C.N.L.R. 159 (Man. Q.B.).

[35] [1990] 1 C.N.L.R. 109 (Man. Prov. Ct.).

such tracts as may from time to time be required or taken up for settlement, mining, lumbering or other purposes by Her said Government of the Dominion of Canada, or by any of the subjects thereof duly authorized therefor by the said Government.

Treaty No. 6 has been considered on various occasions since 1935. Except for the *R. v. Arcand* case,[36] federal legislation has been held to validly abrogate treaty rights. The courts have held that even provincial laws of general application that limit or restrict treaty rights may be valid because the treaty acknowledged that such rights were to be subject to governmental regulation. The right to hunt for food is protected, however, from diminishing provincial legislation by virtue of the Natural Resources Transfer Agreements.[37]

A court has confirmed that the Prairie treaties containing both the words "vocation" and "avocation" protect the right of the signatory First Nations to hunt, trap and fish for commercial purposes, but that the Natural Resources Transfer Agreements have, in effect, gone proxy for treaty provisions guaranteeing hunting and fishing rights over ceded lands and in so doing have limited the commercial aspects to these activities.[38]

Venne's insightful article investigates the understanding of the First Nations who were parties to Treaty No. 6.[39] Her article is written in a narrative style and incorporates interviews that she conducted with chiefs of the Cree society who have been educated by oral tradition about the circumstances surrounding the Treaty No. 6 negotiations. Venne's study focuses on two issues: the negotiating power of the indigenous men who negotiated Treaty No. 6 and the oral basis for interpreting treaties.

Leading up to the signing of Treaty No. 6 in 1876, Aboriginal People residing in the treaty area had heard that the Hudson's Bay Company had sold land to the Crown. The reaction of the indigenous people was that of astonishment and disbelief as they had never recognized that the company could exercise jurisdiction over them. As a result, many First Nations actively sought to prevent surveyors and other non-Aboriginal People from coming onto their land in an attempt to maintain control and jurisdiction over those lands.

---

[36] See *R. v. Arcand*.

[37] See *R. v. Littlewolf; R. v. Potts*, [1992] 3 C.N.L.R. 100 (Alta. Q.B.) reversing [1991] 1 C.N.L.R. 142 (Alta. Prov. Ct.) appeal refused 4 Alta. L.R. (3d) 287 (C.A.), application for leave to appeal to S.C.C. [1992] 4 C.N.L.R. vi. *R. v. Gladue*, [1994] 2 C.N.L.R. 101 (Alta. Q.B.).

[38] *R. v. Horseman*, *supra* note 18 in ch. 2, vi.

[39] Venne, S., "Understanding Treaty 6: An Indigenous Perspective," in Asch, M., ed., *Aboriginal and Treaty Rights in Canada*, UBC Press, Vancouver, 1997.

Venne makes some interesting points in relation to the female Cree and their relationship to the treaty and its negotiations.[40] In Cree tradition, Venne suggests, women hold a unique position. In Cree society, women did not sign treaties for a reason. The reason is not that woman experienced an inferior status; in fact, women in Cree society can be said to hold a special and unique position, particularly in relation to land. Women have what Elders describe as a "spiritual connection" to the land. As women were given the power to create, it is men that are to provide assistance to them. Man is therefore a helper to woman, not woman to man, as is commonly inferred by Eurocentric historians who interpret the absence of female signatures on the treaty as female subservience. Due to the female's ability to create, it is she who owns the land. It is the man's right to use the land, and it is his responsibility to protect and guard it, but ownership of the land resides with women.

Venne's research suggests that this basic Cree understanding placed limits on the negotiating power of the chiefs. Because ownership of the land always resides with Cree females, the chiefs could only *share* the lands. They did not own the land, such that the land could either be sold or surrendered. As mentioned elsewhere, Canadian courts have been more than willing to read into the treaty text oral promises that were made at the time of treaty negotiations and also to take into consideration the Aboriginal understanding of the treaty's meaning. Whether or not the court will allow oral promises and understandings to override the actual text of the treaty has not yet been determined.

Treaty No. 7, No. 163 Blackfeet

Treaty No. 7 merely guarantees the Aboriginal right to "pursue their vocations of hunting." The right to pursue the right to hunt under Treaty No. 7 is restricted to lands that have not been taken up for "settlement, mining, trading or other purposes." The protected right is subject to regulations that may be enacted by the federal government.

One avenue for challenge of Treaty No. 7 may be that the treaty Indians have an exclusive right to harvest vegetation in the treaty area. Some evidence suggests that this was one promise made to certain First Nations that falls outside the scope of the Natural Resources Transfer Agreements:

> [T]he Stoney negotiators were given verbal promises that all benefits in Treaty Six would be understood to be included in Treaty Seven...Certainly we requested and understood that we had been promised, the continuation of our traditional life of hunting, trapping, fishing, and gathering berries, plants and herbs in our traditional hunting grounds.[41]

---

[40] *Ibid.* p. 187.
[41] Snow, Chief J., *These Mountains are our Sacred Places*, Samuel Stevens, Toronto, 1977, p. 33.

Controversy surrounds Treaty No. 7 and some evidence suggests that the Treaty No. 7 First Nations agreed to something other than the text containing the treaty's terms.[42]

Treaty No. 8, No. 428

Note that this treaty has been discussed in the section devoted to treaties in British Columbia (see pages 117-123).

In many cases, the treaties provide that Aboriginal hunting, fishing and trapping rights are to be subject to government regulation. Treaties No. 3 to 8 and Treaty No. 10 all contain such a provision. A report of the Commissioners who negotiated Treaty No. 8 indicates the type of government regulation that would be permitted:

> Our Chief difficulty was the apprehension that the hunting and fishing privileges were to be curtailed. The provision in the treaty under which ammunition and twine is to be furnished went far in the direction of quieting the fears of the Indians, for they admitted that it would be unreasonable to furnish the means of hunting and fishing if laws were to be enacted which would make hunting and fishing so restricted as to render it impossible to make a livelihood by such pursuits. But over and above the proposition, we had to solemnly assure them that only such laws as to hunting and fishing as were in the interest of the Indians and were found necessary in order to protect the fish and fur-bearing animals would be made, and that they would be as free to hunt and fish after the treaty as they would be if they never entered into it.[43]

This passage was cited with approval by Mr. Justice Johnson in *R. v. Sikyea*. There is evidence that these types of assurances were given to the Aboriginal groups at the time the other numbered treaties were also negotiated.

Upon the First Nations' understanding, no government regulation would be allowed that detracted from their right to hunt and fish on lands not used for an inconsistent purpose; rather, that only regulations that preserved and bolstered those rights would be permitted by the treaty. Mr. Justice McGillivray handed down a decision in relation to the regulation provision in Treaty No. 7. He stated:

---

[42] Price, R., *The Spirit of the Alberta Indian Treaties*, Institute for Research on Public Policy, Ottawa, 1979, and Treaty 7 Elders et. al., *The True Spirit and Original Intent of Treaty 7*, McGill-Queen's University Press, Montreal and Kingston, 1996.

[43] Report Of Commissioners For Treaty No. 8 Winnipeg, Manitoba, 22nd September, 1899.

It is true that Government regulations in respect of hunting are contemplated in the treaty but considering the treaty in its proper setting I do not think that any of the makers of it could by any stretch of the imagination be deemed to have contemplated a day when the Indians would be deprived of an unfettered right to hunt game of all kinds for food on unoccupied Crown land.[44]

Ross and Sharvit suggest that Alberta's current regulation of allocation and management of timber harvesting rights over traditional lands of the Cree and Dene Nations are an unjustifiable infringement on the Aboriginal People belonging to those societies' right to hunt, trap and fish. Treaty No. 8, encompassing the largest area of land of the numbered treaties, covers a vast area of land within the boreal forest. Since the 1970s and the advent of utilizing aspen trees to manufacture pulp and paper, there has been a significant increase in the volume of timber allocations in the boreal forests of Alberta. Vast areas inhabited by the Cree and Dene are now subject to forest tenures, with the timber supplying five pulp and paper mills constructed between 1993 and 1998. Accordingly, much concern has been expressed over the impact that such rapid depletion of the boreal forests has had on the constitutionally protected treaty rights of the Aboriginal People in the province.

Ross and Sharvit argue that the rapid depletion of timber in the boreal forests of Alberta can be challenged as a breach of the terms of Treaty No. 8. The treaty, as discussed earlier, grants the Cree and Dene societies the right to gain their subsistence through harvesting activities – hunting, trapping and fishing. Given that such rights are contingent upon the capacity of the environment to support species that may be harvested, the excessive lumbering occurring in the Treaty No. 8 region could be the subject of a challenge. As the authors indicate, the Aboriginal signatories did not agree to permit the government to promote the depletion, degradation or destruction of natural resources and ecosystems, or for the government to put the interests of one group (industrialists) over the interests of the Aboriginal parties. Therefore, a fundamental treaty right is jeopardized by provincial government forestry policy and timber allocations in the treaty region. Provincial laws could be subjected to a justification test under section 35(1) of the *Constitution Act, 1982* to determine whether the rights guaranteed to the Cree and Dene people under Treaty No. 8 are being unjustifiably infringed upon. Based on the test of justification established by *R. v. Sparrow*, the authors conclude that the provincial forestry laws are unconstitutional infringements upon Aboriginal treaty rights.

---

[44] *R. v. Rocher* [1985] 2 C.N.L.R. 151.

Treaty No. 10

Treaty No. 10 was negotiated by the Crown and the Chipewyan and Cree tribes in 1906. The Aboriginal parties agreed to roughly the same terms as the parties to the prior numbered treaties. Harvesting rights, including an exclusive right to trap, were promised on the surrendered territory, except on lands used for mining, forestry, settlement, trading or "other purposes" and in accordance with federal regulations.

A recent case heard in the Saskatchewan Court of Appeal dealt with the Treaty No. 10 guarantees.[45] The case was on appeal from a decision of the Saskatchewan Queen's Bench as to the extent of the right to uncontrolled and unlimited access to the surrendered lands by any means for the purpose of hunting, trapping, fishing and food gathering. In this case the accused was found hunting and camping on an area of land known as the Cold Lake Air Weapons Range that was acquired by National Defence Canada in 1953 for military defence purposes. The treaty itself guaranteed hunting and trapping rights throughout the surrendered land. The Saskatchewan Natural Resources Transfer Agreement ensures that the right to hunt, trap and fish for food is guaranteed at all seasons of the year on all "unoccupied Crown lands and on any other lands to which the said Indians may have a right to access." The Saskatchewan Court of Appeal found that there is no need for there to be obvious and visible signs of occupation for a finding that the land is occupied.[46] The law in Saskatchewan is that, when the Crown in the right of the province appropriates or sets aside certain areas for special purposes, such areas can no longer be deemed to be "unoccupied Crown lands." In coming to this conclusion, the court ignored the recent Supreme Court of Canada decision in *R. v. Badger* that held that for Crown land to be "occupied" there would have to be "visible and obvious incompatible land use." In the words of the unanimous court:

> I do not believe that the Supreme Court of Canada when adopting the term "visible, incompatible use" in *Badger*, intended that the term would be applied to determine when Crown land is occupied. If Crown land is being actively used and if the use to which it is being put is incompatible with hunting, the land must objectively be seen to be occupied.

Accordingly the Aboriginal appellants had their conviction upheld. This decision may be subject to further appeals.

---

[45] *R. v. Catarat*, (2001) S.K.C.A. 50.

[46] Relying on *Rex v. Smith*, [1935] 2 W.W.R. 433 (Sask. C.A.); *R. v. Strongquill*, (1953) 8 W.W.R. (N.S.) 247; *R. v. Sutherland, supra* note 10 in ch. 3; *R. v. Mousseau*, [1980] 2 S.C.R. 89.

General Comment about the Treaties of the Prairie Provinces

There is a strong suggestion that, since the Supreme Court ruling in *R. v. Delgamuukw*, the Prairie treaties are challengeable on the basis that the Aboriginal parties did not share the understanding of the treaty's terms that the Crown did based on oral evidence.[47]

---

[47] Flanagan, T., "The Effect Upon Alberta Land Claims", pp. 173 – 182, in Lippert O. (ed), *Beyond the Nass Valley: National Implications of the Supreme Court's* Delgamuukuw *Decision,* and Zlotkin, N., "Interpretation of the Prairie Treaties," pp. 183 – 195, The Fraser Institute, Vancouver, 2000.

Chapter 10

Alberta

Alberta is the only province to have enacted legislation dealing with the Métis people. The legislation, which provides for both self-government and for a land base for the Métis people, was negotiated by the Alberta provincial government and the Alberta Federation of Métis Settlements. Tenure to the lands conveyed to the Métis people is protected by the *Constitution of Alberta Amendment Act.*[1]

In relation to oil and gas, in 1989 an Accord was signed by the eight Métis settlements and the Alberta provincial government that gave the Métis Settlements General Council the right to negotiate royalty and participation rights on new oil and gas developments. The settlements were then in agreement that a corporation be created to take control of the collective interest held by the General Council. The rights were thus transferred to a corporation owned equally by the eight Métis settlements by the name of Resco Oil and Gas Ltd.

The objective of Resco Oil and Gas Ltd. is to make sure that the settlements receive the most possible long-term benefit from exploitation of the oil and gas reserves under Métis settlement land. In keeping with this objective, Resco performs three basic functions on behalf of the settlements. First, the company negotiates the royalty and participation aspect of new oil and gas projects. Second, it participates by providing the settlements with their own oil company to work as a business partner with other companies drilling oil and gas wells on the settlements. Third, it makes it possible for the settlements who work together to find financing, evaluate prospects and do the other things needed to take a lead role in developing the oil and gas under the Métis land. The right to develop minerals on Métis settlements lands by an operator is governed by a Co-Management Agreement made between the Minister of Energy, the eight Métis settlements and the Métis Settlements General Council.[2]

---

[1] *Constitution of Alberta Amendment Act*, S.A. 1990, c. C-22.2.
[2] Included as Schedule 3 of the *Métis Settlements Act*, S.A. 1990, c. M-14.3.

Mineral Potential on Indian Reserve Lands in Alberta[3]

The Mineral Potential of Indian Reserve Lands report compiled by the Department of Indian and Northern Affairs Canada[4] in Alberta provides overall rating measures of the economic mineral possibilities of each reserve as a whole, on a scale of low/moderate/good. Factors that affect this rating are the size of the reserve, the location with respect to markets, transportation, access, value and type of commodity, social and cultural barriers to mining on certain lands and areas, marketability of a commodity at any given time and other differentials.

The following rating applies in Alberta:

- 73 reserves were given a low rating;
- 20 reserves were given a moderate rating; and
- 7 were given a good rating.

The report indicates that 3 reserves have at least one commodity that has potential for development. At the time of this report, of the total number of reserves, 13 have already surrendered their minerals in some way.

Métis Agreement

The Métis Settlement Act

The *Alberta Métis Settlement Act*[5] was proclaimed on 1 November 1990. The Act establishes Settlement Corporations and a General Council as legal entities. The Settlement Councils deal with matters relating to local government and the needs of each community, while the General Council deals with issues that affect the settlements collectively.

Métis Settlement Land

The Act transferred to the Métis people approximately 1.25 million acres of settlement land. Rights and interests in Métis settlement land can be created in three ways:

- under the *Métis Settlement Act* or any other Act;
- under a General Council Policy; or

---

[3] See Department of Indian and Northern Affairs Canada, online: <http://www.ainc-inac.gc.ca/ntr/alb_e.html>.
[4] Keep in mind that although this site was last updated on the 30 April 2001, the report was actually completed in 1991.
[5] *Métis Settlements Act.*

- under a settlement bylaw that is passed in accordance with a General Council Policy.

Where an interest in land exists that is less than the fee simple estate held by the settlement or a settlement member, it may not be charged, mortgaged or given as security except in accordance with a General Council Policy.[6] Such land is further exempt from seizure or sale under court order, writ of enforcement or other process, again except as provided by a General Council Policy.[7]

Mining and Minerals

The Act provides for the making of agreements in relation to resource access and exploitation on Métis settlement land – specifically, the Act devotes Schedule 3 to the Act in its entirety to the process for negotiating "Co-Management Agreements." The Alberta Métis Settlements Accord[8] contained provisions regarding the co-management of exploration for and development of minerals, including provisions regarding the issue of Resource Agreements in relation to those minerals. The Act therefore lays out procedural guidelines for the Minister and other parties to follow in relation to negotiating such agreements.

Under Article 2 of Schedule 3, section 201, a Settlement Access Committee is to be appointed for each Settlement Area, as defined under the Act. Initially, the Minister is obliged to make a "Notice of Public Offering" in order to solicit bids to acquire resource agreements for rights in any of the minerals on Métis land. Where a request has been made to the government that a Notice of Public Offering be posted (that is, made available to the public) in respect of a particular mineral, the Minister is under an obligation to contact the affected Settlement Access Committee within four days.[9] Under section 302 of the Act, the affected Settlement Access Committee is obliged to respond to the making of a posting request within 42 days of the Minister's referral of the request to the affected Métis Settlement Access Committee.[10] The Settlement Access Committee can recommend that the Minister not post the public offer to solicit bids, or that the minerals that are the subject of the request be posted subject to certain terms and conditions.[11] Accordingly, under section 303 of Schedule 3 to the Act, an affected Métis Settlement Access Committee has the capacity to recommend terms and conditions under which a development can take place concerning the

---

[6] *Ibid.* s. 100.
[7] *Ibid.* s. 101.
[8] 1 July 1989.
[9] *Métis Settlement Act*, s. 301.
[10] *Ibid.* s. 302.
[11] *Ibid.*

environmental, socio-cultural and land use impacts, and employment and business opportunities of exploration for and development of the minerals. The committee may also include terms and conditions concerning reservation to the General Council of an overriding royalty or participation option or both in respect to the development.

Even where the affected Settlement Access Committee has flatly refused the posting request, the Minister can still grant rights in minerals contained on Métis lands to individuals or corporations.[12] However, the Métis General Council and Settlement Council and the Métis occupants retain the right to deny access to those rights holders to Métis land.[13] Ultimately then, the Métis people can control mineral exploitation on their land by withholding consent for the rights holder to access Métis land. The Minister's capacity to grant rights to resources where the Settlement Access Committee has recommended against the posting request is conditional upon disclosure to the grantee.[14]

Where the Settlement Access Committee has agreed to permit the posting, but has recommended that certain terms and conditions be attached to the posting, the Minister is under an obligation to comply with the committee's recommendations. Upon preparing the Notice of Public Offering, incorporating the committee's recommended terms and conditions, he or she must present the Notice of Public Offering to the committee for its approval prior to posting the offering publicly.[15] The Minister can, at any stage, unilaterally decide not to post the Notice of Public Offering,[16] and can also decide to include terms and conditions recommended by the Crown Mineral Disposition Review Committee appointed under the *Land Surface Conservation and Reclamation Act.*[17]

The General Council and the affected Settlement Corporation are to appoint a representative who will consult with potential bidders.[18]

Two days after the public offering, the Minister is to provide the General Council and the affected Settlement Corporation with details of the appropriate bidder – the appropriate bidder is whoever has offered the highest bonus payment and whose bid meets the requirement of the soliciting Notice of Public Offer.[19] Further negotiation between the General Council and Settlement Corporation and the bidder is permitted, but only in respect of the

---

[12] *Ibid.* s. 304.
[13] *Ibid.* see Division 7 "Access to Patented Land."
[14] *Ibid.* s. 304.
[15] *Ibid.* s. 306.
[16] *Ibid.* s. 308.
[17] Incorporated by the *Environmental Protection and Enhancement Act*, Chapter E-13.3.
[18] *Métis Settlement Act*, ss. 401-403.
[19] *Ibid.* s. 501.

topics identified in the terms and conditions included in the Notice of Public Offer.[20] On the basis of those negotiations, the Métis organizations can then recommend that the bidder's bid be rejected, or that the parties have entered into a Development Agreement.[21]

Bylaws – Land and Resource Use

Under the Act, Métis Settlement Councils are permitted to make bylaws. Under section 18, the Settlement Councils are permitted to make bylaws concerning planning, land use and development. This includes the ability to establish a general plan for land use and development in a settlement area, and to prohibit, regulate and control the use and development of land and buildings in the settlement area.

Bylaws can also be made in accordance with General Council Policies. The council is permitted to make general policies in relation to certain activities.[22] General policies must be agreed to by all eight Settlement Councils and are still subject to veto by the Minister.[23] Accordingly, bylaws can be enacted by the Settlement Councils in relation to the following land use activities:

- prohibiting persons who are not settlement members from hunting, trapping, gathering or fishing in the settlement area;
- prescribing the terms and conditions under which a person or class of person is permitted to occupy, hunt, trap, gather or fish in the settlement area;
- prescribing the manner in which and the terms and conditions subject to which a settlement member may acquire
  o the right to trap, hunt or gather in the settlement area;
  o the right to fish in a marsh, pond, lake, stream or creek in the settlement area and the circumstances under which that right may be suspended, limited or revoked;
- as to the use by settlement members of a part of the land allocated for occupation by a Settlement Council in respect of which no person has the exclusive right of occupation;
- respecting the cutting of timber on all or part of the settlement area, including
  o the amount of timber that may be cut,
  o the disposition of the timber cut,

---

[20] *Ibid.* s. 502.
[21] *Ibid.*
[22] *Ibid.* see s. 222.
[23] *Ibid.*

  o the disposition of the proceeds of the sale of the timber cut, and

  o prohibiting the cutting of timber otherwise than in accordance with the bylaws;

- permitting the Settlement Council to engage in certain activities, including engaging in commercial activities.

The Settlement Councils can enforce any type of regime, for example, a licensing scheme, to facilitate operation of the bylaws.[24]

The capacity of the Settlement Councils is restricted by the requirement that consistency exist between the bylaws and provincial laws and regulations. Bylaws made under the Act be of no effect if they are inconsistent with the laws and regulations of Alberta, to the extent of that inconsistency.[25] The only exception to this rule is that bylaws relating to a General Council Policy on hunting, trapping, fishing or gathering that are inconsistent with provincial laws and regulations will nonetheless be valid and of full effect.[26]

Fishing is also dealt with in Part 5 of the Act. Any fishing rights granted in the *Alberta Act* to the Métis people are subject to the federal *Fisheries Act* and associated regulations.[27] Fishing in the Métis settlement area is subject to residential status or persons authorized to fish under the settlement bylaws.[28] The Act also provides that a settlement member who is resident in a settlement area may fish for sustenance in the settlement area or in any watercourse or body of water that adjoins the settlement area.[29] Settlement members are entitled to fish for sustenance at any time of the year, except spawning, and can do so for their own sustenance and also for his or her immediate family.[30] The Act expressly states that settlement members are not authorized by this provision to fish for the purpose of selling, dealing or trafficking in fish.[31] However, at the request of a Settlement Council, the Minister of Environmental Protection may authorize the council to issue Métis Commercial Fishing Licences to settlement members and members of adjacent settlements (with or without conditions) for commercial purposes.[32] The Minister is, furthermore, under an obligation to set aside a portion of the total designated catch for settlement members.[33]

---

[24] *Ibid.*
[25] *Ibid.* s. 72(1).
[26] *Ibid.*
[27] *Ibid.* s. 130.
[28] *Ibid.* s. 131.
[29] *Ibid.* s. 132(1).
[30] *Ibid.*
[31] *Ibid.* s. 132(2).
[32] *Ibid.* s. 133(1).
[33] *Ibid.* s. 133(2).

Chapter 11

Manitoba

Mineral Potential on Indian Reserve Lands in Manitoba[1]

The Mineral Potential of Indian Reserve Lands report compiled by the Department of Indian and Northern Affairs Canada[2] in Manitoba provides overall rating measures of the economic mineral possibilities of each reserve as a whole, on a scale of low/moderate/good. Factors that affect this rating are the size of the reserve, the location with respect to markets, transportation, access, value and type of commodity, social and cultural barriers to mining on certain lands and areas, marketability of a commodity at any given time and other differentials.

The following rating applies in Manitoba:

- 65 reserves were given a low rating;
- 27 reserves were given a moderate rating; and
- 12 were given a good rating.

The report indicates that 15 reserves have at least one commodity that has potential for development. At the time of this report, of the total number of reserves, 14 had already surrendered their minerals in some way.

Treaties of Manitoba

- Treaty No. 1
- Treaty No. 2
- Treaty No. 3
- Treaty No. 5

These treaties are discussed in the section "Treaties in the Prairie Provinces" on pages 194-197.

---

[1] See Department of Indian and Northern Affairs Canada, online: <http://www.ainc-inac.gc.ca/ntr/man_e.html>.

[2] Keep in mind that although this site was last updated on the 30 April 2001, the report was actually completed in 1991.

No. 124

This 1817 treaty was concluded by the Cree and the Chippewa of the Red River District of Manitoba and the Crown. The Cree and Chippewa people agreed that, in return for an annuity and certain goods that would be payable by the Crown, they would adhere to a promise that "the traders hitherto established upon any part of the...tract of land shall not be molested in the possession of the lands which they have already cultivated."

There is no mention of resource or harvestation rights and there has been no court consideration of this treaty.

A recent case dealt with a treaty Aboriginal who was convicted for using a light at night to hunt.[3] The case involved an application for a declaration that sections 71(1) and 78(2) of the Manitoba *Wildlife Act*[4] be declared null and void, or in the alternative that these sections be declared of no force with respect to the applicants. These sections permitted a resources officer to seize items used for night hunting and any wildlife proceeds of night hunting, at the time of apprehending those carrying out night hunting. Turner argued that these provisions were contrary to fiduciary obligations of the province to treaty Aboriginals, that the provisions discriminated against Aboriginal People, and that the government was obligated to consult with the First Nations prior to enacting wildlife legislation. The court found that Turner's case failed on all grounds.

The court held that the fiduciary obligation only applies where the government breaches actual treaty rights. This case was found not to be about breach of treaty rights. Mr. Justice Wright rejected the argument that the effect of the laws was disproportionate impact upon Aboriginal hunters and non-Aboriginal hunters, agreeing instead with the respondent's argument that the *Wildlife Act* applies equally to both Aboriginal and non-Aboriginal People alike. Wright J. noted that the law in question did not remove the right to hunt. It simply imposed restrictions, applicable to everyone, for breach of the law. Thus, so long as the law does not impact or interfere with a treaty right, Aboriginal hunters are subject to the authority of that law. Moreover, the government of Manitoba is only required to consult with First Nations people when a pending law is likely to impinge upon treaty rights.

Land Set Aside by Executive Act

In the 1860s the members of the Dakota (Sioux) Tribe of the United States took refuge in the southern areas of what is now Manitoba and Saskatchewan. They asked that reserve land be set aside by the federal government for their benefit. The Crown agreed and set apart land, but did not recognize any claim

---

[3]   *Turner et. al. v. Government of Manitoba*, [2000] M.J. No. 308.
[4]   R.S.M. 1987, c. W130.

of the Dakota to lands in Canada and did not enter into any treaties with them. Negotiations are, however, finally underway between the Sioux Valley Dakota Nations and the federal and provincial governments.

The Sioux Valley Dakota Nation

The Sioux Valley Dakota Nation and Canada entered into a Framework Agreement in July 1991 agreeing to negotiate in respect of Sioux Valley Dakota Oyate government arrangements. An Agreement In Principle was reached on 2 March 2001 between the Sioux Valley and the Canadian government, and an accompanying Agreement In Principle was concluded between Canada, Manitoba and the Sioux Valley people.

The governments of Canada and Manitoba recognized that the Sioux Valley Aboriginal People had a form of government prior to displacement by settlement in Manitoba and the purpose of the negotiations was to restore the Sioux Valley Dakota Oyate Government. The common objective is to establish a framework for the exercise of law-making powers by Sioux Valley, which would effectively shift the primary political and financial accountability of Sioux Valley Government away from the Minister of Indian and Northern Affairs to the Sioux Valley people.

The Final Agreement, expected in up to two years, will provide the Sioux Valley Government with the ability to make laws on a range of issues that are set out in the Agreement In Principle. The Final Agreement will give the Sioux Valley Government a range of law-making powers relating to the land belonging to the Sioux Valley Dakota Nation.

Natural Resources[5]

The Sioux Valley Government will, upon conclusion of the Final Agreement, be given jurisdiction with respect to natural resources on, or forming part of Sioux Valley lands to varying degrees depending on the resource in question. Generally speaking, that right extends to

- resource use planning, management and conservation;
- granting and transfer of rights and interests in natural resources;
- access to Sioux Valley Lands for the purpose of harvesting, extracting or removing natural resources;
- extraction, removal and disposition on Sioux Valley Lands of natural resources;
- taking of rights and interests in natural resources without the consent of the holder thereof; and

---

[5] *The Sioux Valley Dakota Nation Comprehensive Agreement In Principle*, s. 21.0.

- providing for a system for the registration and recording of rights and interests in natural resources.

The Agreement In Principle states that jurisdiction does not extend to the transfer or assignment of a non-Sioux Valley citizen of any Aboriginal or treaty rights of members of the Sioux Valley recognized and affirmed by subsection 35(1) of the *Constitution Act, 1982* in natural resources on Sioux Valley lands.

Mines and Minerals[6]

The Sioux Valley also has the power to make laws relating to the management and regulation of activities in respect of mining. Laws can be made with respect to prospecting for, extraction, development, refining, disposition and trade, barter or sale of mines and minerals on or under Sioux Valley lands. Minerals means both precious and base, and includes sand and gravel.[7] The right to make laws in relation to minerals and mining does not, however, extend to "atomic energy" and "prescribed substances" as defined in the *Nuclear Safety and Control Act;*[8] or to those matters dealt with in the *Explosives Act.*[9] A Sioux Valley law enacted under this section will be deemed to override any applicable federal or provincial law to the extent of the inconsistency.[10]

Oil and Gas[11]

The Sioux Valley Government has the power to manage and regulate certain activities in relation to oil and gas. Law-making power extends to exploration, extraction, refining, disposition and trade, barter or sale of oil and gas on or under Sioux Valley lands. Again, a law made by the Sioux Valley Government under this section will override a conflicting federal or provincial law to the extent of any inconsistency.

Water[12]

The Agreement In Principle is not conclusive on the jurisdiction of the Sioux Valley with respect to control, use and management of water. The issue has not been resolved as yet, but will be negotiated over the next two years. The only parameters on that debate are that the jurisdiction of the Sioux Valley cannot extend to navigation and shipping.

---

[6] *Ibid.* s. 21.02.
[7] *Ibid.* s. 21.02(1).
[8] *1997,* c.9.
[9] R.S. 1985, c. E-17, *The Sioux Valley Dakota Nation Comprehensive Agreement In Principle,* s. 21.02(1)(c) & (d).
[10] *Ibid.* s. 21.02(3).
[11] *Ibid.* s. 21.03.
[12] *Ibid.* s. 21.04.

Forest Resources[13]

The Sioux Valley Government will be given unfettered jurisdiction with respect to forest resources and activities related thereto, including conservation. Sioux Valley laws will override inconsistent federal or provincial laws to the extent of the inconsistency.

Fish[14]

No agreement has been reached between the three parties as to Sioux Valley jurisdiction over fish and fisheries.

Wildlife[15]

The Sioux Valley has jurisdiction over the protection, harvesting and management of wildlife, which is on Sioux Valley lands. Sioux Valley laws are deemed to prevail against inconsistent provincial and federal laws, with the exception of federal laws concerning migratory birds and their habitat or endangered species and their habitat, in which case the federal law will prevail to the extent of the conflict.

Although the Sioux Valley have jurisdiction over non-citizen access to Sioux Valley lands,[16] the degree to which non-citizens are allowed to access and harvest on Sioux Valley lands has yet to be determined. The Agreement In Principle gives some guidance on this point, however, where it states that future negotiations in relation to non-citizens' right of access to Sioux Valley lands is not to discriminate against them.

Modern Agreements

Nunavut Land Claims Agreement

The Nunavut Land Claims Agreement[17] protects the harvesting rights of Aboriginal People in Manitoba and in specified marine areas.[18] The Agreement states that the cession of Aboriginal rights to land and resources outside of the land specified in the Agreement does not apply to the lands and waters reserved for access by Inuit for harvesting in Manitoba.[19] The Inuit

---

[13]   *Ibid.* s. 21.05.
[14]   *Ibid.* s. 21.06.
[15]   *Ibid.* s. 21.07.
[16]   *Ibid.* s. 48.01.
[17]   Brought into force by the *Nunavut Land Claim Agreement Act*, S.C. 1993, c. 29.
[18]   *Nunavut Land Claims Agreement*, Article 42.
[19]   *Ibid.* s. 42.1.1.

have the right to harvest wildlife in a designated area around Hudson Bay and the Churchill River.[20] Harvesting in such areas can only occur for the purposes of satisfying personal, family or community consumption needs, subject to such restrictions and limitations imposed by management agencies arising from conservation, public health and safety, and humane harvesting concerns, and also international obligations.[21] Other factors that may limit harvest in this area are provision for harvesting by other Aboriginal People pursuant to an Aboriginal treat right, concerns for maintaining any species important for tourism and subject to management of nearby conservation areas.[22]

---

[20] *Ibid.* s. 42.2.1.
[21] *Ibid.* s. 42.2.2.
[22] *Ibid.*

Chapter 12

Saskatchewan

Mineral Potential on Indian Reserve Lands in Saskatchewan[1]

The Mineral Potential of Indian Reserve Lands report compiled by the Department of Indian and Northern Affairs Canada[2] in Saskatchewan provides overall rating measures of the economic mineral possibilities of each reserve as a whole, on a scale of low/moderate/good. Factors that affect this rating are the size of the reserve, the location with respect to markets, transportation, access, value and type of commodity, social and cultural barriers to mining on certain lands and areas, marketability of a commodity at any given time and other differentials.

The following rating applies in Saskatchewan:

- 87 reserves were given a low rating;
- 47 reserves were given a moderate rating; and
- 9 were given a good rating.

The report indicates that 31 reserves have at least one commodity that has potential for development. At the time of this report, of the total number of reserves, 31 had already surrendered their minerals in some way.

Modern Agreements

Meadow Lake First Nations Comprehensive Agreement In Principle and Meadow Lake First Nations Tripartite Agreement In Principle

Meadow Lake First Nations and the governments of Canada and Saskatchewan signed two Agreements In Principle on 22 January 2001. The

---

[1] See Department of Indian and Northern Affairs Canada, online: <http://www.ainc-inac.gc.ca/ntr/sas_e.html>.

[2] Keep in mind that although this site was last updated on the 30 April 2001, the report was actually completed in 1991.

Agreements signify one step further towards completion of negotiations that have been underway since 1991. The Agreements are designed to facilitate the formation of self-government by the Meadow Lake First Nations. One reason why this has been possible is because the Meadow Lake First Nations and the Meadow Lake Tribal Council have received wide recognition for their successful implementation of advancement programs and also for their leadership in economic development. Both organizations have a strong portfolio boasting financially sound businesses.

The Comprehensive Agreement In Principle

This Agreement is a bilateral agreement between the Meadow Lake First Nations, the Meadow Lake Tribal Council and the Government of Canada. The provincial government is also a full party to the negotiations as it signed a Memorandum of Understanding to negotiate areas of jurisdiction with the Meadow Lake First Nations on self-government in 1996. The Agreement In Principle acknowledges that the Final Agreement will provide for the recognition of the government of each Meadow Lake First Nation and also of the Meadow Lake Tribal Council as a regional level of Meadow Lake First Nations Government.[3]

Meadow Lake First Nations Lands, Natural Resources and the Environment

In the event of an inconsistency or conflict between a resource-related law enacted by the Meadow Lake First Nations and any applicable federal or provincial law, in most cases, the Meadow Lake First Nations law is to prevail to the extent of the inconsistency or conflict. One instance when the federal or provincial law will prevail is where the Meadow Lake First Nations is contrary to a federal or provincial law that purports to implement and fulfil Canada's international treaty obligations.[4] The Meadow Lake First Nations has jurisdiction with respect to natural resources on, or forming part of, the Meadow Lake First Nations lands to a certain extent. Jurisdiction is granted over the following (non-exhaustive) areas of land use activities:

- resource use planning, management and conservation;
- granting and transfer of rights and interests in natural resources;
- access to Meadow Lake First Nations lands for the purpose of harvesting, extracting or removing natural resources;
- extraction, removal and disposition on Meadow Lake First Nations lands of natural resources;
- taking of rights and interests in natural resources without the consent of the holder thereof; and

---

[3] *Meadow Lake First Nations Comprehensive Agreement In Principle*, s. 7.
[4] *Ibid.* s. 38.04.

- providing for a system for the registration and recording of rights and interests in natural resources.[5]

Some limitations on the Meadow Lake First Nations jurisdiction in such areas apply, for example:

- no Aboriginal or treaty rights of a Meadow Lake First Nations can be transferred or assigned to a non-Meadow Lake First Nations citizen in natural resources on Meadow Lake First Nations lands;
- Canada is still to have access to the land to fulfil any legal obligation with respect to the collection of information for the production of statistics and reports on natural resources, their use, conservation and related activities; and
- the parties and the government of Saskatchewan also recognize in the Agreement In Principles the mutual advantage of establishing resource management regimes that are compatible with one another.[6]

Mining and Minerals

The Meadow Lake First Nations also have jurisdiction with respect to the management, regulation, prospecting for, extraction, development, refining, disposition and trade, barter or sale of mines and minerals, precious and base, including sand and gravel, on or forming part of Meadow Lake First Nations lands.[7] Jurisdiction does not, however, extend to atomic energy and atomic substances, nuclear substances or energy.[8]

A Meadow Lake First Nation has jurisdiction over the management, regulation, exploration, extraction, refining, disposition and trade, barter or sale of oil and gas that form part of Meadow Lake First Nations lands.[9] Whereupon a Meadow Lake First Nation exercises jurisdiction over oil and gas, the *Indian Oil and Gas Act* is deemed to no longer apply to that Meadow Lake First Nation and Meadow Lake First Nations land.

Water

The Meadow Lake First Nations are to have jurisdiction over the control, use and management of water, although this is still a matter that has been left open for the Meadow Lake First Nations and Saskatchewan to discuss and negotiate upon and attempt to reach an agreement on in the Final Agreement.[10]

---

[5] *Ibid.* s. 21.01.
[6] *Ibid.*
[7] *Ibid.* s. 21.02.
[8] *Ibid.*
[9] *Ibid.* s. 21.03.
[10] *Ibid.* s. 21.04.

Forestry

The Meadow Lake First Nations are to have jurisdiction with respect to forest resources and activities related to forestry, including conservation.[11] The federal government retains ultimate jurisdiction over plant health, however, and its laws are to apply despite inconsistent or conflicting Meadow Lake First Nations laws.

Fish and Fisheries

Jurisdiction of the Meadow Lake First Nations with respect to fish and fisheries is deemed to apply to

- the protection and harvesting of fish and the management of fisheries;
- the giving of non-commercial trade or barter between the Meadow Lake First Nations citizens and the commercial sale of fish harvested in a fishery where a Meadow Lake First Nation has jurisdiction;
- management of the cultivation and rearing of fish or aquatic plants; and
- the protection and management of spawning grounds and any other areas on which fish depend directly or indirectly in order to carry out their life processes, including nursery, rearing, food supply and migration areas.[12]

Fisheries management and regulation is another matter that has been left open to the possibility of joint management and co-operation between the Meadow Lake First Nations and the Saskatchewan government.

Wildlife

A Meadow Lake First Nation is to have jurisdiction with respect to the protection, harvesting and management of wildlife that is on Meadow Lake First Nations lands.[13] The meaning of "wildlife" in this context means a vertebrate animal of any species, excluding fish, that is wild in the province. The term includes: any part, tissue, genetic material, egg, sperm, embryo or other form of developmental life; and any exotic material found on Meadow Lake First Nations lands. Where a Meadow Lake First Nation has enacted a law and it conflicts with either migratory birds and their habitat, or endangered species and their habitat, then the federal law is to prevail to the extent of the inconsistency or conflict.

---

[11] *Ibid.* s. 21.05.
[12] *Ibid.* s. 21.06.
[13] *Ibid.* s. 21.07.

Meadow Lake First Nations Lands[14]

Meadow Lake First Nations lands are to continue to be classified as "lands reserved for Indians" within the meaning of subsection 91(24) of the *Constitution Act, 1867* following the implementation of the Final Agreement.[15] As requested by the Meadow Lake First Nations, title to Meadow Lake First Nations lands as of the date of the Final Agreement will remain in Canada; and any lands that become Meadow Lake First Nations lands following a Final Agreement coming into effect will be vested in Canada for the use and benefit of a Meadow Lake First Nation.[16] Title to Meadow Lake First Nations lands then is something less that legal title. However, a Meadow Lake First Nation is to have full rights, powers, responsibilities and privileges of an owner in relation to such land.[17] A Meadow Lake First Nation may request the transfer of title to land if certain procedures are followed.[18]

Meadow Lake First Nations are also to enjoy full common la riparian rights with respect to the use and occupation of Meadow Lake First Nations lands adjacent to any river, stream, lake, pond, swamp, marsh or other body of water.[19]

Existing interests in Meadow Lake First Nations lands that exist at the date of the Final Agreement will continue to exist.[20]

Meadow Lake First Nations Tripartite Agreement In Principle

The second agreement, the Tripartite Agreement in Principle, incorporates the four parties – the Meadow Lake First Nations, the Meadow Lake Tribal Council, the Government of Canada, and the government of Saskatchewan. This Agreement deals primarily with the relationship of the parties and the interaction and integration of the Meadow Lake First Nations laws into the existing body of laws and governmental framework.

---

14 *Ibid.* s. 44.0.
15 *Ibid.* s. 44.04.
16 *Ibid.* s. 46.01.
17 *Ibid.* s. 46.02(1).
18 *Ibid.* s. 46.03.
19 *Ibid.* s. 46.02(2).
20 *Ibid.* s. 51.02.

Chapter 13

Quebec

Reserves were established in southern Quebec without treaties or agreements. The French effectively asserted and later ceded sovereignty without apparent recognition of Aboriginal title. It was considered that the Royal Proclamation did not require treating with First Nations for the surrender of Aboriginal titles in those areas. Land was, thus, set aside by executive act, without treaty or agreement. By 1854, a total of 230,000 acres had been set apart by order in council for the benefit of First Nations people. Just as no treaties were sought for the surrender of traditional lands, no consent or surrender was sought for the disposition of reserve lands. Commissioners were appointed who were required to protect First Nation land from encroachment. The same Commissioners, however, had the power to dispose of reserve lands to settlers without the consent of the First Nations concerned. Legislation was enacted to that effect in Quebec in 1850.[1]

After Confederation, land was set aside for First Nation people by private purchase by the federal government from Quebec, and in one unique instance, by virtue of a 1922 Quebec statute that authorized setting apart a usufructuary interest in provincial Crown land.[2]

In northern Quebec, land had been reserved for the First Nations under the *Royal Proclamation, 1763*, apart from an area of land within the territory of the Hudson's Bay Company. The federal government recognized the obligation to treat for the surrender of Aboriginal title arising from the Proclamation and the imperial order in council of 1870 that admitted the Hudson's Bay Company's territory into Canada.

When the Quebec boundary was extended to its current position in 1871,[3] the extension was conditional. Quebec was obliged to "recognize the rights of the Indian inhabitants in the territory...and will obtain surrenders of such rights...as the Government of Canada has heretofore recognized such rights and has obtained surrenders thereof."

---

[1] *Crown Lands Act*, S. Prov. C. 1850, c. 42.

[2] *An Act respecting lands set apart for Indians*, S.Q. 1922, 3rd Sess., c. 37.

[3] *Quebec Boundaries Extension Act*, S.C. 1912, c. 45.

No treaties or agreements were entered into in Quebec until 1975. In 1973, Mr. Justice Malouf granted an interlocutory injunction against the James Bay Development Corporation, restraining the construction of the James Bay Hydro Project on the basis that the chiefs of the First Nations of the region had established clear rights of possession and occupancy of the lands affected.[4] Following the judgement, the Quebec government announced its intention to negotiate an agreement with the First Nations concerned. In 1975 the Cree and Inuit of northern Quebec signed the James Bay and Northern Quebec Agreement, which will be discussed below.

There are no agreements regarding minerals on reserves in Quebec, apart from the James Bay and Northern Quebec Agreements.[5] For the most part, Quebec has title to most reserve land within its province. Upon surrender of land to the Crown, the province thus receives the entire benefits of the minerals and mining in the province, subject only to the provisions in the *Indian Act* that may directly relate to land.

Mineral Potential on Indian Reserve Lands in Quebec[6]

The Mineral Potential of Indian Reserve Lands report compiled by the Department of Indian and Northern Affairs Canada[7] in Quebec provides overall rating measures of the economic mineral possibilities of each reserve as a whole, on a scale of low/moderate/good. Factors that affect this rating are the size of the reserve, the location with respect to markets, transportation, access, value and type of commodity, social and cultural barriers to mining on certain lands and areas, marketability of a commodity at any given time and other differentials.

The following rating applies in Quebec:

- 19 reserves were given a low rating;
- 9 reserves were given a moderate rating; and
- 3 reserves were given a good rating.

The report indicates that 8 reserves have at least one commodity that has potential for development. Of the total number of reserves, at the time of this report, none had surrendered their minerals in any way.

[4] *Gros-Louis v. La Societe de Developpement de la Baie James* (1973), 8 C.N.L.C. 188 (Que. Sup. Ct.), reversed on appeal in *James Bay Development Corp. v. Kanatewat* (1974), 8 C.N.L.C. 373.

[5] *James Bay and Northern Quebec Native Claims Settlement Act*, S.C. 1976-77, c.32; James Bay Agreement, S.Q. 1976, c.32; Northern Quebec Agreement, Order in Council, February 23, 1976, F.C. 1978-502; Northern QuebecAgreement S.Q. 1978, c.98.

[6] See the Department of Indian and Northern Affairs, online: <http://www.ainc-inac.gc.ca/ntr/que_e.html>.

[7] Keep in mind that although this site was last updated on the 30 April 2001, the report was actually completed in 1991.

Provincial Legislation

Note that provincial legislation and regulations are deemed to apply to Aboriginal People subject to two conditions:

- provincial legislation cannot apply exclusively to Aboriginal People or to land reserved for their benefit; and
- a provincial law may be declared invalid or inapplicable to Aboriginal People if it infringes upon an established Aboriginal or treaty right that is constitutionally protected.

Where an Aboriginal person has established an Aboriginal or treaty right to hunt or fish then the provincial legislation cannot interfere with that right,[8] unless the limitation can meet the test of justification and is in keeping with the honour of the Crown.[9] A limitation on the exercise of a treaty or Aboriginal right would need to be tested in the courts for clarification. It is clear that sufficient consideration must be given to the Aboriginal interest. Apart from measures implemented by a province to conserve a resource, it is unlikely that any court in Canada would uphold any other provincial legislation that restricts an Aboriginal or treaty right. Recently, provincial laws designed to protect public safety have been permitted to override and limit Aboriginal resource rights.

Fishing in Quebec

A fishing management plan is established annually under the *Act Respecting the Conservation and Development of Wildlife*.[10] The plan must determine the apportionment of fishery resources according to the following order of priorities:

1. the reproductive stock;
2. Aboriginal fishing for food purposes;
3. sport fishing; and
4. commercial fishing.[11]

Under the Act, wildlife conservation officers are responsible for the enforcement of hunting and fishing rights in the James Bay and New Quebec territories and its accompanying regulations.[12] Under the Act, no person is permitted to fish within the province with a line or rod and line in a place specified by regulation unless he holds a licence issued for such a purpose.[13]

---

[8]   *R. v. White and Bob*, supra note 10 in ch. 2; *R. v. Simon*, supra note 2 in ch. 2; and *R. v. Sioui*, supra note 2 in ch. 2.

[9]   *R. v. White and Bob*, supra note 10 in ch. 2; *R. v. Simon*, supra note 2 in ch. 2; and *R. v. Sioui*, supra note 2 in ch. 2; *R. v. Sparrow*, supra note 5 in ch. 1.

[10]   Chapter C-61.1.

[11]   *Ibid.* s. 63.

[12]   Chapter D-13.1, s. 5.

[13]   *Ibid.* s. 41.

The Act contains certain provisions that are specific to Aboriginal communities.[14] The provincial government is authorized to

> better reconcile wildlife conservation and management requirements with the activities pursued by Native people for food, ritual or social purposes, or to further facilitate wildlife resource development and management by Native people, to enter into agreements with any Native community represented by its band council in respect of [certain] matters.[15]

Any agreements concluded by the government and the Aboriginal community in question is to prevail over the provisions of this Act. The province is also authorized to adapt regulations to better reconcile wildlife conservation and management requirements with the activities pursued by Aboriginal people for food, ritual or social purposes.[16]

According to the management plan established under the *Act Respecting the Conservation and Development of Wildlife*, the Minister of Agriculture, Fisheries and Food must devise a program to promote the development of commercial fisheries in and the commerce of aquatic products harvested in tideless waters of the province.[17] The Minister will determine the species and quantity of aquatic products that may be caught or taken.[18] Accordingly, at the Minister's discretion, rights to fish for commercial purposes in tideless waters can be granted to eligible applicants. No harvest of fish or aquatic plants can occur on a commercial basis without the authorization of a licence issued by the Minister.[19] Licences are issued under the Commercial Aquaculture Regulations.[20]

Areas in which fishing and hunting are permitted is regulated under general regulations under the Act.[21] Under the *Parks Act*[22] and its regulations, members of Aboriginal communities in Quebec who engage in an activity within a provincial park for food, ritual or social purposes do not need an authorization to be there.[23]

---

[14] See Chapter II.1.

[15] *Ibid.* s. 24.1. Note that this provision applies to fishing, hunting and trapping.

[16] *Ibid.* s. 24.2.

[17] *An Act Respecting Commercial Fisheries and Aquaculture*, Chapter P-9.01, s. 1.

[18] *Ibid.* s. 6.

[19] *Ibid.* s. 13.

[20] Chapter P-9.01, r.1.

[21] *Fishing and Hunting Areas Regulation*, c. C-61.1, r.0.00001.

[22] Chapter P-9, r.8.

[23] *Parks Regulations*, O.C. 838-2000, s. 6(13).

Hunting in Quebec

No person may hunt in Quebec without the issuance of an authorizing licence.[24] A licence is also required by anyone trapping in the province.[25] Hunting licences are granted under hunting regulations made pursuant to the Act.[26] Hunting licences for certain other species are granted by way of a random draw.

Trapping licences are granted under the *Regulations Respecting Trapping Activities and the Fur Trade.*[27]

As indicated earlier, these laws and regulations are deemed to apply generally to Aboriginal people to the point that interference with an established right to hunt and trap is unjustified.

Modern Agreements

James Bay and Northern Quebec Agreement

The James Bay and Northern Quebec Agreement is recognized as the first modern Canadian treaty.

Land Regime

Under the James Bay and Northern Quebec Agreement, the territory was divided into Category I, II and III lands.

Category I Lands

Subject to limitations specified in the Agreement, Category I lands are described as "an area under the complete and exclusive control of the Native people and for the exclusive use of Native people."[28]

1,348 square kilometres of land was set aside for the exclusive use and benefit of First Nations people.

Mineral and Subsurface Resources. Quebec reserved the mineral and subsurface resources on Category I lands, although the right to mine those mineral or resources is contingent upon consent, which must be obtained from the particular community with rights over such lands.[29] Compensation is also payable to any First Nation person affected. Deposits of steatite (or soapstone) and other similar materials used for traditional arts and crafts

---

[24] *An Act Respecting the Conservation and Development of Wildlife*, s. 38.

[25] *Ibid.* s. 39.

[26] *Regulation Respecting Hunting Activities*, c. C-61.1, r.0.00001.

[27] c. C-61.1, r.3.001.

[28] *James Bay and Northern Quebec Agreement*, s. 24.3.32.

[29] *Ibid.* s. 5.1.10(a).

remain the property of the Aboriginal People.[30] The First Nation signatories to the Agreement also retained the right to use gravel and other analogous material used for "earthworks...personal and community use," although a permit must first be obtained from the Quebec Department of Natural Resources.[31]

Forest Resources. Under the Agreement, the right to use the resources of forests contained within Category I lands was transferred to the First Nations for "personal and community needs," and also for commercial exploitation. The right to exploit forest resources for commercial purposes extends to third parties acting with the consent of the Cree communities. Where a third party is contracted for such a purpose, a cutting permit must be obtained from the Quebec Department of Lands and Forests. The Cree community is not required to pay stumpage dues on timber from Category I lands. The general provincial regime with respect to forest protection remains applicable to forests on Category I lands.

Category II Lands

15,706 square kilometres were transferred to the Aboriginal People as "Category II lands." Upon this land, Aboriginal People have the exclusive right of hunting, fishing and trapping. However, provincial jurisdiction continues over Category II lands, and harvesting will be subject to quotas developed in accordance with the resource management plans developed by the Quebec government. Non-Aboriginal People are not permitted to hunt, fish or trap on Category II lands, unless the consent of the Aboriginal People concerned has first been obtained. Under the Agreement, the Energy Corporation, Hydro-Quebec and the James Bay Development Corporation have specific rights to develop resources on Category II lands, and can do so without paying compensation. Rights to hunt, fish and trap remain subject to this development right.[32]

Minerals and Subsurface Resources. Mineral exploration and technical surveys can be carried out on Category II lands without the need to replace land used for that purpose and without compensation being payable. The only guidance given by the Agreement as to potential conflict between the exercise of Aboriginal rights and mining rights is that such mineral exploration and technical surveys are to be carried out so as to avoid unreasonable conflict with harvesting activities.[33] The right to use soapstone for traditional arts and crafts purposes remains with the Quebec government,

---

[30]   *Ibid*. s. 5.1.10(b).
[31]   *Ibíd*. s. 5.1.10(c).
[32]   *Ibid*. s. 5.5.1.
[33]   *Ibid*. s. 5.2.5(a).

although Aboriginal People can acquire that right by applying for a permit from the Quebec Department of Natural Resources.[34] The permit that will be issued is a "special permit" and extends only to use of such material for traditional arts and craft purposes. Moreover, the Aboriginal right to access and use soapstone will always be subordinated to the rights to other mineral substances in such a way that it will not prevent possible mining developments on that land.

Forest Resources. Commercial cutting programs in Category II lands are to be defined according to management plans devised by the Quebec Department of Lands and Forests. Operations will be governed by Quebec standards and the general regime for forest protection is applicable.[35] Stumpage dues are payable on timber felled in the course of commercial operations.[36]

Category III Lands

Category III lands are Quebec public lands; however, they are a special type of public lands. Both Aboriginal and non-Aboriginal People are able to hunt and fish here. Aboriginal groups retain the exclusive rights to harvest certain aquatic species and furbearing mammals and to participate in the administration and development of the land. Under the Agreement, the Energy Corporation, Hydro-Quebec and the James Bay Development Corporation have specific rights to develop resources on Category III lands. This right overrides the Aboriginal right to hunt, trap and fish.[37]

Mineral Resources. The regime as established for the use of soapstone in Category II lands is applicable to Category III lands.[38]

Forest Resources. Under the Agreement, Aboriginal People can apply to the Quebec Department of Lands and Forests to be able to have wood supplied to develop saw mills. Where commercial utilization of timber rights takes place on Category III lands, stumpage dues are payable.[39]

Hunting, Fishing and Trapping Rights

Section 24 of the Agreement provides detailed regulations for exercise of the right to hunt, fish and trap. Under the Agreement, First Nations people are given the right to harvest any species of wild fauna except species that are

---

[34] *Ibid.* s. 5.2.5(b).
[35] *Ibid.* s. 5.2.5(c).
[36] *Ibid.* s. 5.4.3.
[37] *Ibid.* s. 5.5.1.
[38] *Ibid.* s. 5.3.1.
[39] *Ibid.* s. 5.4.3.

considered to require protection and to ensure the continued survival of a particular species.[40] The right to harvest on the designated lands belongs solely and exclusively to the First Nation parties to the Agreement.[41]

Subject to the principle of conservation, the right to harvest refers to harvesting within the territory, for both personal and community use, and also commercial trapping[42] and commercial fishing.[43] The right extends to trade in and conducting commerce in all the by-products of their lawful harvesting activities.[44] The right to harvest includes the right to possess and use "all equipment reasonably needed to exercise that right"[45] – including both traditional and present methods of harvesting;[46] and the right to travel and establish camps necessary to exercise that right.[47] The general right to harvest is subject to further restrictions and cannot be exercised on lands that are situated within existing or future non-Aboriginal settlements within the territory,[48] in areas where existing lease or permits grant an outfitter exclusive access to fish and game in specified seasons[49] and in conflict with laws enacted to protect public health and safety.[50] In the case of migratory birds, personal use is limited to the gift or exchange of all products of harvesting within the extended family, subject to measures undertaken by Canada to conserve and protect certain species as from time to time may be deemed necessary.[51]

The Agreement also sets aside species that are reserved for Aboriginal People throughout the designated lands.[52] Sole harvesting rights apply to: mustelids (mink, ermine, weasels, marten, fisher, otter, skunk and wolverine); beaver; lynx; foxes; polar bear; muskrat; porcupine; woodchuck; black bear (north of the 50th parallel); wolves and fresh water seals (north of the 55th parallel).[53]

Within Category I and II lands, the Aboriginal People have an exclusive right to establish and operate commercial fisheries. Within Category III lands, the Aboriginal parties have the exclusive right to establish and operate commercial fisheries related to whitefishes, sturgeon, suckers, burbot and

40 *Ibid.* s. 24.3.2.
41 *Ibid.* s. 24.3.3.
42 *Ibid.* s. 24.3.19.
43 *Ibid.* s. 24.3.11(a).
44 *Ibid.* s. 24.3.15.
45 *Ibid.* s. 24.3.12.
46 *Ibid.* s. 24.3.14.
47 *Ibid.* s. 24.3.13.
48 *Ibid.* s. 24.3.7.
49 *Ibid.* s. 24.3.8.
50 *Ibid.* s. 24.3.9.
51 *Ibid.* s. 24.3.11(b).
52 *Ibid.* s. 24.7.
53 *Ibid.* s. 24, Sched. 2.

hiodons.[54] Applications for commercial fisheries permits on all categories of land are to be submitted to a specified body which will assess the application in consideration of the potential impact on harvesting and recreational fishing. The Minister has the final say. However no commercial fishers are to be permitted on Category I and II lands without the consent of the interested Aboriginal People.[55] On Category III lands, non-Aboriginal People have the right to hunt and fish, subject to applicable laws and regulations, but such activities are limited to hunting and fishing for sport.[56]

The Agreement states explicitly that neither the provincial nor federal governments or any other body is to alter the hunting, fishing and trapping regime in such a way as to infringe upon the rights of the Aboriginal People under the Agreement.[57] Where laws and regulations are altered, for example, where harvesting quotes are varied, the Aboriginal right to harvest is to take priority.[58]

Cree-Quebec Final Agreement[59]

A Final Agreement was signed between the Cree and the government of Quebec on 7 February 2002.[60] The Agreement concerns economic development, representing a commitment by the two groups to co-operate and a commitment by the government of Quebec to provide financial assistance to the Cree people, and is intended to renew the relationship between the two parties.

In part, the Agreement is designed to give effect to recommendations made by the Royal Commission on Aboriginal Peoples in 1996. The Report of the Royal Commission states:

Aboriginal Peoples need much more territory to become economically, culturally and politically self-sufficient. If they cannot obtain a greater share of the lands and resources in this country, their institutions of self-government will fail. Without adequate lands and resources, Aboriginal nations will be unable to build their communities and structure the employment opportunities necessary to achieve self-sufficiency. Currently, on the margins of Canadian society, they will be pushed to the edge of economic, cultural and

---

[54] *Ibid.* s. 24.3.26.

[55] *Ibid.* s. 24.3.27.

[56] *Ibid.* s. 24.8.

[57] *Ibid.* s. 24.3.31.

[58] *Ibid.* s. 24.6.

[59] Agreement Concerning a New Relationship Between the Government of Quebec and the Crees of Quebec, 2001.

[60] See the report on the website of the Quebec Government, online: <http://www.premier.gouv.qc.ca/premier/english/press_releases/index_communiques.html>.

political extinction. The government must act forcefully, generously and swiftly to assure the economic, cultural and political survival of Aboriginal nations.[61]

Section 28 of the James Bay and Northern Quebec Agreement of 1975 placed the government of Quebec under an obligation to support and encourage Cree economic and social development. The 1975 Agreement provided for the creation of a corporation by the name of the James Bay Native Development Corporation. It was designed to assist in the development and diversification of resources, properties and industries within the James Bay territory with the paramount objective being to stimulate maximum economic opportunities for Cree people and contribute to their general economic well-being. The corporation had as a further goal to assist and encourage joint ventures between the James Bay Development Society and Cree corporations in activities such as mining exploration and exploitation and forestry exploitation.

Apparently, 25 years after the completion of the 1975 Agreement, very few Crees were involved or employed in development within their own territory and the governments were both refusing to acknowledge any responsibility in the matter. Litigation during the late 1980s and throughout the 1990s brought attention to the economic difficulties faced by the Cree people and to the 1975 Agreement that had promised to help their situation. Accordingly, the new Agreement has been described as "breathing life" into the economic section of the James Bay and Northern Quebec Agreement.

The Agreement In Principle was concluded after a short period of negotiations on 23 October 2001. The signing of the Final Agreement was consented to by 70 percent of the Cree communities.

The Agreement provides for a nation to nation relationship based on mutual respect and co-operation between the Crees and the government of Quebec.

Forestry

Generally, the Agreement promises that the Quebec forestry regime is to apply in the territory in a manner that acknowledges and takes account of the Cree traditional way of life. It aims to integrate concerns relating to sustainable development and to allow greater participation by the James Bay Crees by way of consultation in forest activities, operations, planning and management processes.[62]

---

[61] Royal Commission on Aboriginal Peoples, *Gathering Strength*, Minister of Supply and Services, Ottawa, 1996.

[62] Agreement Concerning a New Relationship Between the Government of Quebec and the Crees of Quebec, s. 3.1.

The Agreement is designed to establish a forestry regime, which will fix regulations and procedures applicable in the territory to take account of the hunting, fishing and trapping activities of the Crees and improved conciliation of forest activities with Cree activities.[63]

Calculation of the annual allowable timber cut is to be determined on the basis of management units, which are to be made of groupings of traplines. A series of discussions are to be carried out by the Crees and the Minister of Natural Resources for Quebec.[64] The regime is to be managed by a Cree-Quebec Forestry Board and will be basically on the basis of the Cree family hunting territory, that is, the "host community and/or the kindred relationship of the tallymen and the Cree users of the traplines."[65]

Five years after the signing of the Agreement at the latest, Quebec is to make 350,000 cubic meters of timber volume within the limits of the commercial forest situated in the territory available to the Cree Enterprises.[66] In the meantime, the government of Quebec agrees to allocate to Cree Enterprises:

- a minimum of 70,000 cubic meters of timber for the 2002 calendar year;
- a minimum of 70,000 cubic meters of timber for the 2003 calendar year;
- a minimum of 125,000 cubic meters of timber is to be made available by 30 June 2004 for the course of 2004 and 2005 calendar years;
- during the course of the 2006 calendar year, a minimum annual volume of 350,000 cubic meters of timber is to be made available.[67]

The minimum timber allocations are guaranteed and will be allocated by means of forest management agreements under the provisions of the *Forest Act*.[68] A distribution of the allocation is to be determined by the Cree Regional Authority, which is to inform the Minister of Natural Resources.[69] Nothing in the Agreement precludes or restricts agreements between Cree individuals or bands and other forestry enterprises.[70]

To ensure that Cree hunters have access to firewood, non-Aboriginal permit holders under the *Forestry Act* are prohibited from harvesting firewood within an area of 75 hectares surrounding each permanent Cree camp.[71]

---

[63] *Ibid.* s. 3.4.
[64] *Ibid.* s. 3.8.
[65] *Ibid.* s. 3.8.2.
[66] *Ibid.* s. 3.55.
[67] *Ibid.* s. 3.59.
[68] *Ibid.* s. 3.56.
[69] *Ibid.* s. 3.58.
[70] *Ibid.* s. 3.65.
[71] *Ibid.* s. 3.63.

Mining

Mining projects are to continue to be subject to the applicable environmental legislation and to the environmental and social protection regimes that are stipulated in the James Bay and Northern Quebec Agreement.[72] The government of Quebec agrees to promote and facilitate participation of the Crees in mineral exploration activities in the territory by setting up a Mineral Exploration Board, which is to be largely composed of Cree representatives. The Board is to be set up before 1 April 2002. The main purposes of the Board is defined as to

- assist the Crees in accessing mineral exploration opportunities;
- facilitate the development of mineral exploration activities by Cree Enterprises;
- facilitate and encourage the access by the Crees and Cree Enterprises to regular Quebec program funding and other encouragements for mineral exploration activities; and
- act as an entry mechanism for offers of services by Crees and Cree Enterprises in the field of mineral exploration.[73]

The government of Quebec promises funding of $24 million in the first calendar year of the Agreement, $46 million in the second and $70 million per year for the following 48 years. That funding is to be put towards community development, economic development, environmental administration, Cree trapping, outfitting and craft associations and other activities to be determined by the Crees.

Current Land Claims

Kahnawake

A draft agreement for formal consultation with members of the Mohawks of Kahnawake was released in the middle of 2001. The draft agreements include a draft Umbrella Agreement and four Sub-Agreements. A process of consultation with members of Kahnawake seeks to negotiate on roughly 30 issues, including land governance, over the next five years. The purpose behind the agreements is to displace the application of the *Indian Act* and to establish a new relationship based on trust and mutual respect. The agreements will empower the Kahnawake to take control of their land and exercise jurisdiction over both land matters and citizens.

---

[72] *Ibid.* s. 5.1.
[73] *Ibid.* s. 5.3.

Mi'kmaq Nation of Gespeg

The Mi'kmaq Nation of Gespeg remains the only Aboriginal band in Quebec without reserve lands or properties. The nation was only recognized as an "Indian band" for the purposes of the *Indian Act* in 1973. Negotiations regarding a land settlement have been ongoing for several years and a Framework Agreement for negotiating self-government for the Mi'kmaq Nation of Gespeg was signed by representatives of Quebec, Canada and the chief of the Mi'kmaq Nation of Gespeg in 1999.

The Framework Agreement aims to permit the Mi'kmaqs to assert more substantial control over their social and economic development. Negotiations are focusing on land matters, including wildlife harvesting activities and resource exploitation. An Agreement In Principle was supposed to have been ready by 2001. However, negotiations are ongoing. Once an Agreement In Principle has been reached, the parties then have a further 12 months in which to negotiate a Final Agreement.

Quebec Algonquin Claim

A number of Algonquin Bands of Quebec submitted a formal comprehensive claim to lands comprising the Ottawa River watershed. Based on extensive research into the history of the Quebec Algonquins, the federal government has confirmed its willingness to commence negotiations with them. Again, negotiations will focus on establishing some form of self-regulation of resources and lands in the future.

Atikamekw and Montagnais Claims

The 12 communities of the Atikamekw and Montagnais have been negotiating with the Crown since 1979. Three groups have so far been treated with. In 2000, Canada and Quebec made the "Common Approach" policy document concluded with the Conseil tribal Mamuitun available to the public. The document contains key elements that will serve as a basis for negotiation of an Agreement In Principle. Those elements include land quantum, resource revenue sharing, natural resource management and conservation, economic development and commitments to self-government.

Kanesatake Land Governance Agreement

The purpose of the Kanesatake Land Governance Agreement is to recognize a land base for the Mohawks of Kanesatake. The Agreement recognizes an interim land base for the Mohawks as well as their legal status under section 91(24) of the *Constitution Act, 1867*. The land of the Kanesatake Mohawks is recognized as "land reserved for Indians" but is not a "reserve" in the sense that it has been understood to date. The Agreement called for the harmonization of Kanesatake laws and the bylaws of the Municipality of Oka in some respects.

The Agreement is not designed to freeze the amount of land made available to the Mohawks of Kanesatake but contemplates the addition of other lands to the interim land base as may be agreed upon by the parties at a later date. The surface area of Kanesatake is 958.05 hectares. The community also includes an area of 7896.2 hectares which is shared with the Mohawks of Kahnawake. There are approximately 1,950 people in the Kanesatake community with 1,300 residents on the actual territory of the Mohawk.

The Agreement indicates that the Kanesatake is a legal entity and as such has the status, capacity, rights, powers and privileges of a natural person.[74] Accordingly, the Kanesatake Mohawks have, among various other rights, the ability to acquire and hold property.

Part VII of the Agreement indicates that the Kanesatake Mohawks are to have jurisdiction over certain matters pertaining to their lands. Included in these matters is a right to regulate: the protection and management of wildlife and fish; trespass; residency; construction and maintenance of local works; and construction and regulation of water supplies. Where the Kanesatake seek to regulate to protect and manage wildlife and fish, those measures must be consistent with, or better than, federal government environmental laws and regulations.[75] The Agreement does not give the Kanesatake Mohawks the right to create, recognize or transfer an interest in Kanesatake lands, although it is recognized that this issue may be negotiated at a later time in a subsequent agreement.[76]

In the event of inconsistency or conflict with provincial laws and regulations, the Kanesatake law or regulation is to override the provincial law.[77] In the event of an inconsistency with a federal law, the federal law will prevail to the extent of the inconsistency with the Kanesatake law.

Caselaw in Quebec

In a 1996 decision, a Mohawk living in the Akwesasne Territory successfully argued that he had an Aboriginal right to fish in the St. Lawrence River.[78] Adams was convicted of fishing with a seine net made of fine mesh, several hundred feet in length, without a licence pursuant to section 4(1) of the Quebec Fishery Regulations. Under the *Quebec Fishery Regulations*, a

---

[74] Agreement with Respect to Kanesatake Governance of the Interim Land Base, Part VI.
[75] *Ibid.* s. 25.
[76] *Ibid.* s. 22.
[77] *Ibid.* Part XII.
[78] *R. v. Adams, supra* note 19 in ch. 1.

licence was in fact unavailable, although under section 5(9) of the Regulations he could have applied for an exercise of Ministerial discretion permitting him to fish for food. This case was an appeal to the Supreme Court of Canada from a judgement that dismissed his appeal from the dismissal of his appeal from conviction. Adams argued that he was exercising an Aboriginal right to fish as recognized by section 35(1) of the *Constitution Act, 1982* and argued that the Regulation was therefore of no force or effect in respect to him.

The Supreme Court allowed Adams' appeal, finding that it is not necessary for an Aboriginal person to prove Aboriginal title to land in order to prove that they retain certain rights to that land. The practical effect of section 35 of the *Constitution Act, 1982* is to afford constitutional protection to the practices, customs and traditions that are integral to the distinctive culture of Aboriginal societies. In this case, Adams effectively demonstrated that fishing for food was an integral part of his people's culture and there was no evidence that the right to fish for food in the area of the St. Lawrence River where he had fished had been extinguished. The court determined that the Mohawks had fished in the area at the point of contact with Europeans, and that there was sufficient continuity in the practice to establish an existing Aboriginal right, even if Aboriginal title could not be established. The court found that the infringement imposed by section 4(1) of the *Quebec Fishery Regulations* was not justified and was therefore of no force or effect in respect of Adams.

In *R. v. Côté*,[79] Côté, a member of the Desert River Band, accompanied a group of young Aboriginal People to educate them about traditional fishing in their traditional fishing territory. The territory fell within a provincially designated "Controlled Harvest Zone" where a licence was required to fish. Côté and five other Algonquin people were charged with entering the area without paying the required fee for his motor vehicle and for fishing without a licence. The appellants argued that they were exercising a constitutionally guaranteed Aboriginal right to fish under section 35(1) and a right guaranteed by a treaty concluded at Swegatchy in 1769.

The court did not specifically address whether a treaty right to fish existed under the Swegatchy Treaty of 1769, which was surrounded by issues of whether or not the French had recognized the right of the Algonquin people to fish in that area prior to British sovereignty. The court found that the appellants could still establish an Aboriginal right to fish under the principles of the *Van der Peet, Gladstone*, and *N.T.C. Smokehouse Ltd* cases. Applying *Van Der Peet*, the court found an Aboriginal right to fish. Lamer C.J. found that food fishing within the lakes and rivers of the restricted zone, in particular Desert Lake, was a significant part of the life of the Algonquins

---

[79]   [1996] 3 S.C.R. 139 (S.C.C.).

from at least 1603 and the arrival of non-Aboriginal settlers. While Côté was not fishing for food at the time he was charged, the court found that education of the other Aboriginal People was incidental to the Aboriginal right to fish for food.

In *R. v. Duguay*[80] the court considered the accused's claim that he could sell fish and game contrary to the provincial *Act Respecting the Conservation and Development of Wildlife* pursuant to his constitutionally protected right to do so. His argument was rejected on the basis that insufficient evidence was submitted to prove that the sale of fish and game was part of the distinct culture of the Algonquins of Kipawa.

The case of *R. v. Ogushing*[81] dealt with a member of the Long Point First Nation who was charged with fishing in a spawning ground for pickerel during a closed season. The court found that such a practice had existed prior to contact with Europeans and a blanket prohibition on fishing during certain times of the year was not a justified infringement of the Aboriginal right.

In *R. v. Paul*[82] the court found that the *Act Respecting the Conservation and Development of Wildlife,* under which the accused (a member of the Kipawa Band) was charged with hunting a moose contrary to certain provisions, was geared towards preserving moose for sports hunters. Accordingly the "conservation measures" could not be justified and did not apply to the accused on the basis of unconstitutionality. To quote the court: "Compared to the number of moose harvested and killed by sportshunters, that of moose harvested by the Aboriginal people of the region seems quite marginal, almost ludicrous, although there is no hard information about this."[83]

---

[80] [1998] 4 C.N.L.R. 183 (C.Q.).
[81] [1998] 4 C.N.L.R. 236 (C.Q.).
[82] [1998] 4 C.N.L.R. 255 (C.Q.).
[83] *Ibid.* p. 253.

Chapter 14

Nunavut

The creation of Nunavut is a result of the 1993 Nunavut Land Claims Agreement (Nunavut Agreement)[1] between the Northwest Territories, the federal government and Inuit. Nunavut is the result of the largest land claim ever settled in Canada and came into being on 1 April 1999. The territory makes up one-fifth of Canada's landmass, approximately 2 million square kilometres.

Nunavut Land Claims Agreement

The Nunavut Agreement purports to place control and management of natural resources back into the hands of the First Nations, at least to the same extent as that of territorial governments. The law-making powers assigned to the Nunavut government are similar to those awarded to the Yukon and Northwest Territories. Under the Agreement, the Inuit agreed to "cede, release and surrender" to the Crown all their claims, rights, title and interests to lands and waters anywhere within Canada.[2] However, the Nunavut Agreement acknowledges that its terms cannot detract from any treaty right that may have pre-existed the Agreement, and which is now afforded constitutional protection.[3] Any land that was previously categorized as "land reserved for Indians," for the purposes of the *Constitution Act, 1867*[4] is no longer subject to federal jurisdiction and reverts to the regulatory capacity of the government of Nunavut.[5]

The Nunavut Agreement is protected from conflicting laws and legislation in several ways. First, the Agreement is given constitutional protection as, by definition, the Agreement is a land claims agreement within the meaning of section 35 of the *Constitution Act, 1982*.[6] Second, in the event of any inconsistency or conflict between any federal, territorial and local

---

[1] Enacted by the *Nunavut Land Claim Agreement Act*, S.C. 1993, c. 29.

[2] Nunavut Land Claims Agreement, 1993, s. 2.7.1.

[3] *Nunavut Land Claims Agreement Act*, s. 2.7.3(a).

[4] *Constitution Act*, 1867, s. 91(24).

[5] Nunavut Land Claims Agreement, 1993, s. 2.17.1.

[6] *Ibid.* s. 2.2.1.

government laws, and the Agreement, the Agreement will be held to prevail to the extent of the inconsistency or conflict.[7]

The Nunavut Agreement establishes and mandates special purpose land and resource bodies in Nunavut. These bodies are referred to as "institutions of public government" as their powers are similar to those that are usually found in government. In Nunavut, there are five institutes of public government: the Nunavut Wildlife Management Board, the Nunavut Planning Commission, the Nunavut Impact Review Board, the Nunavut Water Board and the Nunavut Surface Rights Tribunal. These institutions of public government are established as permanent parts of the system of land and resource management in Nunavut.

Wildlife[8]

The Nunavut Wildlife Management Board

The Nunavut Wildlife Management Board is made up of representatives appointed by each Designated Inuit Organization, and the federal government.[9] The Agreement recognizes that the federal government retains ultimate responsibility for wildlife management, but that the Board is to be the main instrument of wildlife management in the Nunavut settlement area and the main regulator of access to wildlife.[10] The Agreement assigns certain duties to the Board, including:

- the obligation to participate in wildlife research;[11]
- conducting a Nunavut Wildlife Harvest Study, which is designed to establish levels of total allowable harvest, to establish sound practices relating to management and utilization of resources and to determine the basic needs level of Inuit people by documenting levels and patterns of wildlife harvest;[12]
- the Board has the obligation to allocate resources, if available, to residents (apart from the Inuit),[13] and to existing operations;[14]
- recommending allocation of remaining surplus, if relevant;[15]
- establishing, modifying or removing non-quota limitations;[16] and
- setting trophy fees.[17]

[7] *Ibid.* s. 2.12.2, see also, the *Nunavut Land Claims Agreement Act*, s. 6(1).
[8] *Ibid.* Article 5.
[9] *Ibid.*, s. 5.2.1.
[10] *Ibid.* s. 5.2.33.
[11] *Ibid.* ss. 5.2.37 – 5.2.38.
[12] *Ibid.* Part 4.
[13] *Ibid.* ss. 5.6.32 – 5.6.37.
[14] *Ibid.* s. 5.6.38.
[15] *Ibid.* s. 5.6.40.
[16] *Ibid.* ss. 5.6.48 – 5.6.51.
[17] *Ibid.* s. 5.7.41.

Harvesting[18]

Where a total allowable harvest for a stock or population of wildlife has not been established by the Board, an Inuk has the right to harvest that stock or population in the Nunavut settlement area up to the full level of his or her economic, social and cultural needs.[19] The Board is obliged to presume that Inuit peoples need the total allowable harvest of a range of species: all bears, muskox, bowhead whales, migratory birds and their eggs, except for migratory game birds, raptors (including owls), and eiderdown from eider duck nests.[20] This presumption is rebuttable, but can only be subject to review 20 years after the ratification of the Nunavut Agreement.[21]

In order to establish a total allowable harvest, the Board is to investigate the economic, social and cultural needs of the Inuit in the context of actual harvestation levels, availability of and accessibility to wildlife, and the general economic, social and cultural conditions and circumstances of Inuit people.[22] Where the basic needs level is equal to or less than the basic needs level, the Inuit have the right to the entire total allowable harvest.[23] In any given year that there is a surplus, the Board will determine its allocation in the following order of priority: for personal consumption by other residents;[24] for the continuation of sports and other commercial operations;[25] other ventures to support the establishment and continued operation of viable economic ventures sponsored by an Inuit Hunting and Trapping Organization or a Regional Wildlife Organization.[26] These two organizations hold the position as overseers and, in addition to the functions of the Board, will allocate and enforce community and regional basic harvestation needs levels.[27]

Under the Agreement a restricted category of people may harvest fur bearers in the Nunavut settlement area: an Inuk, certain people who had hunting rights in the Nunavut settlement area prior to the Agreement, and those granted permission by an Inuit Hunting and Trapping Organization. [28] Certain other residents of the Nunavut settlement area and Northwest Territories retain hunting and fishing privileges in the Nunavut settlement area.[29]

In the allocation of commercial licences to harvest, preference is given to an applicant who has made his or her principal residence in the Nunavut

---

18   *Ibid.* Part 6.
19   *Ibid.* s. 5.6.1.
20   *Ibid.* s. 5.6.5.
21   *Ibid.* s. 5.6.6.
22   *Ibid.* s. 5.6.9.
23   *Ibid.* s. 5.6.20.
24   *Ibid.* s. 5.6.32 – 5.6.37.
25   *Ibid.* s. 5.6.38.
26   *Ibid.* s. 5.6.39.
27   *Ibid.* ss. 5.7.1 – 5.7.5.
28   *Ibid.* s. 5.6.13.
29   *Ibid.* s. 5.6.43.

settlement area and applications that are likely to provide direct benefits to the local economy.[30] Applications are to be considered on their merits, and an application filed by an Inuk or Inuit entity will not be given preference over other applications.[31]

The Inuit are granted a free and unrestricted right of access for the purpose of harvesting to all lands, water and marine areas within the Nunavut settlement area and to Crown lands, including parks, conservation areas and lands vested in a municipal corporation.[32] This general right of access does not extend, however, to lands dedicated to military or national security purposes; land owned in fee simple prior to the ratification of the Agreement and land granted in fee simple after ratification (where such land is less than one square mile); or subject to a surface lease.[33] Furthermore, the right of access is subject to laws of general application enacted for the purpose of public safety, conservation measures imposed by the Board, agreements involving parks or conservation areas, rights of navigation;[34] and land subject to incompatible use, so long as permitted under the Agreement.[35]

Subject to some exceptions, the general rule is that an Inuk has the right to dispose freely to any person any wildlife lawfully harvested. This right includes sale, barter and exchange inside and outside of the Nunavut settlement area.[36] The Inuit will remain subject to any laws of general application regarding the sale or offer for sale of any migratory bird or migratory bird's egg.[37] Any method or technology to harvest may be employed by the harvester, subject only to laws relating to public health and safety, laws regarding humane killing of wildlife, and environmental protection laws and regulations.[38]

The Designated Inuit Organization affected has the right of first refusal to establish new sports lodges and naturalist lodges in the Nunavut settlement area.[39] Such organizations also have the right of first refusal to establish and operate facilities, other than government facilities, for the purpose of indigenous wildlife and reindeer propagation, cultivation or husbandry.[40] The right of first refusal extends to the marketing of wildlife, wildlife parts and wildlife products in the Nunavut settlement area.[41]

---

[30] *Ibid.* s. 5.6.45.
[31] *Ibid.* s. 5.6.46.
[32] *Ibid.* s. 5.7.16.
[33] *Ibid.* s. 5.7.17.
[34] *Ibid.* s. 5.7.25.
[35] *Ibid.* s. 5.7.18.
[36] *Ibid.* s. 5.7.30.
[37] *Ibid.* s. 5.7.33.
[38] *Ibid.* s. 5.7.42.
[39] *Ibid.* s. 5.8.1.
[40] *Ibid.* s. 5.8.4.
[41] *Ibid.* s. 5.8.7.

Marine Harvesting[42]

The Nunavut Agreement recognizes that Inuit are traditional and current users of certain marine areas, and the legal rights of the Inuit flowing from the Agreement are based on such current and traditional use.[43] There are no Inuit-owned lands in marine areas.[44] Where the federal government grants commercial licences to certain zones near Inuit fishing areas, it is to pay special consideration to Inuit basic needs and concerns, and is to seek the advice of Inuit prior to dealing with such areas.[45] Nothing in the Agreement precludes the right of Inuit to access and harvest in areas adjacent to the marine areas of the Nunavut settlement area.[46]

The harvesting principles in Article 5 are to apply in respect of all harvesting from land-fast ice, and all marine mammals in open waters.[47] In addition, the Inuit have the right to continue to use open waters in the Outer Land Fast Ice Zone for the purpose of harvesting, for domestic consumption, all species other than marine mammals for which activities they will not need a licence, but will be subject to all management regulations imposed by appropriate government authorities.[48]

Water Rights[49]

Under the Agreement, water rights are vested in the Designated Inuit Organization in trust for the use and benefit of the Inuit.[50] Subject to any exceptions, the Designated Inuit Organization has exclusive rights to the water flowing through Inuit-owned lands.[51]

Minerals and Mining

The Agreement transfers title to approximately 35,257 square kilometres of land including mineral rights and the right to mine subsurface resources.[52]

The Agreement provides for royalty sharing under Article 25. The Inuit are to be paid an amount equal to 50 percent of the first $2,000,000 of resource royalty received by the government in that year; and 5 percent of any additional resource royalty received by the government in that year,[53] on and

---

[42] *Ibid.* Article 15.
[43] *Ibid.* s. 15.1.1.
[44] *Ibid.* s. 15.2.3.
[45] *Ibid.* Part 3.
[46] *Ibid.* s. 15.3.8.
[47] *Ibid.* s. 16.1.1.
[48] *Ibid.* s. 16.1.2.
[49] *Ibid.* Article 20.
[50] *Ibid.* s. 20.2.1.
[51] *Ibid.* s. 20.2.2.
[52] *Ibid.* Article 17.
[53] *Ibid.* s. 25.1.1.

under the Nunavut settlement area and the Outer Land Fast Ice Zone as specified in the Agreement.[54] However, where deposits of carving stone are discovered on Crown lands in the Nunavut settlement area, the Designated Inuit Organization is to have the right to obtain an exclusive quarry lease to mine significant deposits, or to acquire title to the land containing the deposits, in exchange for other Inuit-owned lands.[55] Fifty cubic yards of carving stone may be removed annually by the Inuit without a permit on the condition that there is no significant damage to the land, and that interest holders do not have their right to enjoy the land infringed.[56]

Title to land in fee simple, including the mines and minerals that may be found to exist within, upon or under such lands, is transferred to Designated Inuit Organizations to a small portion of land.[57] A description of these lands, which amount to approximately 572 square kilometres in area, are contained in Schedule 41-1 to the Agreement.

Five-Year Review – 1993 to 1998: Implementation of the Nunavut Land Claims Agreement

The five-year review of the implementation of the Nunavut Land Claims Agreement indicates that there have been major disappointments. The most graphic has been the failure of the federal Department of Fisheries and Oceans to respect the rights of Inuit and the role of the Nunavut Wildlife Management Board in regards to the allocation of commercial turbot stocks off Baffin Island, forcing Nunavut people to resort to litigation to obtain relief through the courts.[58]

A claim is currently underway by the Makivik First Nation in relation to an area of offshore Nunavut.

Two recent cases considered the impact of the Nunavut Land Claims Agreement on the Minister of Fisheries and Oceans discretionary authority to set turbot quotas.[59] The first case was an application for judicial review of a decision that set limits on the East Arctic turbot catch. Under the Nunavut Land Claims Agreement, the government recognized Inuit economic reliance on wildlife and assured that fair access to wildlife resources would be promoted. Turbot was caught in waters shared equally by Canada and

---

[54] *Ibid.* s. 25.4.1.

[55] *Ibid.* s. 19.9.2.

[56] *Ibid.* s. 19.9.4.

[57] *Ibid.* s. 41.1.1.

[58] *Nunavut Tunngavik Inc. v. Canada* (Minister of Fisheries and Oceans), (1999) FC T-1135-98, online: <http://www.canlii.org/ca/cas/fc/1999/1999fc25458.html>.

[59] *Nunavut Tunngavik Inc. v. Canada (Ministry of Fisheries and Oceans)*, [1997] 4 C.N.L.R. 193 (F.C.T.D.), and *Nunavut Tunngavik Inc. v. Canada (Ministry of Fisheries and Oceans)*, [2000] 3 C.N.L.R. 136 (F.C.T.D.); affirmed [2001] 1 C.N.L.R. iv (F.C.A.).

Greenland. The share allocated to Canada was allotted to licensed fishermen in the Atlantic provinces. Under the federal *Fisheries Act* the Minister retained the power to set and allocate quotas for the 200-mile fishing zone beyond the 12-mile Territorial Sea. However, the Agreement specified that the Minister was under an obligation to consider recommendations in respect of fishery matters made by the Board established under the Agreement. The Nunavut Wildlife Management Board, constituted under the Nunavut Land Claims Agreement, sought additional licences for Inuit fishermen for the entire Atlantic fishery from the federal Department of Fisheries and Oceans. The board also sought a 27 percent allocation of the Canadian catch to Nunavut fishermen. The Board's recommendations in setting the catch levels and allocation of the Canadian share were in large part ignored by the Minister in subsequent decision making. Nunavut argued that the Minister had interfered with the Board's authority to establish catch levels and that the Minister failed to consider the Board's recommendations or to give special consideration to Inuit economic dependence and proximity to the resource.

The Nunavut application was allowed and the Minister's quota decision was set aside and declared illegal. The Federal Court found that the Minister had failed to give full, careful and conscientious attention to the recommendations of the Wildlife Board and observed that the Minister's primary concern in setting quota allocations appeared to be non-Nunavut fishermen. The Board's primary responsibility to set catch levels within Nunavut's territorial area had been infringed upon and the Minister was found to have failed to have fulfilled his obligation to justify the dismissal of the Board's proposals and also to give special consideration to the principle of Inuit economic dependence and proximity to the resource in setting its quota levels. Mr. Justice Campbell held that the Minister could not simply receive and examine the advice given by the Board, and was under an obligation to maintain a "mandatory, close, cooperative and highly respectful" relationship with the Board.[60] The Crown must therefore take a proactive stance when dealing with Aboriginal interests and advice with respect to decisions and actions arising from activities that have the potential to adversely affect Aboriginal People. The Federal Court indicated "the Minister's discretion in section 7 of the [federal] *Fisheries Act* is no longer absolute when the exercise of that discretion affects the wildlife and the marine areas of the [Nunavut settlement area] and the wildlife management."[61] The matter was subsequently remitted to the Minister for reconsideration.

---

[60] *Nunavut Tunngavik Inc. v. Canada (Ministry of Fisheries and Oceans)*, Ibid. at 210.

[61] *Ibid.* at 633.

The second case of 2000 involved a challenge to the authority of the Minister.[62] The application in this case was for judicial review of a decision by the Minister of Fisheries and Oceans to establish turbot quotas for the Davis Strait fishery for 5 years. The Nunavut sought larger quotas, a request that was rejected by the Minister. At issue in this case was whether the Minister's determined quota violated the Agreement.

This time the application was dismissed. The Federal Court found that the Minister had the discretion to set quotas under the Agreement that allowed the Minister to take into consideration other matters such as the growth and decline of available stock. Accordingly the quota did reflect the special consideration given to Nunavut residents pursuant to the Agreement and was a fair distribution between Nunavut and non-Nunavut residents of Canada. "Fairness" in this sense was based on the specific circumstances that governed the available Atlantic fishery resource. The court found that on their interpretation of the Agreement the Minister did not act in bad faith or on the basis of irrelevant factors. In this case, substantial evidence was submitted to the court that the Minister had taken into account all of the relevant considerations and had received and regarded all applicable advice and material.

In 2001, an Inuit applicant sought judicial review of a decision by the Nunavut Minister of Sustainable Development to disallow a decision by the Nunavut Wildlife Management Board on polar bear hunting.[63] Kadluk had applied to the Board for permission to hunt a bear using a spear or harpoon. The Board approved the application and the Minister subsequently overturned the Board's decision on the basis that it was contrary to concerns for public safety. The appeal was allowed and the Minister's decision was quashed and remitted back to the Ministry for further consideration. The court held that the Inuit right of harvest within the Nunavut Land Claims Agreement was constitutionally protected by virtue of the Agreement's incorporation into section 35 of the *Constitution Act, 1982*. The court held that the decision to restrict the harvesting right was based on a valid legislative objective to protect public safety; however, the Minister's decision to overturn the Board's decision did not satisfy the principle of minimal interference with the Aboriginal right to hunt. The court found that reasonable conditions could have been imposed on the licence to hunt the bear in order to address the Minister's safety concerns.

---

62 *Supra*, note 71 in ch. 13.
63 *Kadlak v. Nunavut (Minister of Sustainable Development)*, [2001] 1 C.N.L.R. 147 (Nun. Ct. J.).

Chapter 15

Nova Scotia, New Brunswick and Prince Edward Island

From 1713 to 1763, the Maritimes were central to the struggle between the French and the British over control of North America. The Mi'kmaq and the Maliseet, the two Aboriginal groups that currently reside in the Maritimes, were caught in the middle of this conflict. When the British acquired sovereignty over most of the Maritimes, a series of peace and friendship treaties were signed between the British and the two First Nations.[1] The treaties did not surrender land to the Crown, but were merely designed to ensure that peaceable relations continued between the Aboriginal and non-Aboriginal occupants of the provinces. The British in Atlantic Canada continued the French practice of establishing reserves without treaties or agreements. It was considered that the Royal Proclamation of 1763 did not require treating with Aboriginal People for the surrender of Aboriginal title in those areas. The Royal Proclamation affirmed that Aboriginal lands were reserved for them until the Aboriginal Peoples were inclined to surrender them. Until a reserve policy was established in the Maritimes, settlers or the Crown occupied the land without first seeking the permission of the Aboriginal inhabitants. Eventually the encroachment of non-Aboriginal settlers onto lands occupied by Aboriginal People was so extreme that the Maritime provinces and subsequently Canada enacted legislation to protect these lands and organize the process of disposition of those lands.[2] Land reserved for the Mi'kmaq and the Maliseet was accordingly not set apart following the process laid out by the Royal Proclamation, but instead by executive orders issuing licences of occupation or by orders-in-council. [3]In most cases consent of the Aboriginal inhabitants was not obtained prior to reserve creation. According to one commentator, the reason why the interests of the Aboriginal People in the Maritimes were ignored, in comparison to the

---

[1] For background on these treaties, see Wicken, W., "The Mi'kmaq and Wuastukwiuk Treaties" (1994) 44 *University of New Brunswick Law Journal*, 241.

[2] See these statutes reproduced in Isaac, T., *Pre-1986 Legislation Concerning Indians*, University of Saskatchewan Native Law Centre, Saskatoon, 1993.

[3] See Bartlett, R., *Indian reserves in the Atlantic Provinces of Canada*, University of Saskatchewan Native Law Centre, Saskatoon, 1986, p. 14.

deference given to Aboriginal rights in Ontario, for example, was that politically speaking, Aboriginal issues in Atlantic Canada were of less pressing importance than those in Ontario.[4]

In Nova Scotia, land was set apart by order in council in trust for the Aboriginal People "to whom they are to be hereafter considered as exclusively belonging."[5]

In New Brunswick, reserve lands were set apart mainly by licence of occupation and subsequently confirmed by order in council.

Prince Edward Island was granted in full to British landowners and no land was reserved for the Aboriginal People. The First Nations in residence on Lennox Island were, however, permitted to continue occupancy by the island's proprietor. The four reserves that currently exist on the island were acquired by private purchase of land by the Crown.[6]

No permission, consent or surrender was ever sought, therefore, from the original inhabitants of these areas of Canada. Commissioners were appointed in each province to protect First Nations land from encroachment by settlers. However, the Commissioners also had the power to dispose of reserve lands for the purpose of settlement without having to seek the consent of the Aboriginal People affected. Due to the fact that land cession treaties were not signed in the Maritime provinces, traditional Aboriginal rights have only begun to be defined in the Maritimes in the preceding two decades.

The majority of Aboriginal residents in Nova Scotia reside on reserve land that was set aside by virtue of federal government purchases in the 1940s.

Prior to 1958 it seemed that Nova Scotia and New Brunswick held title to the reserve land within the provinces. In 1958, Canada entered into an agreement respecting Aboriginal land with New Brunswick and Nova Scotia.

Resource Transfer Agreements in New Brunswick and Nova Scotia[7]

These agreements transferred reserve lands, apart from those lands that were under public highways and minerals, from the provinces to Canada. In Nova Scotia and New Brunswick, the transfer of title of reserves from the province to Canada results in the proceeds of mineral disposition on reserves going to

---

4   See Harring, S., *White Man's Law: Native People in Nineteenth-Century Canadian Jurisprudence*, University of Toronto Press, Toronto, 1998, p. 185.

5   Hutton, E., "Indian Affairs in Nova Scotia: 1760-1834," in McGee, H., ed., *The Native Peoples of Atlantic Canada*, McClelland and Stewart, Toronto, 1974, p. 78, cited in Bartlett., p. 15.

6   Cumming, P. and Mickenberg, N., *Native Rights in Canada*, 2d ed., General, Toronto, 1972, p. 98.

7   *An Act to Confirm an Agreement between the Government of Canada and the Government of the Province of Nova Scotia Respecting Indian Reserves*, S.C. 1959, c.50; *An Act to Confirm an Agreement between the Government of Canada and the Government of the Province of New Brunswick Respecting Indian Reserves*, S.C. 1954, c.4.

the federal government for the benefit of the affected Aboriginal People. Minerals and mining developments are done under the *Indian Act.*

Mineral Potential on Indian Reserve Lands in the Atlantic Provinces[8]

The Mineral Potential of Indian Reserve Lands report compiled by the Department of Indian and Northern Affairs Canada[9] in the Atlantic Provinces provides overall rating measures of the economic mineral possibilities of each reserve as a whole, on a scale of low/moderate/good. Factors that affect this rating are the size of the reserve, the location with respect to markets, transportation, access, value and type of commodity, social and cultural barriers to mining on certain lands and areas, marketability of a commodity at any given time and other differentials.

The following rating applies in the three provinces:

- 46 reserves were given a low rating;
- 19 reserves were given a moderate rating; and
- 3 reserves were given a good rating.

The report indicates that 11 reserves have at least one commodity that has potential for development. Of the total number of reserves, at the time of this report, none had surrendered their minerals in any way.

Provincial Legislation

Note that provincial legislation and regulations are deemed to apply to Aboriginal People subject to two conditions:

- provincial legislation cannot apply exclusively to Aboriginal People or to land reserved for their benefit; and
- a provincial law may be declared invalid or inapplicable to Aboriginal People if it infringes upon an established Aboriginal or treaty right that is constitutionally protected.

Where an Aboriginal person has established an Aboriginal or treaty right to hunt or fish, then the provincial legislation cannot interfere with that right[10] unless the limitation can meet the test of justification and is in keeping with the honour of the Crown.[11] A limitation on the exercise of a treaty or Aboriginal right would need to be tested in the courts for clarification. It is clear that sufficient consideration must be given to the Aboriginal interest.

---

[8] See the Department of Indian and Northern Affairs on line: <http://www.ainc-inac.gc.ca/ntr/atl.html>.

[9] Keep in mind that although this site was last updated on the 30 April 2001, the report was actually completed in 1991.

[10] *R. v. White and Bob, supra* note 10 in ch. 2; *R. v. Simon, supra* note 2 in ch. 2; and *R. v. Sioui, supra* note 2 in ch. 2.

[11] *R. v. White and Bob, supra* note 10 in ch. 2; *R. v. Simon, supra* note 2 in ch. 2; and *R. v. Sioui, supra* note 2 in ch. 2; *R. v. Sparrow, supra* note 5 in ch. 1.

Apart from measures implemented by a province to conserve a resource, it is unlikely that any court in Canada would uphold any other provincial legislation that restricts an Aboriginal or treaty right. Recently, provincial laws designed to protect public safety have been permitted to override and limit Aboriginal resource rights.

Under the *Wildlife Act*[12] all property in wildlife resides with the province.[13] The Minister of Natural Resources has responsibility for overseeing the protection, management and conservation of wildlife in the province.[14] There is a mechanism under the Act whereby the Minister in right of the province can enter into agreements with any person or group for the purpose of wildlife management.[15]

Fishing in Nova Scotia

Under the *Wildlife Act*, no person is permitted to fish within provincial waters without a valid licence issued pursuant to the Act.[16] The Minister has absolute discretion as to whom a licence, permit or certificate will be issued to.[17] Licences are issued under the accompanying *Fishing Regulations*.[18]

Hunting in Nova Scotia

The Minister of Natural Resources is responsible for regulating hunting in the province. No person is permitted to hunt wildlife without a valid licence or permit issued under the Act and its accompanying regulations (*Bear Harvesting Regulations*;[19] *Deer Hunting Regulations*;[20] *Fur Harvesting Regulations*;[21] *General Wildlife Regulations*[22]).[23] The Minister is responsible for establishing bag limits in relation to species that may be hunted during the open season for that species.[24]

Under the *Endangered Species Act*[25] the Minister can regulate to protect species that are determined to be at risk. The list of species that are to be protected appears in the Species at Risk List Regulations.[26] The Act and its Regulations do not override Aboriginal or treaty rights.[27]

---

[12] R.S., c. 504, s. 2.
[13] *Wildlife Act*, s. 4(1).
[14] *Ibid.* s. 6(1).
[15] *Ibid.* s. 11.
[16] *Ibid.* s. 53(3).
[17] *Ibid.* s. 30(1).
[18] N.S. Reg. 50/2000.
[19] N.S. Reg. 77/2001.
[20] N.S. Reg. 74/2001.
[21] N.S. Reg. 76/2001.
[22] N.S. Reg. 73/2001.
[23] *Wildlife Act*, s. 26.
[24] *Ibid.* s. 39(2).
[25] S.N.S. 1998, c. 11.
[26] N.S. Reg. 109/2000.
[27] *Endangered Species Act*, s. 2(2).

Fishing in New Brunswick

Under the *Fish and Wildlife Act*,[28] property of all wildlife and fish within the province is vested in the Crown in right of the province.[29] The Minister is responsible for issuing angling licences within the province.[30] An angling lease that is issued to a band is to be for a period of five years or less and will cost the band an annual rental fee of one dollar.[31] An angling lease permits the lessee to fish with a rod and line. Licences are issued under the *General Angling Regulation – Fish and Wildlife Act*.[32]

Hunting in New Brunswick

Under the *Fish and Wildlife Act*, any person hunting for moose, deer, bear beaver, bobcat, fisher, marten, mink, otter, racoon or red fox must be the holder of a valid licence issued by the Minister.[33] The licence will dictate the number of species that may be harvested in the province. Under the *Fur Harvesting Regulation – Fish and Wildlife Act*[34] the Minister can issue a licence to an individual for the purpose of fur harvesting of certain species. Licences are issued under the *Hunting Regulation – Fish and Wildlife Act*[35] and the *Moose Hunting Regulation – Fish and Wildlife Act*.[36]

Fishing on Prince Edward Island

Residents of Prince Edward Island must buy a Trout Fishing License along with a Wildlife Conservation License. A trout licence enables the angler to fish for brook and rainbow trout only. Separate licences must be obtained for fishing for Atlantic salmon and for winter ice fishing.

Hunting on Prince Edward Island

An Aboriginal person does not require a hunting license on the island. Aboriginal person means a person who is registered as an Indian pursuant to the *Indian Act* or is a registered member of a *bona fide* Aboriginal organization that has as a condition of membership proof of Aboriginal ancestry.

---

[28] Chapter F-14.1.
[29] *Fish and Wildlife Act*, s. 3(1).
[30] *Ibid*. s. 63.
[31] *Ibid*. s. 64. and s. 66.
[32] O.C. 82-473.
[33] *Ibid*. s. 32(1) and s. 34(2).
[34] O.C. 84-462.
[35] O.C. 84-480.
[36] O.C. 94-235.

As indicated earlier, these laws and regulations are deemed to apply generally to Aboriginal People to the point that interference with an established right to hunt and trap is unjustified.

Treaties of the Maritimes

Peace and Friendship Treaties

Although no land was ceded to the Crown in the Maritimes by treaty, several peace and alliance treaties were negotiated with original Aboriginal occupants of certain areas.

- On 11 August 1693 a treaty was negotiated between the British Crown and the Penobscot, Kennebeck, Amrascogen and Saco tribes to cover the area of Massachusetts Bay in the then province of New England. The purpose of the treaty was to make peace and to ensure alliance between the Crown and the Aboriginal inhabitants. The treaty does not, therefore, refer to any surrender of lands or rights to that land. Although the treaty makes no reference to the resource access rights of the Aboriginal People concerned, the treaty does acknowledge the consent given by the First Nations to have all future trade and commerce regulated by the government of the province. Moreover, the treaty states that the negotiating Aboriginal parties thereby submitted to be "ruled and governed by their Majesties' laws."[37]

- On 13 July 1713 a treaty was negotiated between the British Crown and the Norrigawake, Narrakamegock, Amascontoog, Piwocket, Pennecook and Indian Plantations on Rivers St. Johns, Penobscot, Kenybeck, Amascogen, Saco and Merrimack tribes. The area covered is the eastern parts of the then provinces of Massachusetts Bay and New Hampshire. Again, the intention of the Crown was to sustain peace and alliance among the Aboriginal and non-Aboriginal residents of the district. Both the Crown and Aboriginal participants agreed to certain terms. The Aboriginal participants agreed to submit to Crown regulation of all trade and commerce between "the English and Indians," and more generally, to submit to the rule and governance of "her Majesty's Laws." In return for the agreement of the Aboriginal parties to respect the right of the non-Aboriginal settlers to certain occupation rights, the Crown agreed to save "unto the said Indians their own Grounds, and free liberty for Hunting, Fishing, Fowling, and all other their Lawful Liberties and Privileges" as of 11 August 1693.[38]

---

[37] Reproduced in Reiter, R., *The Law of Canadian Indian Treaties*, Juris Analytica Publishing Inc., Edmonton, 1995, Part III, I.

[38] *Ibid.*

- On 12 August 1717, the British Crown entered into a treaty with the Kennebeck, Penobscot, Pegwackit, Saco and other First Nations not specified within that area regarding land mass to the east of the then provinces of Massachusetts Bay and New Hampshire. The effect of this treaty was to ratify the terms of the earlier treaty, saving the "restraint and limitation of Trade and Commerce," which, according to the treaty, was by this time "now otherwise managed."[39] The treaty therefore incorporated the earlier Crown promise to guarantee unto the Aboriginal signatory groups their "own Grounds, and free liberty for Hunting, Fishing, Fowling and all other their Lawful Liberties and Privileges" as of 11 August 1693.

- On 15 December 1725, the Crown entered into a further treaty with the Aboriginal People belonging to the Penobscot, Naridgwalk, St. John, Cape Sables and other unspecified Aboriginal groups in the territories of New England and Nova Scotia. Although the purpose of the treaty is to maintain peace and alliance with the Aboriginal occupants at that time, the treaty does refer to Aboriginal land and resource rights. The treaty reads:

    > Saving unto the Penobscot, Naridgwalk and other Tribes within His Majesty's province aforesaid and their natural Descendants respectively all their lands, Liberties and properties not by them convey'd or sold to or possessed by any of the English Subjects as aforesaid. As also the priviledge of fishing, hunting, and fowling as formerly.[40]

    The Aboriginal signatories agreed that, henceforth, all trade and commerce between the "English and Indians" would be governed by the Crown, and more generally, agreed to submit to be ruled and governed by "His Majesty's Laws."

    A further treaty to ratify the 1725 treaty was negotiated on 13 May 1728 between the Crown and the St. Johns, Cape Sables and other tribes inhabiting Nova Scotia and Acadia at the time. The terms of the treaty are the same as those expressed in the 1725 treaty, although some are not expressly stated.

    The treaty of 1725 was further renewed by way of a treaty between the Crown and the Chineto people of Nova Scotia and Acadia on 15 August 1749. The terms of this treaty are the same as those contained in the 1725 treaty. However, some terms are not expressly stated. Renewal of the 1725 treaty occurred between the St. Johns tribe and the Crown on 4 September 1749. The terms of the original treaty again remain the same.

---

[39] *Ibid.*
[40] *Ibid.*

Reaffirmation of the 1725 treaty occurred again on 22 November 1752 with the Mi'kmaq people of the eastern coast of Nova Scotia. In this case, the Crown guaranteed to the Mi'kmaq signatories that

[the Mi'kmaq] not be hindered from, but have the liberty of hunting and fishing as usual; and that if they shall think a Truckhouse needful at the River Chibenacadie they shall have the same built and proper merchandise lodged therein, to be exchanged for what the Indians shall have to dispose of, and that in the meantime the said Indians shall have free liberty to bring for sale to Halifax or any other settlement in this Province, skins, feathers, fowl, fish or any other thing they shall have to sell, where they have the liberty to dispose thereof to the best advantage.

Canadian courts have had various opportunities to interpret the meaning of these peace and alliance treaties of the Maritimes. The courts have been willing to recognize the binding nature of the peace and alliance treaties and have affirmed Aboriginal harvesting rights contained within them in certain circumstances. The court determined that the treaty of 1713 did not involve any surrender of Aboriginal rights by the Mi'kmaq people of New Brunswick and that Aboriginal hunting rights still exist.[41]

The 1994 *R. v. Paul* decision in New Brunswick concerned three Maliseet individuals who were charged with unlawfully possessing deer meat. The Crown argued that the animals had been shot in an unsafe manner as the accused were hunting on private lands near a highway. The Maliseet men argued that they had an unfettered right to hunt anywhere in New Brunswick at any time. The court determined that, although a treaty right was found to exist, treaty rights must be exercised with regard to the safety of others. The 1994 case of *R. v. McCoy*[42] involved a Maliseet man who was a member of the St. Mary's Band. He was acquitted of unlawfully hunting wildlife with the aid of a light. The New Brunswick Court of Appeal found that the Maliseet and the Mi'kmaq of New Brunswick had never surrendered any Aboriginal rights. Thus, the court found that the Indians had retained hunting rights, stating that "the expeditions by Moncton and Murray were for settlement and did not conquer Indian title." Interestingly, the court found that there had been no symbolic conquest of Aboriginal title during the Seven Years War and that neither the treaty of 1713 nor the Dummer's Treaty in 1726 at Annapolis Royal had involved a surrender of Aboriginal rights in New Brunswick. Accordingly, the provincial Act failed to recognize those rights and therefore did not apply to them.

---

[41] *R. v. McCoy*, [1994] 2 C.N.L.R. 129 (N.B.C.A.), [1993] 1 C.N.L.R. 135 (N.B.Q.B.); *R. v. Paul*, [1994] 2 C.N.L.R. 167 (N.B.C.A.).

[42] [1994] 2 C.N.LR. 129 (N.B.C.A.), [1993] 1 C.N.L.R. 135 (N.B.Q.B.).

In *R. v. Fowler,*[43] another decision relating to the treaty of 1725 was determined. The court found that Maliseet, who are not registered under the *Indian Act,* are entitled to benefits under the treaty.

In *R. v. Paul,*[44] the court determined that neither the treaty of 1725 nor the *Royal Proclamation, 1763* take precedence over federal legislation, and in particular that section 35 of the *Constitution Act, 1982* does not revive or restore such rights.

In 1998 the New Brunswick Court of Appeal discussed the Drummer Treaty of 1725, the Drummer Proclamation of 1725 and other such treaties negotiated by the Crown with the Mi'kmaq and Maliseet First Nations of eastern Canada in the early eighteenth century.[45] A member of the Mi'kmaq First Nation of New Brunswick had removed logs from Crown land and had sold them and was subsequently charged under the *Crown Lands and Forest Act.*[46] In his defence he presented seven treaties, proclamations or promises in support of his assertion that he possessed a treaty right to harvest and sell timber. The judge of first instance undertook private historical research after the hearing, and based upon that research and His Honour's interpretation of the documents that were uncovered during his personal study or during the hearing determined that the Crown had never obtained title to land that belonged to the Mi'kmaq and Maliseet. On appeal however, the Court of Appeal overruled Mr. Justice Turnbull's decision on the basis that he was not entitled to rely on evidence not submitted during the course of the trial. Independent research conducted post-trial, no matter what it indicated, was contrary to the *Provincial Offences Procedure Act,* and the decision was thereby void on this and several other grounds. Accordingly, the Court of Appeal found that the respondent had not presented evidence to the effect that the commercial harvesting of timber was a practice, tradition or custom that was an integral part of his culture. Thus he did not succeed in establishing that he possessed an Aboriginal right to harvest and sell timber. Leave to appeal to the Supreme Court of Canada was refused.

In 1928 a Court of Nova Scotia found that the treaty of 1752 was not in reality a treaty made between competent contracting parties and did not extend to the Aboriginal People of Cape Breton. Those Aboriginal People therefore acquired no rights to hunt under the treaty and were thereby subject to the general game laws of Nova Scotia.[47] (Note that this is no longer the case – treaty rights supersede any negatively impacting provincial laws.[48]) In

---

[43] [1993] 3 C.N.L.R. 178 (N.B. Prov. Ct.).

[44] (1988), 232 A.P.R. 231, [1989] 1 C.N.L.R. 135 (N.B.Q.B.).

[45] *R. v. Paul,* [1998] 3 C.N.L.R. 221 (N.B.C.A.).

[46] S.N.B. 1980, c. 381, s. 67(2).

[47] *R. v. Syliboy* (1928), 4 C.N.L.C. 430 (N.S.C.C.).

[48] Overturned by *R. v. White and Bob, supra* note 10 in ch. 2.

Simon v. The Queen[49] the New Brunswick Court of Appeal found that the 1752 treaty did not extend to a Mi'kmaq from the Big Cove reservation who was convicted under provincial fisheries legislation. The Mi'kmaq person could not produce evidence to satisfy the court that a connection existed between the accused and the First Nations with whom the original treaty was made. In 1978 a New Brunswick Court held that the treaties of 1725 and 1752 were in effect land cession treaties, and therefore the federal fisheries legislation applied to Aboriginal People fishing in an area that had been surrendered to the Crown.[50] However, in 1985, in *R. v. Simon*,[51] the Supreme Court ruled that these treaties did convey rights and allowed an appeal of a hunting conviction. In *R. v. Atwin*[52] a New Brunswick court held that the 1725 and 1752 treaties protected the Aboriginal right to hunt muskrat off-reserve; therefore, the accused Aboriginal was acquitted of hunting without a licence contrary to the New Brunswick *Game Act*.

In 1990, 14 Aboriginal People charged with hunting moose contrary to the Nova Scotia hunting scheme were acquitted.[53] The accused claimed that Aboriginal and treaty rights under the treaties of 1725, 1752, 1760-61 and the Royal Proclamation took precedence over the *Wildlife Act* that prohibited hunting out of season and without a licence. The court found that unextinguished Aboriginal rights existed and that therefore the provincial hunting scheme did not apply to the Aboriginal People charged with hunting offences.

In *R. v. Denny*[54] three Mi'kmaq men from Eskasoni and Afton River were charged with a variety of fishing offences. The Eskasoni charges related to fishing without a licence for cod and salmon, and possessing salmon illegally. The Afton River case involved using a snare for fishing for salmon. The accused argued that their Aboriginal right to fish for food took precedence over fisheries regulations. The Court of Appeal of Nova Scotia agreed with their position, and stated that an Aboriginal right to fish for food took precedence over fisheries regulations and that "an Aboriginal right to fish for food in the waters in question" had "not been extinguished through treaty, other agreement or competent legislation." In recognizing the "legitimate food needs" of First Nations fishers, the court further indicated that this Aboriginal right to fish for subsistence purposes stood only behind conservation as a priority in terms of resource use. This decision made it clear that Mi'kmaq food fishing rights were recognized by law and took precedence over commercial or sport fishing. The *Denny* decision came in the

---

49 (1958), 5 C.N.L.C. 617 (N.B.C.A.).

50 *R. v. Nicholas* (1978), 39 A.P.R. 285, [1979] 1 C.N.L.R. 69 (N.B. Pr.Ct.).

51 *R. v. Simon* (1985) 2 S.C.R.

52 [1981] 2 C.N.L.R. 99 (N.B.Pr.Ct.).

53 *Nova Scotia Moose Harvesting Cases*, [1990] 3 C.N.L.R. 87.

54 [1990] 2 C.N.L.R. 115 (N.S.C.A.).

middle of a trial of 14 Mi'kmaq charged with illegal moose hunting. As discussed above, that case was dismissed on the grounds that the fishing judgement created "a presumption of Aboriginal rights" that made it clear First Nations people had the right to hunt as well as fish for subsistence purposes.

In *R. v. Tomah*,[55] two Maliseet appealed a charge of unlawful fishing. The New Brunswick Court of Queen's Bench dismissed the appeal on the basis that they were not satisfied that any evidence had been submitted supporting the proposition that fishing on the Miramichi River for food was a tradition, custom, or practice of the Maliseet people.

Caselaw to date has determined that no Aboriginal right to exploit natural resources for commercial purposes exists on the basis of the treaties discussed above. Where Aboriginal rights to hunt, fish and trap have been established, there is a general reluctance by the courts to extend that right to any more than subsistence harvesting. Nevertheless, it is a factual reality that no treaty or other documents records any Aboriginal group in the Maritimes ever selling or surrendering their rights in land to the Crown.

- In 1760 the Crown negotiated treaties with the Passamaquody and St. Johns tribes and, in a separate document, with the Richebucto people of Nova Scotia. The objective of the treaties was to renew prior treaties and to establish a future of peace and amity between the Aboriginal and non-Aboriginal inhabitants of Nova Scotia. The treaty provided that the Aboriginal signatories were entitled to traffic and barter commodities, but "at all times" with the "managers of such Truckhouses as shall be established for that purpose by His Majesty's Governors." *R. v. Marshall* addressed the implications of the inclusion of the treaty term permitting trade and barter at truckhouses and is discussed below.

- Two other treaties were concluded between the Crown and Aboriginal People of Nova Scotia: in 1761 with the Merimichy people, and in 1779 with the Merimichy, Pagumske, Restigouche and Mi'kmaq tribes. Again, these treaties were negotiated with the intention of securing peaceful alliances with the Aboriginal People. The 1761 treaty included the provision that Aboriginal People were only to traffic, barter and exchange commodities at government established truckhouses. The 1779 treaty contains no comparable provision, and instead provides that

> ...the said Indians and their constituents shall remain in the districts before mentioned quiet and free from any molestation of any of His Majesty's troops or other his good subjects in their hunting and fishing...

---

[55] [1999] 3 C.N.L.R. 311 (N.B.Q.B.).

That immediate measures shall be taken to cause traders to supply them with ammunition, clothing and other necessary stores in exchange for their furs and other commodities.

In *R. v. Francis*,[56] the court held that the treaty of 1779 did not confer fishing or hunting rights. However that decision was overturned in *Paul v. The Queen*, which recognized that the treaty did in fact protect such rights. In *Augustine v. R.*[57] the court considered whether the Mi'kmaq treaty of 1779 conferred immunity from prosecution for unlawful night hunting. Apparently the trial judge took judicial notice of the assertions of the Mi'kmaq people that their right to hunt at night was a protected right based on testimony of a chief as to tribal history. The Queen's Bench refused to allow the chief's testimony on the basis that he was not qualified as an expert and could only give evidence within his personal knowledge. The Court of Appeal held that it was beyond the capacity of a judge to allow submission of inadmissible evidence, even if there had been no objection to it. Having been established in *Delgamuukw* and the later case of *R. v. Marshall* that Aboriginal oral history is admissible in evidence, this case may be decided quite differently if re-litigated.

The most recent litigation regarding the court's approach to the interpretation of the Maritime peace and friendship treaties is that of *R. v. Marshall*.[58] This case involved an appeal by Marshall from a Court of Appeal decision that had upheld his convictions for selling eels without a licence, fishing without a licence, and fishing during the close of season with illegal nets, contrary to the federal fishery regulations. Marshall, a Mi'kmaq from the Membertou Band of Cape Breton Island, was convicted of fishing for eels contrary to federal fishing laws. He was charged with fishing without a licence and selling eels without a licence as well as fishing in a closed season. Marshall claimed that he had a right to fish and to sell his catch, as such a right had never been surrendered to the British Crown. The treaty argument was based on treaties signed with the Crown in 1760 and 1761. Marshall alleged that these agreements guaranteed to the Mi'kmaq the right to fish for commercial purposes. Under those treaties, the Crown placed an obligation on the Mi'kmaq of Nova Scotia not to "traffic and barter commodities with the persons or the managers of such Truckhouses in any manner but with such persons...as shall be appointed or established by His Majesty's Governors."

The Supreme Court of Canada found for Marshall and he was acquitted of all charges. The court found that the trade arrangement under the Agreement, that the Mi'kmaq be permitted to undertake trade at "Truckhouses," had to be interpreted in light of the oral promises made by the

---

56 (1969), 10 D.L.R. (3d) 189, 6 C.N.L.C. 327 (N.B.C.A.).

57 [1987] 1 C.N.L.R. 20, 74 N.B.R. (2d) 156 (C.A.).

58 *R. v. Marshall*, supra note 93 in ch. 4.

Crown during the treaty negotiations. The court accepted on the evidence that the Crown's promise of the Mi'kmaq's access to necessaries through trade in wildlife was the deciding evidence and that, where that right had been granted, there had to be more than a disappearance of the mechanism created to allow the exercise of the right (i.e., truckhouses) in order to conclude that the right had been extinguished. The fact that truckhouses no longer exist in the Maritimes is not relevant where the surviving substance of the Mi'kmaq's treaty rights was the right to obtain commodities through the trade of hunting and fishing products. Marshall's treaty rights to fish for trading purposes and to trade for sustenance would be interfered with if the discretionary licensing system and the ban on sales were to be enforced against him. To determine otherwise would go contrary to the obligation on the Crown to act with integrity and honour when dealing with Mi'kmaq people. The Supreme Court determined that the commercial use of natural resources was guaranteed by the treaties, but subject to certain limitations. First Nations covered by the treaty are entitled to earn a "moderate income" from the sale of harvests and are under an obligation to operate within the federal legislative and regulatory framework. What the court said was that the treaty rights are limited to securing necessaries, and do not extend to the open-ended accumulation of wealth. The definition of "moderate income" was: "such basics as food, clothing and housing, supplemented by a few amenities, but not the accumulation of wealth. It addresses day-to-day needs. This was the common intention in 1760. It is fair that it be given this interpretation today."

Beyond fishing for the purpose of maintaining a "moderate income," the court indicated that fisheries legislation and regulations would apply.

The court interpreted the "truckhouses" clause and promises made to the Mi'kmaq at the time of negotiations to be designed to provide them with an opportunity to provide sustenance for the family.

The right conveyed to the First Nations by virtue of these treaties is not one of ownership or control of resources within the treaty area. Rather, the court acknowledged that it is the federal government and not the First Nations that has stewardship over ocean resources. Therefore it is within the powers of the federal government to regulate ocean fisheries. The Crown is still under an obligation to prove that any infringement of Aboriginal rights is reasonable and justifiable and in keeping with the fiduciary relationship between Aboriginal People and the Crown. Compensation may be payable by the Crown where this treaty right is infringed upon. Moreover, the right to exploit resources commercially does not mean to the exclusion of all others.

In November 1999 the Supreme Court publicly issued a clarification (in the opinion of some, a drastic expansion upon and reinterpretation of the issues at hand)[59] of its original decision. The court clarified that the original

---

[59] See Wildsmith, B., "Vindicating Mi'kmaq Rights: the Struggle before, During and after Marshall" (2000) 19 *Windsor Yearbook of Access to Justice* 203.

decision "did not rule that the appellant had established a treaty right to 'gather' anything and everything physically capable of being gathered. The issues were much narrower and the ruling much narrower." What the court was saying in its declaratory statement was that this ruling only applied to eel harvesting, which means that, in reality, treaty Indians can be charged with harvesting other types of fish or resources, and would then have to appeal the conviction to have new rights recognized and have the charge lifted. The court indicated that evidence would need to be brought before it on issues such as logging, mining and other exploitation activities before the Mi'kmaq could exercise any rights over the targeted resources. The court also clarified that the government is quite capable of imposing regulations over Aboriginal treaty rights. The right to fish was, therefore, secondary to government efforts to conserve fishery resources. Moreover, the Aboriginal treaty right did not automatically displace non-Aboriginal users of fishing resources.[60]

An interesting result of the *R. v. Marshall* decision can be seen in New Brunswick in relation to moose harvesting. Under the assumption that *R. v. Marshall* applies to all products that can be harvested for commercial profit, according to provincial Natural Resources Department officials, Mi'kmaq and Maliseet hunters shot over 1,000 moose during the 1999-2000 hunting season without a licence. This figure represented almost half the allowed provincial harvest of 2,000 animals in that year. Aboriginal hunters shot more moose than were needed for food and were secured for sale. The New Brunswick government, which operates a tightly controlled moose harvest that attracts over 60,000 applications for the 4,500 permits issued annually, publicly stated its intention not to charge Aboriginal People with hunting moose illegally. The provincial government expressed a desire to meet with First Nations leaders to negotiate band quotas so that the government would not impose a regulatory system that would meet with hostility. Natural Resources Minister Jeanot Volpe is quoted as having said: "I don't want to force anything on them. [Native hunters] don't want it to be imposed. I want to work with them. They want to work with us. We're all working for the same objective."[61]

During the period that conflict raged over Aboriginal lobster harvesting, Mi'kmaq leaders were demanding that the government and industry take their new rights more seriously. Chief Benjamin Paul of the Union of New Brunswick Indians appeared before the National Energy Board to demand a share of royalties on natural gas transported on the new Sable Island pipeline.[62] The Mi'kmaq eventually took this matter to court and lost in their attempts to delay construction. Some Aboriginal loggers also commenced

[60] For a good discussion see Coates, K., *The Marshall Decision and Native Rights*, McGill-Queen's University Press, Quebec City, 2000.

[61] "Minister won't force moose rules on natives," Saint John *Times Globe*, 10 April 2000.

[62] "Natives want gas money," Saint John *Times Globe*, 13 October 1999.

logging in New Brunswick, believing that the *R. v. Marshall* decision applied to timber harvests as well.

The proposition that the Maritime treaties protected commercial forestry activities was tested in *R. v. Bernard*[63] in 2000. The accused was a Mi'kmaq who was convicted for possessing timber contrary to section 67(1)(c) of the *New Brunswick Crown Lands and Forests Act*.[64] The accused alleged that he was protected by treaty to commercially harvest and sell forest products and that such a right was part of his community's Aboriginal title. The court came to the following conclusions:

1. Applying the principles in *R. v. Marshall* to commercial harvesting of forestry products does not amount to an evolution of Miramichi Mi'kmaq gathering activities and does not attract the protection of section 35 of the *Constitution Act, 1982*. No evidence was presented to suggest that log harvesting was part of the distinctive culture of the Miramichi Mi'kmaq at the time of contact, and no evidence was submitted to indicate that the Mi'kmaq had ever harvested or traded logs with either the British or French and no basis for such a right could be found in the treaties to be applicable to Bernard.

2. No evidence was provided to indicate that language posed a difficulty in the ability of the Mi'kmaq to understand and appreciate the written documents as well as the oral representations made prior to and after the treaties were made.

3. The treaties of 1761 and 1779 were signed by the Miramichi Mi'kmaq as a hunting, fishing and gathering society. An interpretation of the right to "gather" as a right to participate in the "wholesale uncontrolled exploitation of natural resources would alter the terms of the Treaty" and "wholly transform" the rights conferred.

This was reversed on appeal and the accused was acquitted. The Court of Appeal found by majority that the accused's treaty rights had been infringed.[65]

A later case decided in Nova Scotia, another by the name of *R. v. Marshall*,[66] also dealt with Mi'kmaq people charged with cutting and removing timber from Crown lands without authorization, contrary to the *Crown Lands Act*.[67] The accused alleged that their ancestors had Aboriginal title to all of Nova Scotia and that they have inherited it. They also claimed that treaties entered into between 1760 and 1761 gave them a right to harvest

---

[63] [2000] 3 C.N.L.R. 184.
[64] R.S.N.B. 1973 c. C-38.1.
[65] N.B.C.A [2003], N.B.T. No. 320, 2003 N.B.C.A 55.
[66] [2001] 2 C.N.L.R. 256.
[67] R.S.N.S. 1989, c.114, s. 29.

forest products and included a right to harvest timber commercially. Mr. Justice Curran found that there was insufficient evidence to conclude that the Mi'kmaq had occupied any land to the extent required for Aboriginal title and that on the balance of probabilities the accused had not proven that their ancestors had Aboriginal title to the cutting sites. Finally, Justice Curran found that the Mi'kmaq treaties of 1760 and 1761 did not establish any right of which harvesting timber for sale is the modern equivalent. In other words, commercial logging is not a logical evolution of Mi'kmaq use of forest resources in daily life, even if in 1760 those resources were sometimes traded.

In *Shubernacadie Indian Band v. Canada (Min. of Fisheries and Oceans)*,[68] the Federal Court, Trial Division, considered an application by the Shubernacadie Indian Band for an interlocutory injunction preventing the Department of Fisheries and Oceans Canada from seizing lobster traps and other equipment used to harvest lobster, fishing vessels and lobsters harvested by the band. Further, the band sought an injunction from the court preventing the Department from any future interference with the band's lobster harvesting activities. The government action arose due to a statement made by the band's chief that the band proposed to harvest lobster in St. Mary's Bay using 800 traps from 3 July until 15 October. This period fell within the closed season according to the *Atlantic Fishing Regulations*. Ultimately the band's application for an injunction was dismissed on the grounds that approval of an injunction would have very likely affected the final disposition of the matter, and would have affected rights beyond those of the immediate parties. The injunction had the potential to harm the rights of 33 other Aboriginal communities that claimed to be entitled to the benefits of Aboriginal fishing rights pursuant to treaties. To quote Justice Pelletier:

> [T]he public interest is against creating a vacuum of authority with respect to the fishery resource until the necessary negotiations and consultations have taken place. To grant this injunction to this Band is to grant it to every other Band which is entitled to claim the benefit of the Peace and Friendship treaties. It may be that this is exactly what will happen once the issue is decided on its merits. If that is what the law requires, it shall be done. But such a determination can only be made after all the issues are fully canvassed, including the issue of justification.[69]

First Nations leaders assumed that *R. v. Marshall* would apply more widely to minerals, land and natural resources. Where a compromise agreement is not negotiated, First Nations will probably press for an extension of their treaty right to exploit all natural resources for commercial purposes. As Chief Lawrence Paul of the Assembly of Nova Scotia Mi'kmaq

---

[68] [2001] 1 C.N.L.R. 282 (F.C.T.D.).

[69] *Ibid.* at para. 75.

Chiefs asserted in relation to the government of Nova Scotia: "Right now the province is giving us no choice but to fight this matter in the courts…They don't want to recognize anything until the courts force them."[70]

The *R. v. Marshall* decision potentially affects 34 Mi'kmaq and Maliseet First Nations in Nova Scotia, New Brunswick, Prince Edward Island and the Gaspé region of Québec.

In light of these decisions and the Supreme Court's clarification of the original decision in Marshall, it would seem that the courts will attempt to maintain a tight reign on the possibility of *R. v. Marshall* conveying any real commercial harvesting rights on the Aboriginal People who are covered by the peace and friendship treaties of the Maritimes. Undoubtedly the future promises much more litigation, as all participants test the boundaries of the treaty right to harvest for commercial purposes in *R. v. Marshall*.

A General Comment about the Maritime Treaties

- The land in the Maritimes changed hands between the British and the French on several occasions such that the validity of the treaties is questionable.

- Many of the treaties are clearly not land cession treaties, which gives rise to the questionable acquisition of land in the Maritimes by the Crown.[71] If the land was never surrendered voluntarily as per the Royal Proclamation then Aboriginal title may persist. The court has held on several occasions that the Royal Proclamation does apply to the Maritimes.[72] As commented by Professor Brian Slattery:

  > [T]he question of Aboriginal title in New Brunswick and Nova Scotia is very much alive and will continue to preoccupy the courts of those provinces for some years to come. Perhaps thegovernments of New Brunswick and Nova Scotia would be wise to read the judicial writing on the wall and take steps to resolve the matter by timely negotiations.[73]

- Implications from the 1999 Supreme Court decision in *R. v. Marshall* seem to be that, for one thing, Aboriginal People will need to take their claims to commercial harvesting rights to the courts to get lawful recognition of such a treaty right if one is found to exist, and also that the provinces seem to be more motivated to initiate negotiations with First Nations with respect to resource sharing rather than leaving this issue solely in the hands of the courts.

---

[70] "Mi'kmaq loggers to stay off Crown land," *Chronicle-Herald*, Halifax, 8 November 1999.
[71] See Chief Justice MacKeigan in *R. v. Isaac* (1975), *supra* note 11 in ch. 1.
[72] *Warman v. Francis* (1958), 20 D.L.R. (2d) 627, 43 M.P.R. 197; *R. v. Isaac, Ibid.*
[73] Slattery, B., "Some Thoughts on Aboriginal Title" (1999) 48 *University of New Brunswick Law Journal* 19 at 40.

Appendix

List of Bands

Ontario

Band No.	Band Name	Band No.	Band Name
172	Aamjiwnaang	138	Chippewas of Georgina Island
142	Albany		
160	Alderville First Nation	171	Chippewas of Kettle and Stony Point
163	Algonquins of Pikwakanagan		
		139	Chippewas of Mnjikaning First Nation
194	Animbiigoo Zaagi'igan Anishinaabek		
		122	Chippewas of Nawash First Nation
153	Anishinabe of Wauzhushk Onigum		
		166	Chippewas of the Thames First Nation
125	Anishnaabeg of Naongashiing		
		182	Constance Lake
242	Aroland	126	Couchiching First Nation
143	Attawapiskat	161	Curve Lake
180	Aundeck•Omni•Kaning	237	Deer Lake
198	Batchewana First Nation	218	Dokis
207	Bearskin Lake	183	Eabametoong First Nation
141	Beausoleil	148	Eagle Lake
124	Big Grassy	227	Flying Post
197	Biinjitiwaabik Zaaging Anishinaabek	215	Fort Severn
		187	Fort William
228	Brunswick House	199	Garden River First Nation
165	Caldwell	185	Ginoogaming First Nation
216	Cat Lake	149	Grassy Narrows First Nation
221	Chapleau Cree First Nation	188	Gull Bay
229	Chapleau Ojibway	231	Henvey Inlet First Nation

Band No.	Band Name	Band No.	Band Name
162	Hiawatha First Nation	204	North Caribou Lake
154	Iskatewizaagegan #39 Independent First Nation	238	North Spirit Lake
		151	Northwest Angle No.33
210	Kasabonika Lake	152	Northwest Angle No.37
325	Kee•Way•Win	147	Ochiichagwe'babigo'ining First Nation
212	Kingfisher		
209	Kitchenuhmaykoosib Inninuwug	258	Ojibway Nation of Saugeen
		131	Ojibways of Onigaming First Nation
189	Lac Des Mille Lacs		
127	Lac La Croix	192	Ojibways of the Pic River First Nation
205	Lac Seul		
184	Long Lake No.58 First Nation	169	Oneida Nation of the Thames
174	Magnetawan	191	Pays Plat
186	Martin Falls	195	Pic Mobert
219	Matachewan	208	Pikangikum
226	Mattagami	236	Poplar Hill
326	McDowell Lake	130	Rainy River
181	M'Chigeeng First Nation	193	Red Rock
225	Michipicoten	214	Sachigo Lake
203	Mishkeegogamang	179	Sagamok Anishnawbek
223	Missanabie Cree	196	Sandpoint
200	Mississauga	211	Sandy Lake
140	Mississauga's of Scugog Island First Nation	123	Saugeen
		132	Seine River First Nation
120	Mississaugas of the Credit	201	Serpent River
159	Mohawks of Akwesasne	137	Shawanaga First Nation
164	Mohawks of the Bay of Quinte	176	Sheguiandah
		178	Sheshegwaning
144	Moose Cree First Nation	155	Shoal Lake No.40
135	Moose Deer Point	121	Six Nations of the Grand River
167	Moravian of the Thames		
168	Munsee•Delaware Nation	259	Slate Falls Nation
213	Muskrat Dam Lake	133	Stanjikoming First Nation
128	Naicatchewenin	145	Taykwa Tagamou Nation
158	Naotkamegwanning	222	Temagami First Nation
239	Neskantaga First Nation	202	Thessalon
241	Nibinamik First Nation	150	Wabaseemoong Independent Nations
129	Nicickousemenecaning		
220	Nipissing First Nation	156	Wabauskang First Nation

Band No.	Band Name
157	Wabigoon Lake Ojibway Nation
233	Wahgoshig
232	Wahnapitae
134	Wahta Mohawk
170	Walpole Island
206	Wapekeka
136	Wasauksing First Nation
235	Washagamis Bay
234	Wawakapewin
240	Webequie
146	Weenusk
224	Whitefish Lake
230	Whitefish River
190	Whitesand
175	Wikwemikong
217	Wunnumin
173	Zhiibaahaasing First Nation
32	Mushuau Innu First Nation
33	Sheshatshiu Innu First Nation
47	Miawpukek

Newfoundland and Labrador

Band No.	Band Name
32	Mushuau Innu First Nation
33	Sheshatshiu Innu First Nation
47	Miawpukek

British Columbia

Band No.	Band Name
684	Adams Lake
659	Ahousaht
558	Aitchelitz
709	Alexandria
710	Alexis Creek
685	Ashcroft
640	Beecher Bay

Band No.	Band Name
547	Blueberry River First Nations
686	Bonaparte
700	Boothroyd
701	Boston Bar First Nation
590	Bridge River
619	Burns Lake
549	Burrard
622	Campbell River
713	Canim Lake
723	Canoe Creek
623	Cape Mudge
591	Cayoose Creek
583	Chawathil
584	Cheam
559	Chehalis
641	Chemainus First Nation
620	Cheslatta Carrier Nation
693	Coldwater
604	Columbia Lake
624	Comox
694	Cook's Ferry
642	Cowichan
635	Da'naxda'xw First Nation
662	Ditidaht
548	Doig River
561	Douglas
634	Ehattesaht
711	Esketemc
644	Esquimalt
543	Fort Nelson First Nation
592	Fountain
531	Gitanmaax
537	Gitanyow
535	Gitsegukla
536	Gitwangak
533	Glen Vowell
724	Gwa'Sala-Nakwaxda'xw
627	Gwawaenuk Tribe

Band No.	Band Name	Band No.	Band Name
534	Hagwilget Village	695	Lower Nicola
645	Halalt	598	Lower Similkameen
546	Halfway River First Nation	646	Lyackson
675	Hartley Bay	705	Lytton
538	Heiltsuk	647	Malahat First Nation
661	Hesquiaht	629	Mamalilikulla•Qwe' Qwa'Sot'Em
703	High Bar		
552	Homalco	565	Matsqui
664	Hupa4asath First Nation	618	McLeod Lake
663	Huu-ay-aht First Nations	673	Metlakatla
683	Iskut	530	Moricetown
638	Ka:'yu:'k't'h'/ Che:k:tles7et'h' First Nations	557	Mount Currie
		630	Mowachaht/Muchalaht
		550	Musqueam
688	Kamloops	612	Nadleh Whuten
704	Kanaka Bar	614	Nak'azdli
563	Katzie	631	Namgis First Nation
532	Kispiox	649	Nanoose First Nation
676	Kitamaat	720	Nazko
540	Kitasoo	726	Nee•Tahi•Buhn
672	Kitkatla	690	Neskonlith
680	Kitselas	566	New Westminster
681	Kitsumkalum	696	Nicomen
553	Klahoose First Nation	671	Nisga'a Village of Gingolx
721	Kluskus	679	Nisga'a Village of Gitwinksihlkw
610	Kwadacha		
626	Kwakiutl	678	Nisga'a Village of Laxgalt'sap
564	Kwantlen First Nation		
580	Kwaw-kwaw-Apilt	677	Nisga'a Village of New Aiyansh
628	Kwiakah		
625	Kwicksutaineuk-ah-kwaw-ah-mish	699	Nooaitch
		691	North Thompson
560	Kwikwetlem First Nation	556	N'Quatqua
607	Lake Babine Nation	639	Nuchatlaht
643	Lake Cowichan First Nation	539	Nuxalk Nation
674	Lax-kw'alaams	616	Okanagan
579	Leq' a: mel First Nation	669	Old Massett Village Council
611	Lheidli T'enneh	692	Oregon Jack Creek
689	Little Shuswap Lake	596	Osoyoos
606	Lower Kootenay	541	Oweekeno

Band No.	Band Name	Band No.	Band Name
658	Pacheedaht First Nation	555	Squamish
652	Pauquachin	574	Squiala First Nation
650	Penelakut	602	St. Mary's
597	Penticton	613	Stellat'en First Nation
586	Peters	717	Stone
585	Popkum	578	Sumas First Nation
544	Prophet River Band, Dene Tsaa Tse K'Nai First Natn	682	Tahltan
		608	Takla Lake First Nation
651	Qualicum First Nation	593	T'it'q'et
633	Quatsino	660	Tla•o•qui•aht First Nations
715	Red Bluff	632	Tlatlasikwala
615	Saik'uz First Nation	617	Tl'azt'en Nation
567	Samahquam	712	Tl'etinqox•t'in Government Office
542	Saulteau First Nations		
568	Scowlitz	637	Tlowitsis Tribe
581	Seabird Island	603	Tobacco Plains
551	Sechelt	718	Toosey
569	Semiahmoo	666	Toquaht
595	Seton Lake	653	Tsartlip
698	Shackan	636	Tsawataineuk
605	Shuswap	654	Tsawout First Nation
587	Shxw'ow'hamel First Nation	577	Tsawwassen First Nation
706	Siska	609	Tsay Keh Dene
562	Skatin Nations	665	Tseshaht
582	Skawahlook First Nation	655	Tseycum
687	Skeetchestn	594	Ts'kw'aylaxw First Nation
670	Skidegate	657	T'Sou•ke First Nation
729	Skin Tyee	575	Tzeachten
571	Skowkale	667	Uchucklesaht
707	Skuppah	668	Ucluelet First Nation
573	Skwah	722	Ulkatcho
570	Skway	588	Union Bar
554	Sliammon	697	Upper Nicola
648	Snuneymuxw First Nation	599	Upper Similkameen
716	Soda Creek	545	West Moberly First Nations
656	Songhees First Nation	601	Westbank First Nation
572	Soowahlie	725	Wet'suwet'en First Nation
600	Spallumcheen	702	Whispering Pines/Clinton
708	Spuzzum	719	Williams Lake

Band No.	Band Name
714	Xeni Gwet'in First Nations Government
576	Yakweakwioose
589	Yale First Nation
728	Yekooche

Yukon

Band No.	Band Name
491	Carcross/Tagish First Nations
507	Champagne and Aishihik First Nations
504	Dease River
495	First Nation of Nacho Nyak Dun
503	Kluane First Nation
500	Kwanlin Dun First Nation
502	Liard River
492	Little Salmon/Carmacks First Nation
497	Ross River
498	Selkirk First Nation
508	Ta'an Kwach'an
501	Taku River Tlingit
499	Teslin Tlingit Council
494	'Tr'on dëk Hwëch'in
496	Vuntut Gwitchin First Nation
506	White River First Nation

Northwest Territories

Band No.	Band Name
758	Acho Dene Koe
755	Aklavik
771	Behdzi Ahda" First Nation
774	Dechi Laot'i First Nations
760	Deh Gah Gotie Dene Council
754	Deline

Band No.	Band Name
762	Deninu K'ue First Nation
765	Dog Rib Rae
752	Fort Good Hope
773	Gameti First Nation
753	Gwicha Gwich'in
780	Inuvik Native
770	Jean Marie River First Nation
768	Ka'a'gee Tu First Nation
761	K'atlodeeche First Nation
757	Liidlii Kue First Nation
764	Lutsel K'e Dene
766	Nahanni Butte
756	Pehdzeh Ki First Nation
759	Salt River First Nation #195
767	Sambaa K'e (Trout Lake) Dene
751	Tetlit Gwich'in
750	Tulita Dene
772	West Point First Nation
769	Wha Ti First Nation
763	Yellowknives Dene First Nation

Alberta

Band No.	Band Name
438	Alexander
437	Alexis
463	Athabasca Chipewyan First Nation
445	Beaver First Nation
460	Beaver Lake Cree Nation
458	Bigstone Cree Nation
435	Blood
470	Chipewyan Prairie First Nation
464	Cold Lake First Nations
448	Dene Tha'
450	Driftpile First Nation
451	Duncan's First Nation

Band No.	Band Name	Band No.	Band Name
440	Enoch Cree Nation #440	261	Brokenhead Ojibway Nation
443	Ermineskin Tribe	265	Buffalo Point First Nation
467	Fort McKay First Nation	301	Bunibonibee Cree Nation
468	Fort McMurray #468 First Nation	289	Canupawakpa Dakota First Nation
465	Frog Lake	309	Chemawawin Cree Nation
469	Heart Lake	276	Cross Lake First Nation
449	Horse Lake First Nation	288	Dakota Plains
452	Kapawe'no First Nation	295	Dakota Tipi
466	Kehewin Cree Nation	316	Dauphin River
447	Little Red River Cree Nation	280	Ebb and Flow
476	Loon River Cree	264	Fisher River
439	Louis Bull	262	Fort Alexander
453	Lubicon Lake	305	Fox Lake
461	Mikisew Cree First Nation	294	Gamblers
442	Montana	297	Garden Hill First Nations
431	O'Chiese	296	God's Lake First Nation
441	Paul	310	Grand Rapids First Nation
436	Piikani Nation	263	Hollow Water
462	Saddle Lake	286	Keeseekoowenin
444	Samson	268	Kinonjeoshtegon First Nation
454	Sawridge		
430	Siksika Nation	271	Lake Manitoba
477	Smith's Landing First Nation	275	Lake St. Martin
471	Stoney	260	Little Black River
455	Sturgeon Lake Cree Nation	270	Little Grand Rapids
456	Sucker Creek	274	Little Saskatchewan
434	Sunchild First Nation	287	Long Plain
457	Swan River First Nation	302	Manto Sipi Cree Nation
446	Tallcree	328	Marcel Colomb First Nation
432	Tsuu T'Ina Nation	311	Mathias Colomb
459	Whitefish Lake	312	Mosakahiken Cree Nation
	Woodland Cree First Nation	313	Nisichawayasihk Cree Nation

Manitoba

Band No.	Band Name	Band No.	Band Name
		317	Northlands
		278	Norway House Cree Nation
308	Barren Lands	279	O-Chi-Chak-Ko-Sipi First Nation
266	Berens River		
284	Birdtail Sioux	315	Opaskwayak Cree Nation
267	Bloodvein	327	Pauingassi First Nation

Band No.	Band Name
269	Peguis
272	Pinaymootang First Nation
282	Pine Creek
277	Poplar River First Nation
300	Red Sucker Lake
291	Rolling River
273	Roseau River
283	Sandy Bay
314	Sapotaweyak Cree Nation
303	Sayisi Dene First Nation
307	Shamattawa First Nation
290	Sioux Valley Dakota Nation
281	Skownan First Nation
298	St. Theresa Point
293	Swan Lake
306	Tataskweyak Cree Nation
292	Tootinaowaziibeeng Treaty Reserve
323	War Lake First Nation
299	Wasagamack First Nation
285	Waywayseecappo First Nation Treaty Four • 1874
324	Wuskwi Sipihk First Nation
304	York Factory First Nation

Saskatchewan

Band No.	Band Name
406	Ahtahkakoop
369	Beardy's and Okemasis
399	Big Island Lake Cree Nation
404	Big River
403	Birch Narrows First Nation
359	Black Lake
398	Buffalo River Dene Nation
394	Canoe Lake Cree First Nation
378	Carry The Kettle
401	Clearwater River Dene
366	Cote First Nation 366
361	Cowessess

Band No.	Band Name
350	Cumberland House Cree Nation
389	Day Star
400	English River First Nation
390	Fishing Lake First Nation
395	Flying Dust First Nation
351	Fond du Lac
391	Gordon
352	Hatchet Lake
397	Island Lake First Nation
370	James Smith
362	Kahkewistahaw
393	Kawacatoose
367	Keeseekoose
377	Kinistin
353	Lac La Ronge
379	Little Black Bear
340	Little Pine
341	Lucky Man
396	Makwa Sahgaiehcan First Nation
374	Mistawasis
354	Montreal Lake
342	Moosomin
343	Mosquito, Grizzly Bear's Head, Lean Man First.Nations.
381	Muscowpetung
375	Muskeg Lake
371	Muskoday First Nation
392	Muskowekwan
380	Nekaneet
408	Ocean Man
363	Ochapowace
382	Okanese
373	One Arrow
344	Onion Lake
383	Pasqua First Nation #79
384	Peepeekisis

Band No.	Band Name	Band No.	Band Name
405	Pelican Lake	75	Cree Nation of Mistissini
355	Peter Ballantyne Cree Nation	60	Cree Nation of Wemindji
409	Pheasant Rump Nakota	65	Eagle Village First Nation • Kipawa
385	Piapot	57	Eastmain
345	Poundmaker	80	Innu Takuaikan Uashat Mak
356	Red Earth		Mani•Utenam
346	Red Pheasant	70	Kahnawake
364	Sakimay	73	Kitigan Zibi Anishinabeg
347	Saulteaux	87	La Nation Innu
357	Shoal Lake of the Cree Nation		Matimekush•Lac John
386	Standing Buffalo	53	La Nation Micmac de Gespeg
387	Star Blanket	78	Les Atikamekw de Manawan
360	Sturgeon Lake First Nation	82	Les Innus de Ekuanitshit
348	Sweetgrass	51	Listuguj Mi'gmaq First Nation Council
368	The Key First Nation	67	Long Point First Nation
349	Thunderchild First Nation	52	Micmacs of Gesgapegiag
358	Wahpeton Dakota Nation	69	Mohawks of Kanesatake
402	Waterhen Lake	83	Montagnais de Natashquan
365	White Bear	88	Montagnais de Pakua Shipi
372	Whitecap Dakota First Nation	84	Montagnais de Unamen Shipu
407	Witchekan Lake	76	Montagnais du Lac St.•Jean
388	Wood Mountain	86	Montagnais Essipit
376	Yellow Quill	81	Naskapi of Quebec

Quebec

Band No.	Band Name	Band No.	Band Name
		63	Nation Anishnabe du Lac Simon
71	Abénakis de Wôlinak	50	Nation Huronne Wendat
74	Algonquins of Barriere Lake	59	Nemaska
79	Atikamekw d'Opitciwan	72	Odanak
85	Betsiamites	95	Première nation de Whapmagoostui
62	Communauté anicinape de Kitcisakik	54	Première Nation Malecite de Viger
55	Conseil de la Première Nation Abitibiwinni	64	Timiskaming First Nation
77	Conseil des Atikamekw de Wemotaci	61	Waskaganish
		56	Waswanipi
58	Cree Nation of Chisasibi	68	Wolf Lake

Nova Scotia

Band No.	Band Name
18	Acadia
20	Annapolis Valley
21	Bear River
22	Chapel Island First Nation
23	Eskasoni
30	Glooscap First Nation
26	Membertou
27	Millbrook
19	Paq'tnkek First Nation
24	Pictou Landing
25	Shubenacadie
28	Wagmatcook
29	Whycocomagh

New Brunswick

Band No.	Band Name
3	Big Cove
4	Buctouche
5	Burnt Church
7	Eel Ground
8	Eel River
9	Fort Folly
10	Indian Island
11	Kingsclear
6	Madawaska Maliseet First Nation
14	Metepenagiag Mi'kmaq Nation
12	Oromocto
13	Pabineau
15	Saint Mary's
16	Tobique
17	Woodstock

Prince Edward Island

Band No.	Band Name
1	Abegweit
2	Lennox Island

Bibliography

Books and Reports

Abel, K., and Friesen, J. (eds.), *Aboriginal Resource Use in Canada*, University of Manitoba Press, Winnipeg, 1991.

Arnot, D., *Statement of Treaty Issues: Treaties as a Bridge to the Future*, Office of the Treaty Commissioner, Saskatoon, 1998.

Asch, M. (ed.), *Aboriginal and Treaty Rights in Canada*, UBC Press, Vancouver, 1997.

Bartlett, R., *Indian Reserves and Aboriginal Lands in Canada: A Homeland*, University of Saskatchewan Native Law Centre, Saskatoon, 1990.

————., *Aboriginal Water Rights in Canada: A Study of Aboriginal Title to Water and Indian Water Rights*, Canadian Institute of Resources Law, University of Calgary, 1986.

————., *Indian reserves in the Atlantic Provinces of Canada*, University of Saskatchewan Native Law Centre, Saskatoon, 1986.

Chartrand, P., *Manitoba's Metis Settlement Scheme of 1870*, Native Law Centre, University of Saskatchewan, Saskatoon, 1991.

Coates, K., "The *Marshall* Crisis and East Coast Confrontations," *The Marshall Decision and Native Rights*, McGill-Queen's University Press, Montreal and Kingston, 2000.

————., *The Marshall Decision and Native Rights*, McGill-Queen's University Press, Montreal and Kingston, 2000.

Cumming, P., *Canada: Native Land Rights and Northern Development*, York University Law Library, Downsview, 1977.

Cumming, P., and Mickenberg, N., *Native Rights in Canada*, 2nd ed., General, Toronto, 1972.

Daniel, R., "The Spirit and Terms of Treaty Eight" in Price, R., (ed.), *The Spirit of the Alberta Indian Treaties*, Institute for Research on Public Policy, Toronto, 1979.

Elliot, D., *Law and Aboriginal Peoples in Canada*, 4th ed., Canadian Legal Studies Series, Captus Press, 2000.

Frideres, J., *Aboriginal Peoples in Canada: Contemporary Conflicts*, 5th ed., Prentice Hall, Scarborough, 1998.

Fumoleau, R., *As Long as This Land Shall Last*, McClelland and Stewart, Toronto, 1973.

Harring, S., *White Man's Law: Native People in Nineteenth-Century Canadian Jurispriducen*, University of Toronto Press, Toronto, 1998.

Imai, S., *Indian Act and Aboriginal Constitutional Provisions*, Carswell, 2001.

Isaac, T., *Aboriginal and Treaty Rights in the Maritimes: The Marshall Decision and Beyond*, Purich Publishing Ltd., Saskatoon, 2001.

————., *Aboriginal Law*, Purich Publishing, Saskatoon, 1999.

————., *Pre-1986 Legislation Concerning Indians*, University of Saskatchewan Native Law Centre, Saskatoon, 1993.

Keeping, J., *The Inuvialuit Final Agreement*, Canadian Institute of Resources Law, University of Calgary, 1989.

Lippert O. (ed.), *Beyond the Nass Valley: National Implications of the Supreme Court's* Delgamuukw *Decision*, The Fraser Institute, Vancouver, 2000.

Mainville, R., *An Overview of Aboriginal and Treaty Rights and Compensation for their Breach*, Purich Publishers, Saskatoon, 2001.

McGee, H. (ed.), *The Native Peoples of Atlantic Canada*, McClelland and Stewart, Toronto, 1974.

McNab, D., *Circles of Time: Aboriginal Land Rights and Resistance*, Wilfred Laurier University Press, 1999.

————., *Earth, Water, Air & Fire: Studies in Canadian Ethnohistory*, Wildfred Laurier University Press, 1998.

McNab, D., and Standen, D. (eds.), *Gin Das Winan Documenting Aboriginal History in Ontario*, Occasional Papers of the Champlain Society No. 2, The Champlain Society, Toronto, 1996.

McNeil, K., *Indian Hunting, Trapping and Fishing Rights in the Prairie Provinces of Canada*, University of Saskatchewan Native Law Centre, 1983.

Morris, A., *The Treaties of Canada with the Indians of Manitoba and North-West Territories*, Belfords, Clarke & Co., Toronto, 1980.

Morrison, J., *Treaty Research Report: Treaty Nine (1905-1906): The James Bay Treaty*, Treaties and Historical Research Centre, Ottawa, 1986.

Notzke, C., *Aboriginal People and Natural Resources in Canada*, Captus University Press, North York, 1994.

Ojibeway-Cree Cultural Centre, *Nishnawbe-Aski Nation: A History of the Cree and Ojibway of Northern Ontario*, Ojibeway-Cree Cultural Centre, Timmins, 1986.

Ponting, J. (ed.), *Arduous Journey: Canadian Indians and Decolonization*, McClelland and Stewart, Toronto, 1986.

Price, R., *The Spirit of the Alberta Indian Treaties*, Institute for Research on Public Policy, Ottawa, 1979.

Reiter, R., *The Law of Canadian Indian Treaties*, Juris Analytica Publishing Inc., Edmonton, 1995.

————., *The Fundamental Principles of Indian Law*, First Nations Resource Council, 1991.

Snow, Chief J., *These Mountains are our Sacred Places*, Samuel Stevens, Toronto, 1977.

Sprague, D., *Canada's Treaties with Aboriginal People*, Canadian Legal History Project, University of Manitoba, Winnipeg, 1991.

Treaty 7 Elders et al., *The True Spirit and Original Intent of Treaty 7*, McGill-Queen's University Press, Montreal and Kingston, 1996.

Articles

Arnot, D., "Article treaties as a Bridge to the Future" (2001) 50 *University of New Brunswick Law Journal* 57.

Asch, M., and Macklem, P., "Aboriginal Rights and Canadian Sovereignty" (1991) 26:2 *Alberta Law Review* 502.

Bell, C., and Buss, K., "The Promise of Marshall on the Prairies: A Framework for Analyzing Unfulfilled Treaty Promises" (2000) 63 *Saskatchewan Law Review* 667.

Binnie, W., "The Sparrow Doctrine: Beginning of the End or End of the Beginning?" (1991) 15 *Queen's Law Journal* 217.

Borrows, J., "Contemporary Traditional Equality: The effect of the Charter on First Nation Politics" (1994) 43 *University of New Brunswick Law Journal* 19.

Curran, D., and M'Gonigle, M., "Aboriginal Forestry: Community Management as Opportunity and Imperative" (1999) 37 *Osgoode Hall Law Journal* 771.

Dufraimont, L., "Justifiable Infringement of Aboriginal Rights at the Supreme Court of Canada" (2000) 58(1) *University of Toronto Faculty Law Review* 1.

Edwards, B., "Note Toward A Bilateral Fiduciary Relationship: Recognizing Mutual Vulnerability In *R. v. Marshall*" (2001) 59 University of Toronto Faculty of Law Review 107.

Elliot, D., "Fifty Dollars of Fish: A Comment on *R. v. Van Der Peet*" (1996) 35:3 *Alberta Law Review* 759.

————., "In the Wake of *Sparrow*" (1991) 40 *University of British Columbia Law Journal* 23.

Harris, D., "Territoriality, 'Aboriginal Rights, and the Heiltsuk Spawn-on-Kelp Fishery'"(2000) 34 *University of British Columbia Law Review* 195.

Henderson, J., "Constitutional Powers and Treaty Rights" (2000) 63 Saskatchewan Law Review 719.

Hunter, J., "Consent and Consultation After *Delgamuukw:* Practical Implications for Forestry and Mining in British Columbia," Aboriginal Title Update, Continuing Legal Education Society of British Columbia, Vancouver, 1998.

Imai, S., "Treaty Lands and Crown Obligations: The 'Tracts Taken Up' Provision" (2000) *Queen's Law Journal* 1.

Isaac, T., "The Courts, Government, and Public Policy: The Significance of *R. v. Marshall*" (2000) 63 *Saskatchewan Law Review* 701.

Joffe, P., "Assessing the *Delgamuukw* Principles: National Implications and Potential Effects in Quebec" (2000) 45 *McGill Law Journal* 155.

Kyle, R., "Aboriginal Fishing Rights: The Supreme Court of Canada in the Post-Sparrow Era" (1997) 31 *University of British Columbia Law Review* 293.

Lambert, D., "*Van der Peet* and *Delgamuukw*: Ten Unresolved Issues" (1998) 32 *University of British Columbia Law Review* 249.

Lonf, J., "No Bases for Argument: The Signing of Treaty 9 in Northern Ontario, 1905-1906" (1989), 5 *Native Studies Review* 19.

McNab, D., "A Few Thoughts on Understanding Propaganda After Oka," Social Sciences and Humanities Aboriginal Research Exchange, 1, 1, Fall-Winter, 1993.

————., "Treaties and Official Use of History," *Canadian Journal of Native Studies*, XII, 1, 1993.

Normey, R., "Angling for "Common Intention": Treaty Interpretation in *R. v. Marshall*" (2000) 63 *Saskatchewan Law Review* 645.

Reid, J. et al., "History, Native Issues and the Courts: A Forum" (1998) 28 *Acadiensis* 3.

Ross, M., and Sharvit, C., "Forest Management in Alberta and Rights to Hunt, Trap and Fish Under Treaty No. 8," (1998) 36:3 *Alberta Law Review* 645.

Rotman, L., "Taking Aim at the Canons of Treaty Interpretation in Canadian Aboriginal Rights Jurisprudence" (1997) 46 *University of New Brunswick Law Journal* 11.

Schulze, D., "The Murray Treaty of 1760: The Original Document Discovered" [1998] 1 *Canadian Native Law Review* 1.

Schulze, D., and Grant, P., "Governing Lands and Waters: Limits to Reserve Title and Indian Act Powers in British Columbia, and Proposals for Reform" (2001) 34 *University of British Columbia Law Review* 415.

Slattery, B., "Some Thoughts on Aboriginal Title" (1999) 48 *University of New Brunswick Law Journal* 19.

Walter, E., M'Gonigle, M., and McKay, C., "Fishing around the Law: the Pacific Salmon Management System as a "Structural Infringement" of Aboriginal Rights" (2000) 45 *McGill Law Journal* 263.

Walters, M., "According to the old customs of our nation: Aboriginal Self Government on the Credit River Mississauga Reserve, 1826-1847" (1998-1999) 30 *Ottawa Law Review* 1.

————., "Aboriginal Rights, Magna Carta and Exclusive Rights to Fisheries in the Waters of Upper Canada" (1998) 23 *Queen's Law Journal* 301.

Wicken, W., "The Mi'kmaq and Wuastukwiuk Treaties" (1994) 44 *University of New Brunswick Law Journal*, 241.

Wildsmith, B., "Vindicating Mi'kmaq Rights: the Struggle before, during and after *Marshall*" (2000) 19 *Windsor Yearbook of Access to Justice* 203.

Yukich, K., "Aboriginal Rights in the Constitution and International Law" (1996) 30 *University of British Columbia Law Review* 235.

Zalewski, A., "From *Sparrow* to *Van Der Peet*: The Evolution of a Definition of Aboriginal Rights" (1997) 55 *University of Toronto Faculty of Law Review* 435.

Online Resources

Department of Indian and Northern Affairs, Canada: <http://www.ainc-inac.gc.ca>

Department of Fisheries and Oceans, Canada: <http://www.dfo-mpo.gc.ca/index.htm>

Department of Natural Resources, Canada: <http://nrcan.gc.ca>

Canadian Government Information on the Internet (CGII), Aboriginal Peoples – Federal Information: <http://cgii.gc.ca/f-AB-e.html>

Statistics Canada: <http://www.statcan.ca/>

Government of Canada, Digital Resources: <http://collections.ic.gc.ca/>

Government of Alberta: <http://www.gov.ab.ca>

Government of British Columbia: <http://www.gov.bc.ca>

Government of Manitoba: <http://www.gov.mb.ca>

Government of New Brunswick: <http://www.gov.nb.ca>

Government of Newfoundland and Labrador: <http://www.gov.nf.ca>

Government of Northwest Territories: <http://www.gov.nt.ca>

Government of Nova Scotia: <http://www.gov.ns.ca>

Government of Nunavut: <http://www/gov.nu.ca>

Government of Ontario: <http://www.gov.on.ca>

Government of Quebec: <http://www.gouv.qc.ca>

Government of Saskatchewan: <http://www.gov.sk.ca>

Government of Yukon: <http://www.gov.yk.ca>

Aboriginal Canada Portal: <http://aboriginalcanada.gc.ca>

Canlii Legal Resources: <http://www.canlii.org>

Quicklaw Legal Resources: <http://www.quicklaw.com>

Westlaw Legal Resources: <http://www.westlaw.com>

University of Saskatchewan, Aboriginal Law Resources:
    <http://library.usask.ca/native/cnlch.html>

Institute of Indian Governance: <http://www.indigenous.bc.ca/>

Native American Law: <http://www.indianz.com/nal/>

Royal Commission on Aboriginal Peoples:
    <http://www.ainc-inac.gc.ca/rcap/index.html>

Aboriginal Connections:
    <http://www.aboriginalconnections.com/links/Law/>

Canadian Native Law Reporter: <http://www.usask.ca/nativelaw/cnlr.html>

Native Law Centre of Canada: <http://www.usask.ca/nativelaw/index.html>

Bill Henderson's First Nations Law Resources:
    <http://www.bloorstreet.com/200block/brintro.htm>

Wasekun People's website, Aboriginal Law and Legislation in Canada:
    <http://www.waseskun.net/law.htm>

Congress of Aboriginal People, Bill C-31 – Indian Act:
    <http://www.abo-peoples.org/programs/c-31.html>

Donovan and Company Barristers and Solicitors, Aboriginal Law:
    <http://www.aboriginal-law.com/>

Fast & Cocoran Legal Services, Native Law Resources:
    <http://www.nativelaw.com/website/fwp01.nsf>

Indian Land Transactions:
    <http://www.pushormitchell.com/nf/articles/indian.html>

Native Web, Aboriginal Legal Resources: <http://www.nativeweb.org/>

Internet School Library Media Center Native American Legal Resources: <http://falcon.jmu.edu/~ramseyil/native.htm>

Native American Documents Project: <http://www.csusm.edu/nadp/nadp.htm>

Oneida Indian Nation Treaties Project: <http://oneida-nation.net/treaties.html>

Indian Law Overview – US: <http://wwwsecure.law.cornell.edu/topics/indian.html>

Internet Law Library Indian Nations and Tribes: <http://www.lawguru.com/ilawlib/31.htm>

Native Americas: Hemispheric Journal of Indigenous Issues: <http://nativeamericas.aip.cornell.edu/>

Communities First: First Nations Governance: <http://www.fng-gpn.gc.ca/index_e.asp>

Assembly of First Nations: <www.afn.ca>

Congress of Aboriginal Peoples: <http://www.abo-peoples.org>

Aboriginal Relations: <http://www.conferenceboard.ca/aboriginal/>

AGMV Marquis

MEMBER OF SCABRINI MEDIA

Quebec, Canada
2004